Learning Language and Culture via Public Internet Discussion Forums

Learning Language and Culture via Public Internet Discussion Forums

Barbara E. Hanna and Juliana de Nooy

First published 2009 by
PALGRAVE MACMILLAN

Palgrave Macmillan in the UK is an imprint of Macmillan Publishers Limited, registered in England, company number 785998, of Houndmills, Basingstoke, Hampshire RG21 6XS.

Palgrave Macmillan in the US is a division of St Martin's Press LLC, 175 Fifth Avenue, New York, NY 10010.

Palgrave Macmillan is the global academic imprint of the above companies and has companies and representatives throughout the world.

Palgrave® and Macmillan® are registered trademarks in the United States, the United Kingdom, Europe and other countries.

ISBN-13: 978-0-230-57630-8 hardback

This book is printed on paper suitable for recycling and made from fully managed and sustained forest sources. Logging, pulping and manufacturing processes are expected to conform to the environmental regulations of the country of origin.

A catalogue record for this book is available from the British Library.

Library of Congress Cataloging-in-Publication Data
Hanna, Barbara E., 1964–
    Learning language and culture via public internet discussion forums /
    Barbara E. Hanna, Juliana de Nooy.
        p.   cm.
    Includes bibliographical references and index.
    ISBN-13: 978-0-230-57630-8 (alk. paper)
    1. Intercultural communication.   2. Electronic discussion groups.
    3. Second language acquisition.   4. Culture—Study and teaching.
    I. De Nooy, Juliana.   II. Title
    P94.6.H365 2009
    418'.002854678—dc22   2008052852

10   9   8   7   6   5   4   3   2   1
18   17   16   15   14   13   12   11   10   09

Transferred to Digital Printing 2011

In memory of Abdi Kazeroni

Contents

List of Tables

Acknowledgements

The research for this book would not have been possible without the precious input of a series of research assistants and the financial support of the institutional structures which made it possible to employ them.

In the first category, that of the research assistants whose monitoring of forums identified many of the critical examples used in the development of our arguments, we thank Lara Cain-Gray, Peter Cowley, Diana Newport-Peace, Wendy Ward, Carol Wical, Sonia Wilson and Emma Woodley.

In the second, we gratefully acknowledge the support of the departments and research centres in which we have worked at Queensland University of Technology and the University of Queensland.

We also thank colleagues whose examples and conversation have influenced this work, in particular Béatrice Atherton, whose unit on argumentation, with its use of Internet forums, was one of the inspirations for the project, and Guy Ramsay, who explored sites in Mandarin. We express our appreciation, too, to our students for their interactions on discussion forums which have provided such rich examples for analysis and commentary.

Early versions of Chapters 3, 6, 7 and 8 were published in *Multilingua* 23 (4) 2004; *Language Learning and Technology* 7 (1) 2003; *Australian Journal of French Studies* 41 (3) 2004; and *Language, Society and Culture* (19) 2006. Our thanks to these journals for permission to reproduce material.

Finally we thank our families and friends for their support and contributions to our sanity.

Note on Quotations from Internet Forums

All extracts from electronic messages appear as originally posted, with no modification to syntax or spelling: errors and incorrect usage have been reproduced to show exactly what appears on the screen. Examples in languages other than English have been translated idiomatically by the authors of the book, who have, however, made no attempt to reproduce any linguistic errors that may appear in the original. Where we have added emphasis to the original messages, this is noted in the text.

1
Introduction

Public Internet forums: A neglected genre?

Public Internet discussion forums appear to offer limitless opportunities for communication across linguistic, geographical and cultural borders. Newspaper websites propose forums on a vast range of topics from current affairs to crosswords. More specialized sites provide the hobbyist or professional with discussion on everything from Fender guitars to giant pumpkin-growing to cardio-thoracic surgery. Whatever your penchant, Internet discussion proffers the prospect of interaction with people from around the world, in a myriad of languages.

This apparent wealth of possibilities for authentic language practice and intercultural contact was the starting point for this book. Clearly, public Internet discussion forums provide language teachers and learners with a valuable and accessible educational resource. Curiously, however, we found very few references to these vibrant cultural spaces in the literature on language learning and technology, and very little awareness of the possibilities for their pedagogical use. While language educators have been quick to take up some of the opportunities for intercultural contact provided by the Internet, notably learner-to-learner exchanges, the possibilities offered by public Internet discussion remain largely overlooked.

This neglect suggests that taking advantage of opportunities to move out of the classroom and become part of online communities in a foreign language may not be as straightforward as it at first appears. While asynchronous written communication online makes some things easier – from finding available interlocutors in the foreign language to consulting a verb table mid-sentence – it seems to exacerbate or produce other difficulties. For teachers and students of foreign languages and cultures, the issue is how to alleviate these and foster successful online participation. But simultaneously, the pitfalls and obstacles encountered allow us to plot the form of the problems and so elucidate more general questions of negotiating intercultural communication in an online environment.

The book has thus shaped itself around the question 'How is intercultural communication negotiated in online discussion?'

While the answers are of interest to those in many fields – from armchair travellers to managers of multinationals – we explore the particular implications for those in the business of teaching and learning intercultural communication, and specifically foreign language communication. In contradistinction, however, to many other studies of online communication in the area of language learning, our focus is not on learner-to-learner interaction. Rather, choosing a specific genre of computer-mediated communication (CMC) – discussion forums attached to media websites – we examine it as an authentic, culturally grounded practice. We study instances of intercultural communication on these sites, some of which involve self-identified learners, in order to derive principles of how such interaction actually takes place. It is only then that we can suggest some guidelines for teaching with and for the use of such sites. That is, our starting point will be understanding online discussion forums as cultural practices. Successful participation in such practices, we might hope, is that to which learners aspire.

In order to arrive at such an understanding, we must consider the interconnections between culture, genre and technology. While new information and communications technologies (ICTs) have made possible novel forms of human contact, the technologies of themselves do not determine the ways in which they are understood and exploited. Technological innovation is necessarily accompanied by cultural innovation as the technologies are appropriated by users and integrated into their repertoire of genres of communicative practices. Our project works at this interface between culture and technology, at the pivot points where cultures take up technological innovations, adapt them and adapt to them. It seeks to understand better the processes by which cultures modify existing genre-related and communicative conventions to accommodate new technologies and, conversely, put pressure on technological constraints to accommodate existing cultural practices. It is through understanding that uniformity of technology does not mean uniformity of cultural practice that we can start to understand some of the adaptations necessary when communicating interculturally online.

This brief introductory chapter outlines the book's scope and its usefulness to teachers of language and intercultural communication. It explains the methodology: a detailed ethnographic observation of the online discussion forums attached to media websites and the analysis of critical incidents, particularly in relation to intercultural communication. And it sets out the division of the book into two parts:

- *Part I (Chapters 2–4)* provides the theoretical basis for the book, analysing cultural differences in online communication and the ways in which they can be understood, and raising doubts as to whether these differences can be expected to disappear over time.
- *Part II (Chapters 5–10)* explores ways in which Internet discussion forums can be used to develop intercultural communication competence among language learners. We focus on specific examples of real learners using public Internet forums in a foreign language, and analyse the questions and difficulties that arise. From these very particular examples are elucidated principles which can be applied elsewhere, in other teaching/learning contexts.

Those readers whose interest is more in the area of cultural difference in engagement with emerging genres can read Part I before Part II. Those whose concern is predominantly pedagogical practice are invited to start with Part II, before turning back to Part I to investigate the underpinnings of the approaches advocated.

Public discussion sites

From the multiplicity of genres of CMC, we have selected public Internet discussion forums attached to media websites as our field of enquiry. Firstly, for reasons outlined below, the genre lends itself to the kind of interrogation necessary to answer our research questions. Secondly, and again for reasons which will be developed more fully later in this section, this is a genre of discussion to be recommended to learners and other interculturalists.

Media organizations today require a web presence and that presence typically involves some facility for readers to share their views. This may amount to little more than an electronic version of letters to the editor: a selection of messages is published on the website with very limited opportunity for discussion between contributors. The term 'discussion forum', however, usually indicates that reader-participants are able to post to an ongoing discussion, with the expectation that all messages compliant with site rules will be published. Across the sites surveyed and over the length of our study, forum rules vary (for example, with respect to contributions from non-subscribers; contributors' rights to start discussions and choose topics; the period during which a discussion is open or is available in read-only mode), but all the forums are characterized by asynchronous, threaded, publicly available discussion. While there may be official moderators, some of whom make their presence felt more than others, discussions are dominated by interactions between peers who do not represent the media organizations concerned. Similarly, the forums with which we are concerned do not feature question and answer sessions or debate with special guests or experts (although such discussions may be offered separately from 'reader' forums). Finally, it should be noted that although online newspapers have become multimodal, the public discussion forums they host remain resolutely text-based: they do not contain images, videos or audio-files. At the most, a participant may include a hyperlink to a page featuring multimedia in order to comment on it.

As would be expected, the 'core business' of such forums is the discussion of issues related to current affairs, and several of the sites studied make some explicit commitment to 'quality debate'. However, the extent to which contributions confine themselves to news-related topics varies, and indeed, some sites have shown changes over the period covered by this study. From our observations, it seems that for many publications the run-away success of the discussion forums entirely exceeded original expectations about the volume of messages which would be contributed. The profusion of postings clearly has become an issue to be managed, with not insignificant resource implications. Thus, we see some sites introducing a subscriber-only policy for contributors; attempts to enforce adherence to moderator-imposed topics; or, most radically, closure. User reaction to these changes, which ranges from the migration of discussion elsewhere to inventive attempts at flouting the rules is testament to the extent to which forum discussion has quickly established itself as a part of many lives.

Our investigation centres on high-profile Francophone and Anglophone discussion sites, particularly those of media organizations that might be considered logical ports of call for outsiders seeking cross-cultural contact (see Table 1.1). The postcolonial legacies of France and the UK ensure multicultural readerships for many of these sites, as does high immigration to the US. The status of French and English as international languages, and widely taught foreign languages, also encourages participation by non-native speakers. While regional spin-offs are

Table 1.1 Media sites monitored

	English language	**French language**
Newspaper and magazine sites	UK daily newspapers • *The Guardian • *The Independent	French daily newspapers • *Libération* • *Le Monde
	US daily newspapers • *New York Times* • *Washington Post*	French weekly magazines • *Le Nouvel Observateur*
Radio and television network sites	UK • *BBC	France • TF1 • M6

Note: The sites marked with an asterisk provide the bulk of the examples for discussion. *The Independent* no longer offers forums. The column headings 'English language' and 'French language' indicate the predominant or default language of the sites. Some accept contributions in other languages.

possible – *The Independent* readers organizing a face-to-face (FTF) meeting in Utrecht, for example – these localized subgroups are not typical. More visible are the disparate individuals with little in common bar a desire to communicate with others about matters of interest to them.

For teaching purposes and in terms of an investigation of culturally determined behaviour online, such media-site discussion facilities recommend themselves for a variety of reasons. Firstly, they are general interest forums hosting discussion on a wide range of topics between participants from a diversity of backgrounds and so very specifically subcultural norms are avoided in favour of more general patterns of usage. These highly visible sites attract a high turnover of participants, meaning that there is an ongoing process of initiation of new members, along with the observable instruction that initiation entails. More generally, the high volume of discussion provides a rich source of data. Furthermore, this discussion is archived (for at least a year in most cases) and therefore is available to the teacher, learner and researcher. Finally, these forums are in the public domain, which provides two sets of advantages. For the researcher, many of the usual ethical difficulties associated with studying interpersonal communication are avoided. For the language teacher, the use of these sites requires neither the creation of the discussion facility nor negotiations with online partners. Having justified our choice of sites, we now move on to look more closely at the use of such sites by language learners.

Public discussion sites and advanced learners

In terms of teaching and learning, public Internet discussion has much to offer more advanced language learners. The book will review some of the technical/procedural features of the sites, pointing out how they share the affordances of other non-FTF forms of CMC which have proved appealing to learners and teachers, principally the opportunity for 'authentic' communication with native speakers. Unlike the two modes of CMC dominating language learning, 'keypal' exchanges and web-based discussions between classes in different countries, the public discussion forum offers learners the opportunity to move beyond the relative shelter of activities designed specifically for them. Here they can engage with native speakers who are seeking interaction on topics of mutual interest: at any time of the day or night – in whatever time zone you happen to be – there are discussions available on an immensely varied set of topics. Extraordinary opportunities exist, therefore, for students to build on their own expertise and interests to engage with wider communities of target-language users, developing linguistic and rhetorical competences while also being exposed to other cultures' 'takes' on the topic of discussion and their points of reference in the debate. Finally, it is not only the prospects for learning of useful skills which advocate for the use of Internet discussion forums. Thorne (2006, p. 20) reminds us that 'for many students, performing competent identities in second and additional language(s) may now involve Internet-mediation as often as or more often than face-to-face and non-digital forms of communication'. The focus shifts from what you can learn through discussion on Internet forums to quite simply learning to participate in a widespread and popular cultural practice in another language.

Exploiting this potential is, however, not a matter of simply indicating addresses to students as if ignorance of specific URLs were the only barrier to successful participation in discussion. Differences in cultural conventions need to be intelligently negotiated for learners to make the most of the opportunities. What are the obstacles, how can they be surmounted and is it worth the effort? What do we need to teach our students, and how do we need to frame an activity in order for it to result in learning? Most importantly, what makes for successful engagement both in terms of acceptance by other participants and in terms of learning? These are questions which will be taken up in the second part of the book. In attempting to answer them for teachers and learners, we endeavour to encourage reflective practice, rather than to provide a tool kit of ready-made activities; exactly how instructors and learners engage with forums will depend on their particular objectives.

Throughout, rather than maintaining a neat division between forums for the general public and educational forums, the book shows how forums for the general public can be used for language learning. Rather than separating the sociological from the educational, the book shows how understanding the cultural conventions of a public Internet forum can become an important pedagogical task, with pay-offs for intercultural learning. Finally, rather than dividing instructed learning from non-institutional learning, the book focuses on the continuity of these situations, and the ways in which instructed learning can prepare students for effective non-institutional learning.

Approach and design of study

Our project is shaped by three main principles. Firstly, it is informed by contemporary theorizations of culture, genre, identity and difference. Secondly, we pay close attention to the ways in which Internet users represent their own practices and make sense of what they do, in order to study the cultural uptakes of the technology. Thirdly, the work is driven by a commitment to explore the practical consequences of our findings for educators and trainers. Our primary interest as teachers contemplating the use of forums for foreign language instruction was the idea of involving students in an accessible cultural practice. Successful involvement requires an understanding of how the chosen practice and intercultural communication function. Such an understanding can be gained only through observations of the forums in use.

Our approach combines elements of ethnography, cultural studies and discourse analysis. The method is dominated by a search for critical incidents in the lives of the forums studied. This provides the basis for qualitative analysis of predictably overlapping data sets related to the three themes which emerge as important: genre, identity and culture. A series of research assistants regularly monitored a total of a dozen public discussion sites from 2000 to 2004, with later updates from the authors, in search of such incidents (see Table 1.1).

A first source of data can be found in the site rules/user guides/codes of conduct, which are not part of the forums themselves but are published on the sites to regulate discussion: these are the official versions of how forum participation is construed and constructed. We are interested in moments when rules change, and how these changes are explained and justified. Our major data source is, however, the forums themselves and the contributions posted by discussants. Here discussion of the *genre* might take the form of

- *Explicit commentary on the appropriateness of contributions*: intervention by a moderator (official or self-appointed); identification and discussion of offensive behaviour; discussion of appropriate length, subject matter or style; mention of expectations regarding forms of debate; discussion of a forum's purpose.
- *Implicit commentary on appropriateness of contributions*: responding to a message but not engaging with its content.
- *Informal induction of newcomers to the forum by seasoned contributors*: explanation or justification of cultural/generic practices; attempts to make explicit unwritten conventions.
- *Comparisons made with other genres and situations*: is the forum seen to resemble a soapbox or a letters page, a café or a boxing ring, the French *Minitel* or SMS messaging?
- *Instances of protest or conflict*: site users explicitly react to changes in forum appearance/policy/function, and so on.

At the same time, an absence of commentary can also be significant: complete lack of engagement with a message suggests its unsuitability for the forum. On the other hand, if an apparently aberrant message attracts no comments on its non-standard nature, we can make some assumptions about tolerance of difference in discursive conventions, regarding, for example, digression, register (formality/informality), explicitness, framing of personal opinion, authority to speak on an issue.

Moments of negotiation of the appropriate forms of participation on the sites allow us to understand

- the ways generic conventions are adapted to cultural conventions of participants (cultural variation between apparently similar sites);
- the ways cultural conventions are adapted to suit the generic and material/technological constraints of Internet discussion platforms;
- the ways material/technological constraints are stretched by cultural and genre-related pressures;
- the ways particular forums are culturally and institutionally defined.

From our study it appears that one of the points of greatest difficulty for learners is that of personal *identity*, and its relations to the speaking positions created by the genre. For this reason, we collect data on the assertion, deployment and challenging of identity on the forums. The emergence of identity as a focus is unsurprising given that one of the often-cited differences of CMC with respect to FTF interactions is the apparent liberty the former provides where identity is concerned. The insistence with which these claims are made, and their at times startlingly revolutionary nature means that we will return to questions of identity repeatedly in the following chapters.

In particular, we are interested in clues to identity which lead us to view particular exchanges as *intercultural*. Identification relies on a combination of indicators such as non-native errors, speaking position, pseudonym and explicit self-identification (see Table 1.2).

Given widespread expectations about online fraudulence, it could be argued that our methods for determining cultural affiliation are unreliable: surely false claims about identity are easily made. However, problems of accurate identification are not limited to CMC and may occur in any study where researchers rely on their subjects' word. Conceding then, that we can never be entirely sure if (for example) 'Alain Rudaz' is who he says – 'a Frenchman living in the UK' (Independent Argument, 2003–2004) – the successful deployment of this persona nonetheless relies on accurately reproducing cultural and linguistic traits. These are so varied and numerous that it is often just as

Table 1.2 Indicators used to identify intercultural exchanges

Markers used to identify intercultural exchanges include

- *Explicit self-identification as a cultural outsider:* information provided on participant profiles; apologies for linguistic errors; questions as to the eligibility of foreigners as participants; expressions of ignorance of cultural practices.
- *Implicit self-identification:* speaking position, use of 'us' and 'them'.
- *Linguistic behaviour:* atypical language errors; use of non-standard language; use of a foreign language; comments on linguistic accuracy.
- *Cultural labelling by other participants:* for example, 'That's sooo Parisian!' 'You're clearly no Brit!'.
- *Names, pseudonyms.*
- *Knowledge of current affairs and cultural practices.*
- *Cultural allusions:* repertoires of assumed cultural knowledge.
- *Instances of miscomprehension of a message.*

difficult falsely to assume another cultural identity online as offline. The question of online fraudulence in a genre where participation is largely anonymous is discussed at length in Chapter 7.

Moving beyond the issue of purposeful deceit, it must still be admitted that none of our indicators is entirely trustworthy alone. Yet a cluster of such clues points to outsider status, even if the precise cultural affiliation may remain unclear. Now it is true that, in the absence of self-identification, an accomplished linguist may go unnoticed as a non-native speaker/writer. On the other hand, prolonged discussion can lead to disclosure of relevant personal experiences and other identifying information, enabling the study of communication between interlocutors of different cultures.

Focusing then on the specifically intercultural aspect of interactions, we can ask,

- When does cultural identity become an issue? How is it asserted, requested or challenged?
- Are there cultural patterns in strategies for dealing with intercultural interaction?

Working in the knowledge gap identified above with respect to intercultural communication online, our aim is not to deliver detailed descriptions of cybercultures associated with, say, *The Guardian* or *Libération* or even of Francophone or Anglophone online behaviour as discrete forms of practice. Rather, we choose to look at what happens when culture becomes an issue online. This, we imagined at the outset of our project, would manifest itself when cultural conventions clashed or were questioned, when cultural affiliation was invoked or challenged, that is, when cultures online had to deal with the intercultural. We therefore aimed to analyse the kinds of problems that arose and their consequences, whether and how they were resolved, and the role of other contributors (official or self-appointed moderators) in determining the outcome. What emerged, however, was a much lower rate of observable protracted intercultural exchange than we had anticipated. This can be explained through interactions between genre and culture and their effects on noticeability and frequency of intercultural communication.

Firstly, intercultural encounters may simply go unmarked and unnoticed, one reason for this being the way in which identity, including cultural identity, is deployed. In these discussion sites, revelation of personal detail tends to be used sparingly and strategically: successful exchange between participants of different intercultural origins does not necessarily require those origins being signalled or discussed.

Our data suggest, however, that it is not a mere matter of a hidden world of flourishing intercultural encounters. Despite the similarities listed above, these forums are ruled by very different cultural conventions. Getting to the stage of challenging cultural norms, spurring clashes and so on requires some form of participation. However, the nature of those differences may be enough to dampen keenness for cross-cultural excursions. To take but one example, that of message length, if your delight in debate lies in the exchange of witty brevities, you may be inclined to view 500-word contributions as boorish pontification. On the other hand, if what you value is thoughtful exposition, rapid-fire one-liners may smack of buffoonery and will certainly not seem interesting enough to encourage attempts at intercultural communication. Judging these differences by the standards of one's own culture and not seeing them as part of the intercultural experience sought will discourage participation.

And thirdly, our analyses will show that successful participation is rather more difficult than it appears at first glance for reasons to do with three recurrent themes which we have indicated above: genre, culture and the identities which learners are prepared to assert.

Preview of chapters

This book falls into two parts: the theoretically oriented Part I, where the aim is to arrive at a comparative cultural understanding of the genre of Internet discussion forums; and the more practice-oriented Part II, which seeks both to understand successful intercultural participation on the sites and to see how this understanding might facilitate successful forays into such discussion boards by advanced language learners. As stated earlier, Part I can be read before or after Part II depending on the reader's centre of interest.

Following the present introductory chapter, Chapter 2 offers a critical survey of the substantial amount of work on intercultural CMC which has emerged since 2000. It reveals divergent understandings of how these differences arise, how culture and technology interact and thus of the role culture plays in shaping online communication. Questioning these assumptions enables us to elaborate our understanding of 'culture' and our theoretical approach regarding the interaction between culture, genre and technology.

This approach is then applied in Chapter 3, a detailed cross-cultural study based on ethnographic observation of Internet discussion forums on four high-profile media sites (*Le Monde, Le Nouvel Observateur, The Guardian* and the BBC). Significant differences in the cultural conventions of communication are revealed. However, and crucially, these differences are not simply predictable from a knowledge of other French and British communicative practices. Rather, we find different cultures using different generic templates as a basis for participation. Data from the period when the Internet discussion forum was still relatively new allow us to witness first hand the negotiation of cultural practices, particularly in contributors' explicit commentary on their participation. And in the complex interaction between cultural, technical and contextual constraints, we see new, culturally specific ways of communicating emerge from more established genres, leading to an understanding of the means by which cultural differences arise in supposedly global forms.

But has Internet discussion use evolved since its rather self-conscious early use? Chapter 4 examines the evolution of online practices and, specifically, the hypothesis that the passage of time will see the convergence of cultural conventions: perhaps cultures started out engaging differently with the technology, but exposure to these other practices through the cross-cultural communication they make possible has dulled difference? Returning to the French and British media websites mentioned in Chapter 3, we see that while there has been change over the five years of our study (in response to the huge success of the discussion facilities and rise of other online genres such as blogs), this has not had the effect of erasing cultural difference.

Internet discussion forums therefore remain sites of vibrant and lively practice which appear to offer limitless opportunities for communication across linguistic, geographical and cultural borders. We thus turn in the second part of the book to the question of language learners and intercultural Internet discussion. Chapter 5 considers the uptake of Internet-based technologies in foreign language education, and discusses the additional possibilities offered by public Internet discussion forums, their distinguishing features and specific affordances, along with potential obstacles to their use. The chapter also functions as an introduction to a series of case studies of learner-participants on discussion forums in the following chapters.

Chapter 6 goes to the heart of the topic of language learners online, presenting a case study of four self-identified cultural 'outsiders' on the forums of *Le Monde*. The two participants who attempt to deploy the rules of many tandem/telecollaboration partnerships – introduce oneself and invite language practice – are rather less successful in gaining acceptance as forum members than two other outsiders who position themselves as debaters. Whereas the earlier chapters made theoretical points about the importance of genre for understanding cultural practices, this case study shows the practical application of these ideas by forum users, whose commentary to our newcomers relies on mutually defining notions of genre and culture. We also see successful participation critically dependent on engagement with the aims and conventions of forum discussion. Neither language proficiency nor overtures of friendship (often the priorities in learner exchanges) will compensate for a failure to do so.

Chapter 7 pursues more thoroughly the question of self-positioning raised in Chapter 6, exploring the ways in which identity is constructed and used. Using examples of 'identity challenges', we suggest that the identity which can be asserted on a forum is bound up with the genre's stakes and that when debate takes hold, these are about making a case. That is, identity becomes a tool used to prove a point. Noting how rarely the type of self-presentation inculcated in language classes is used in online debate, we suggest ways of alerting learners to alternative, more strategic modes of self-description. Such exploration of speaking positions not only enables them to engage productively in online intercultural discussion but also develops their interactional skills in a second language.

Successful use of identity in online intercultural discussion is however no simple matter. Chapter 8 will show independent learners on a 'learner site' so obsessed with their status as language novices that rather than talk the language they would prefer to talk about it. Unable to imagine other ways of being in their new language, they elect practice, in the sense of rehearsal, over performance. We explain this in terms of default speaking positions. While they exert a powerful attraction because so obviously available, they are not necessarily the most useful for sustained and enriching intercultural contact. If learners are to survive beyond the sheltered waters of learner-only sites, they need more flexibility in the way they position themselves. Analysis of a prolonged and productive intercultural discussion on one of the forums of *The Independent* shows speakers positioning and repositioning themselves in response to the postings of other contributors. The interactional strategies identified provide a model for successful intercultural communication in general.

Chapter 9 reports on an advanced university-level French course, implementing the principles for teaching suggested by preceding analyses. Following discussion of the integration of forum participation into the course, the alignment of assessment requirements with the forum genre and the description of preparatory tasks, the chapter focuses on the responses students received to the messages they posted, and the intercultural and linguistic lessons available from this feedback. Particular attention is paid to the need to train students to recognize and learn from the feedback offered. Finally, suggestions are made regarding the application of the pedagogical principles to other teaching contexts.

In the last decade, the focus of research in language learning and technology has shifted from an emphasis on improving language proficiency to a concern for simultaneously developing interactional and intercultural competence. Part of this shift has been a new focus on identity issues, with identity seen as mediating the communicative practices of language learners online. Chapter 10, which concludes the book, stresses the opportunities provided by public Internet discussion forums for developing awareness and skills in all these areas.

Wider applications of this study

If new technologies merely connect up people who are unequipped to manage communication appropriately, their potential remains unrealized. While widespread access to the Internet opens up intercultural contact to new groups of users, this ease of access gives the illusory impression that intercultural communication online is similarly unproblematic. We assume that 'they' will just be like us online, ignoring the possibility of cultural variation. This book suggests that we ignore such variation at our peril.

One site for learning about cultural variation in communicative practices should be the language classroom. And while our most pedagogically oriented chapter, Chapter 9, takes as its context tertiary language courses, this is certainly not the only place where this project can be applied, particularly in a context of increasing globalization. The lessons of this book could, for example, find their place in modules on intercultural CMC built into business training courses.

Although we are working in our languages of expertise, benefits are not limited to French–Anglophone relations: our case studies in these international languages involve a range of cultural backgrounds and the principles elucidated are of wide application. For example, interlocutors who might have confidently supposed that all participants in online negotiations model their messages on verbal interaction may learn to look for clues in others' postings to see if this is indeed the case, or whether instead the expectation is that intelligent contributions should be patterned on writing. Sensitized to issues such as degrees of formality, optimal lengths of contribution and inclusion of the personal, online communicators will be equipped to relativize 'atypical' online communication patterns in terms of other standards of culturally appropriate behaviour rather than as negative individual traits (such as overfamiliarity, pomposity, standoffishness, rudeness). While work exists on cultural difference in many other aspects of intercultural contact, its inflection of CMC is rarely if ever discussed in intercultural training manuals.

In elucidating these dynamics, the book contributes to our understanding of communication in an era of globalization. The utopian discourse of the borderless world predicts that ease of communication through shared technologies will erase cultural difference. Studying intercultural Internet exchanges gives the lie to this myth.

Part I
Cultural Differences Online

2
Culture and Online Communication

Intercultural CMC: A nascent field of research

Approaching the year 2000, a chorus of complaints arose about the lack of research on intercultural CMC. Jarvenpaa and Leidner's (1998) lament that '[w]hile there is a wealth of research on computer-mediated communication and research on cross-cultural communication, there is a paucity of research on cross-cultural computer-mediated communication' was echoed by Hart (1998); Kim, Hearn, Hatcher, and Weber (1999, p. 144); Ess (2001, p. 9); St Amant (2002, p. 212); and in Herring's (2001a) evaluation that 'there has been little scholarship that evaluates critically the effects of computer networking on the world's cultures' (p. viii).

By the late 1990s, cultural studies scholars were producing a wealth of detailed research on Internet practices, on topics such as cybercultures and subcultures, the formation of online communities, online identities, race, gender, class, sexuality and (dis)ability in cyberspace, and cyberdemocracy.[1] There was, however, relatively little work available on what happens when participants do not seek to belong to the same 'imagined community' (Anderson, 1983) but attempt to engage with 'the other'. Despite the much touted opportunities to communicate with other cultures through CMC, the bulk of research at that time focused on Internet exchanges occurring primarily within rather than across cultures. Meanwhile, research in Computer-Assisted Language Learning (CALL) was primarily focused on facilitating networked contact between students and devising tasks for their language development rather than on questions of culture.

The situation has changed radically since the turn of the millennium, with a rapid increase in scholarly attention devoted to intercultural

CMC from a number of disciplines, primarily second-language learning, business communication and cultural studies. Early impetus to this nascent and much needed field of investigation was provided in 1998 by the first of the biennial CATaC conferences (*Cultural Attitudes towards Technology and Communication*), and since 2002 we have witnessed a veritable explosion of research in the area, with special issues in a number of prominent journals devoted to CMC across and between cultures.[2]

Clearly this rapid expansion of research has occurred due to increasing recognition that simply making keyboard contact with people from other cultures – whether students of another language background, employees in an overseas office, potential business partners or visitors to a corporate website – is insufficient to ensure effective communication.

The aim of this chapter is to sift through the research to date on culture and Internet-based CMC, not only exploring the kinds of cultural differences to be found in online communication, but also analysing this work to discover the underlying conceptions of the role of culture in cyberspace. For the studies reveal a variety of conflicting assumptions about the way in which culture and technology interact, assumptions that in turn inform communicative practice, business practice and teaching practice.

The role of culture in Internet communication: Conflicting views

Is our use of the Internet independent of culture, determined above all by technological factors? Or do cultural factors come into play? If so, does Internet communication reflect the cultural background of the user or of the designer of the technology? Does it give unfiltered access to other cultures? Or does the Internet itself have a culture? Does it flatten or accentuate cultural difference between users? Do cultural conventions determine Internet use? Or is there a more complex interaction between cultural and technological constraints?

These are the questions raised by the literature, sometimes explicitly, sometimes through unexamined assumptions. We rehearse the major lines of thought below and explore their implications.

The borderless world: The Internet removes cultural difference

Early utopian visions suggested that the Internet constituted a culture-free zone, a space where old rules and identities could be left behind. This view was epitomized by the celebrated 1993 cartoon by Peter

Steiner in the *New Yorker*, in which a dog at a keyboard claimed that 'On the Internet, nobody knows you're a dog.' Rheingold (1993), Negroponte (1995), and Turkle (1995) provided enthusiastic academic elaborations of this hypothesis, according to which Internet communication is disembodied and independent of human conventions, a liberation from familiar constraints:

> You can be whoever you want to be. You can completely redefine yourself if you want. You don't have to worry about the slots other people put you in as much. They don't look at your body and make assumptions. They don't hear your accent and make assumptions. All they see are your words.
>
> (Turkle, 1995, p. 184)

It turns out, of course, that words can be very revealing of one's identity, and particularly of cultural identity, as more recent research demonstrates only too clearly.[3]

The supposed erasure of national boundaries has led to the popular metaphor of the 'borderless world' of global communication, which gives the impression of unrestricted access to our cultural others, without the encumbrance of passports, immigration controls and customs procedures.[4] But although the Internet notionally transcends national and cultural boundaries, as soon as communication occurs, cultural practices and values are necessarily activated. However malleable the limits are, we do not leave our values and attitudes, our turns of phrase, our judgements of appropriateness, behind at the logon screen. Internet users are therefore still likely to have to contend with customs of the social kind, and we should remain suspicious of the idea of the removal of cultural difference.

Superhighway to the other: The Internet gives direct access to cultural difference

The goal of many who log on is direct and instant access to other cultures, with the Internet serving as the superhighway to cultural difference. While physical boundaries may be irrelevant, the existence of cultural borders continues to be asserted. This impulse has been particularly strong in educational contexts (language learning, business communication) as the rationale behind courses aimed at diversifying students' cultural experiences. A typical example of the discourse from 1990s research reads,

By using the Internet and the World Wide Web (WWW), students can have almost instantaneous access to a range of foreign experiences in their target language. The computer then serves as a gateway to the virtual foreign world where 'real people' are using real language in 'real context'.

(Osuna & Meskill, 1998, pp. 71–72)

Ironically, however, an assumption of cultural sameness often prevails despite the eagerness for alterity. The contradiction plays out as follows: through CMC we have access to our linguistic and/or cultural other, but this other is assumed to be doing the same thing as we are – chatting, debating, courting, negotiating – in the same way. The cultural aspect of communication is restricted to the message content, as participants swap information about their respective countries, and the question of cultural difference shaping CMC conventions does not arise. Early CALL research on the use of email, with its focus on providing learners with opportunities for language practice, abounds with examples of this approach (for example, Gunske von Kölln & Gunske von Kölln, 1997; Wong, 1995).

Unlike the discourse of the borderless world, in which the technology was seen to override cultural factors in determining communicative practice, here the entire communication process becomes a transparent conduit, and neither technology nor culture is seen to inflect it. Although giving access to other cultures, CMC is once again assumed to be culture-free.

Internet culture: The Internet imposes a culture

An apparently contradictory view to that of the Internet as culture-free is the idea of the Internet as a culture in itself. In fact, these two positions have something in common, in that both assume the flattening out of cultural difference within cyberspace. The culture identified may be multifarious (Scheuermann & Taylor, 1997) or in flux (Johnston & Johal, 1999), but is still seen as sufficiently unified to be described as 'Internet culture'. Using Hofstede's (1980) terminology, Johnston and Johal describe this culture as characterized by low power distance, low uncertainty avoidance, and moving from collectivism towards individualism. Evans (1998) describes it as non-hierarchical, decentralized and based on the principle that information should be available to all. From this basis, he is able to explain such phenomena as the comparatively slow initial uptake of the Internet in France by an apparent incompatibility between Internet culture and French national and corporate culture. Although reference is made in these articles either to the large proportion of US users of the technology at this time or to its US origins, Internet culture itself is seen as universal.

Other researchers who see the Internet as having a culture do not view it as non-aligned with respect to national cultures. Reeder, Macfadyen, Roche and Chase (2004) argue that the values of Western industrialized societies are embedded in the whole conception and functioning of the Internet, and in the design of various Internet-based communications platforms. They observe that

> the communicative space or platform created by the Internet is not a culturally neutral or value-free space in which culturally diverse individuals communicate with equal ease.
>
> (p. 91)

This is – they suggest – because the technical constraints of the Internet embody the cultural values of its creators (Anglo-American engineers and scientists) in promoting 'communications characterized by speed, reach, openness, quick response, questions/debate and informality' (2004, pp. 91–92). Similarly, Dragona and Handa contend that the logic and navigation of hypertext links reflect Anglophone thought processes (2000, p. 53) such that '[t]he Web [...] is not a neutral space, either rhetorically or culturally' (p. 69).

Like Reeder et al., St Amant (2002) points out the potential for culture clash between existing Internet culture and those unfamiliar with it: dominant online practices are derived from US mores to which other cultures will be able to adapt with greater or lesser success. Potential sources of cross-cultural difficulty in online communication include explicitness, assertiveness, lack of status cues and use of humour. The ideal of the borderless world, however, dies hard. His suggested solution to cross-cultural confusion – the rapid introduction of an international online protocol (his comparison is with Aviation English) – is effectively a plea for enforcement of a supposedly culturally neutral cyberspace.

Considerably less cheered by the prospect of online uniformity is Ess, for whom the Western cultural values embedded in CMC technologies give rise to a form of 'computer-mediated colonization' that threatens to 'impos[e...] a specific set of cultural values and communicative preferences upon diverse cultures' (2002, p. 12). He is not entirely pessimistic, however, noting that it is possible for these cultures to 'resist and reshape' Western technologies (p. 12).

The idea that Internet technology embodies and imposes particular norms and values is, then, not simply – or not always – a form of technological determinism. For several of these writers, CMC does not elide culture, but, due to its cultural origins, favours certain communicative practices. Cultural difference still comes into play in the clash between a dominant Internet culture and the cultural conventions of diverse Internet users. There is considerable variation, however, in the extent to which they consider this clash able to 'resist and reshape', to lead to transformation and variation in the way the technology is used. There is thus a certain area of overlap between proponents of this view and those of the following one.

Internet communication is shaped by culture

Remedying the previous lack of scholarly interest in the subject, since 2000 a large body of research has accumulated, focusing on the ways in which various cultures approach and communicate via the Internet. The research ranges from broad applications of intercultural theory to analysis of the impact of very local factors. It includes both cross-cultural studies (comparisons of online practices) and intercultural studies (analyses of online interactions between people from different backgrounds) to highlight differences and potential sources of intercultural misunderstandings. Cultural differences are identified in attitudes to particular technologies, in overarching values such as individualism, in discursive strategies such as those for expressing disagreement, and in the manner in which particular online affordances (such as subject lines, layout, images) are adopted and adapted in different cultural environments.[5]

Table 2.1 provides an overview of the themes and orientation of the research to date regarding the wide variety of ways in which cultural difference is manifested in CMC. The bulk of the research tabled concerns text-based CMC, and the cultures investigated reflect the concerns of researchers in language learning and business communication, with a predominance of data from Europe, Western Anglophone countries (the US, Canada, Australia) and East Asia (Japan, Korea, China). Clearly, for these writers, standardized technology does not mean standardized communication practices (cf. Chase et al., 2002).

At their very broadest, cultural differences are identified in attitudes towards ICTs and the purposes for which they might be used. Comparisons are made of predispositions towards ICTs such as email or videoconferencing and towards technological innovation generally. These attitudes are in turn related to whether particular technologies are used widely by students/employees/the general public, or whether they continue to have novelty value.

Differences in approaches to Internet communication tools are discussed by Zorn (2005) in terms of 'technology scripts', assumptions about how technologies are to be used, by whom and for what purpose. These are infinitely varied. For example, among such scripts identified by Miller and Slater (2000) is the use of personal home pages by Trinidadians to educate the world about their nation and expand its reputation. In other Cultural Studies research, Morris and Meadows (2004) describe how the Internet is being used to perpetuate traditional knowledge by indigenous Australians.

Much research from the field of Communications focuses on correlations between online communication and the kinds of patterns in cultural behaviour described by intercultural theorists such as E. T. Hall and Geert Hofstede. Koeszegi, Vetschera and Kersten (2004), for example, analyse the extent to which business negotiation simulations carried out by students using a web-based support platform reflect differences between high-context and low-context cultures as defined by Hall (1976). They find that 'users from high-context cultures exchange significantly more messages and offers during negotiations than users from low-context cultures' (p. 79). On the other hand, in keeping with a task-centred approach, students from low-context cultures use the platform's analytical support tools considerably more than their counterparts from high-context cultures. Hofstede's (1980) dimensions of culture provide a basis for Kim and Papacharissi's (2003) analysis of Korean and US personal home pages. Self-presentation in the former is realized through links to special interests and through manipulated graphics, while the US pages offer a more direct and personal presentation of the self together with still pictures. These differences are interpreted as manifestations of collectivism and individualism respectively.

The issue of directness of communication is repeatedly raised in research, in particular with regard to emails, where the absence of non-verbal cues can make directness appear even balder, and asynchronous turn-taking often means a considerable delay before any adjustment can be made in response to feedback. Differences in approaches to expressing criticism and disagreement and in ways of obtaining information are common sources of intercultural misunderstanding in both business and student emails. Belz (2003) demonstrates this in her linguistic analysis of an email exchange between German and American students. She compares the frequency of positive and negative appraisals, and the ways in which opinions are softened or intensified, to explain why the

German participants were seen as confrontational and the Americans as non-committal.

Analyses of directness often lead to discussion of the understanding of the relationship being developed online. An important question here concerns expectations about the extent to which communication will be centred on accomplishing a particular task or will incorporate a personal/affective element. Kramsch and Thorne (2002) show that even understanding of the task (of discussion, for example) can differ widely between cultures in the extent to which it includes the personal. They analyse a student email exchange on a film portraying urban youth, and the disappointment experienced by both parties when the French messages consist of dispassionate, factual arguments while those of the American students are characterized by emotional identification and reference to personal experience.

A related set of questions concerns attitudes towards self-disclosure: what counts as personal information; to whom and in what circumstances it is appropriate to reveal such information; and what disclosure indicates about the nature of the relationship. The issue is linked with notions of private/public space and arises with respect to email communication, discussion boards, personal home pages, and in studies of student, business and personal/romantic exchanges. Reeder et al. (2004) discuss Canadian Aboriginal, non-Aboriginal and immigrant perceptions of these issues and their effect on online participation in a distance adult education course. They contrast culturally inflected modes of student self-presentation, which in their examples range from resume-style to genealogical, and note the indigenous students' reluctance to communicate with facilitators publicly online.

There is a particular focus on the evolution of online relationships in email exchanges among language learners, where the investment in the relationship is seen as crucial to the success of intercultural learning. Misinterpretation of a factual message or of a slow reply as unfriendly, or of an off-topic message as indicative of a lack of interest or commitment can lead to the partnership becoming unworkable. All too often, the mediating distance of email enables learners to retreat from participation, with negative stereotypes of the other culture reinforced by the experience. Belz (2001, 2002, 2003, 2005), Belz and Müller-Hartmann (2003), Ware (2005), Ware and Kramsch (2005), Thorne (2003), Kramsch and Thorne (2002) and O'Dowd (2006) all analyse examples of such miscommunication between language students and the consequences for both the online relationship and the image of the partner's culture that is retained.

The wealth of research outlined above and in Table 2.1 all seems to point in the same direction: towards the conclusion that cultural differences in CMC are profound and wide-ranging. On closer examination, however, we once again find divergent understandings of how these differences arise, and thus of the role culture plays in shaping online communication.

Cultural differences are replicated online

We discussed earlier the perspective of 'technological determinism', whereby technology is seen to determine communication to such an extent that cultural difference is erased online and Internet practices are universal. At the opposite extreme we find a form of cultural determinism, whereby culture is the overriding factor in determining communication, and technology becomes transparent. This translates into the idea that pre-existing cultural differences simply reappear online, and that CMC mirrors FTF communication in, for example, formality, rhetorical strategies and underlying values. Thus, in early examples of research, Coverdale-Jones (1998) applies Hofstede's dimensions of culture to CMC in broad-brush fashion, and Chen (1998) sees the expression styles of various cultures (linearity, directness, low context and so on) as dictating participation in email debate. Broad national tendencies are used to explain the differences observed, and 'culture bumps' (Archer, 1986) that occur online are simply virtual versions of FTF mismatches in cultural expectations.

From this point of view, Internet communication is understood to be inflected by pervasive norms of cultural behaviour, whilst the reverse – the impact of the mode of communication on this behaviour – is dismissed. Cultural practices are understood to be directly transferred into cyberspace.

Cultural conventions are manifested online in modified form

In fact, the above is rarely found in extreme form. Instead we commonly find the view that while CMC conforms to more general tendencies in cultural behaviour, these are modified – either quantitatively or qualitatively – to fit the exigencies of the medium. Here CMC is still seen as following wider cultural patterns, but the impact of technology is recognized to a greater or lesser extent. This impact ranges from a filtering effect to a transformation.

Cultural conventions are filtered by CMC. One strand of thought sees CMC as filtering out certain aspects of cultural behaviour. From this perspective, inconsistencies between Internet and FTF communication are due to the 'reduced social dimension' (Coverdale-Jones, 1998) or 'restricted channels of communication' (Rice, 1996, pp. 61–62) of CMC: in other words, the text-based nature of the exchanges in question is understood to limit the aspects of behaviour that are culturally determined. There is no face, nor tone of voice, nor gesture. With no non-verbal cues evident, there will be fewer ways for cultural difference to emerge. CMC is seen to resemble FTF communication – without the faces.

For some, the filtering of cultural practices by CMC results in a tendency towards greater uniformity than in FTF communication. Others suggest that it may have the opposite effect, magnifying cultural differences. St Amant (2002), for example, proposes that 'such technology, in its removal of more traditional communication obstacles such as distance and time, may amplify cultural rhetorical differences' (p. 196), while Murray (2000a) points out that these two positions are not incompatible, that CMC 'amplifies some characteristics of communication and reduces others' (p. 407).

According to the 'filter' hypothesis, then, aspects of cultural difference may be dampened or exaggerated by CMC, but to a large extent still mirror broader cultural patterns. The difference is above all a quantitative one, rather than a qualitative one.

Discussion.   Let us dwell for a moment on the idea of reduced channels of communication in CMC, and especially text-based CMC. In the eyes of many, this reduction results in simplification: online communication is not different in kind, but deficient; it is the skim milk to the full cream richness of FTF communication. This widespread view is associated with 'social presence theory' and the work of Short, Williams and Christie (1976) on 'reduced social cues', and with Daft and Lengel's (1984) 'media richness theory', according to which FTF communication is the richest form of human communication in terms of the types of information that can be transmitted via the medium, while text-based forms such as email rank well below. Both these theories suggest that CMC results in a lack of relational information and thus impersonal messages.

But is text-based communication necessarily lacking or impersonal? Literary genres are rarely thought of in this way. And is it unfailingly enriched by extra channels? A cursory comparison of novels and their film adaptations would suggest not.

Challenges to the discourse of CMC's poverty of expression have been mounted along the lines that users will adapt creatively to the material constraints of CMC in order to afford themselves the range of expressive possibilities they require. Here Walther's (1992, 1996) work stands out. He outlines ways in which relational messages are encoded in text-based CMC, both verbally and through textual mechanisms such as typographical manipulations, spatial arrangements, non-standard spellings and emoticons (1992, pp. 79, 82, and we could add use of font and colour and pictorial representations of one's online identity to the list). These have resulted in new stylistic conventions. Herring (1999) similarly emphasizes the capacity of users to devise alternative means of communicating information – signalling listenership and negotiating turn-taking, for instance – that do not rely on non-verbal channels. In addition, 'some users exploit the potential of loosened coherence [between messages] for the purposes of play and to enjoy intensified interactivity', using the less transient nature of CMC to 'extend the limits of what is possible in spoken conversation'.

Like Herring, Walther points to areas where CMC can exceed the capacity of FTF communication. He argues that in some cases the absence of physical proximity in CMC facilitates the idealization of one's interlocutor, leading to 'hyperpersonal communication', which 'surpasses normal interpersonal levels' (1996, p. 3). In this way, 'not only do CMC senders overcome the limits of the media to express personal cues, they may actually do so in ways that FtF communicators cannot' (1996, p. 19).

In a similar vein, Raybourn (1997) maintains that 'computer-based environments may provide a richer communication medium in certain contexts than face-to-face interaction', and refers specifically to the capacity of simulation games to 'facilitat[e] more truthful communication while minimizing player risk and emotional discomfort' during exploration of potentially threatening topics.

These contestations of the 'filter model' support the next hypothesis: the idea that cultural conventions, like relational cues, will emerge online in ways adapted to that environment, and remodelled to fit the medium.

Cultural values and conventions are expressed in qualitatively different ways in CMC environments. According to this view, the constraints of CMC impact on cultural practices in ways other than simply dampening or amplifying them: the affordances of the technology include new means of expression of cultural values and conventions. For example, we can see in Sugimoto and Levins' (2000) discussion of Japanese email conventions the suggestion that signature files allow users new ways to indicate their status (pp. 141–142). Kim and Papacharissi (2003) explore the ways in which values such as individualism and collectivism can be expressed on a personal home page (types of graphics, use of links). And Würtz (2005) looks at the ways in which high- and low-context communication strategies are manifested through the use of visuals. Using Hall's (1976) categorization of cultures, she compares McDonald's websites across the world, and finds that those from countries categorized as high context tend to use more imagery and animation and less text than low-context cultures. They also use imagery differently: picturing products together with people rather than in isolation, and reflecting collectivist pastimes such as family gatherings rather than individual leisure activities and lifestyles. Moreover, their layout is more layered, less linear, with more menus and sidebars, inviting exploratory rather than goal-oriented navigation.

Discussion.   In the positions outlined thus far regarding the ways in which culture shapes Internet practices, there is an assumption of the consistency and predictability of cultural differences across the full range of modes of communication. In the examples of the positions 'Cultural differences are replicated online' and 'Cultural conventions are manifested online in modified form' explained above, cultural values and practices may be reproduced, attenuated, amplified or otherwise modified to fit the online environment, but remain recognizably an extension of their FTF counterparts, tending unquestionably in the same direction. This view is aligned with branches of intercultural theory, evoked above, that classify cultures in terms of poles of behaviour such as individualism or collectivism (Hofstede, 1980), low- or high-context communication (Hall, 1976), monochronism or polychronism (Hall, 1976). Thus cultures categorized as collectivist are expected to manifest collectivism online in one way or another.

This assumption has also been influential in areas of education where Internet exchanges are used to teach languages and intercultural communication. An indication of the scale of this activity is the success of Internet services such as the *International Tandem Network, Intercultural E-mail Classroom Connections, ePALS Classroom Exchange* and *The Mixxer*, which link prospective 'key-pal' partners (both individuals and school and university classes of various ages and levels). This extensive teaching practice often looks upon CMC as training for in-country encounters, assuming its intercultural lessons to be generally applicable, as exemplified in Rice's (1996) statement that '[t]hough International and intercultural e-mail encounters are no substitute for study-abroad and person-to-person cross-cultural experiences, they can play a powerful role in bringing such encounters into the classroom' (p. 60). A two-way extrapolation operates here: teachers expect wider cultural norms to manifest themselves online, and students expect what they learn online to apply to other modes of encounter.

At first glance, this assumption seems self-evident. It seems to go without saying, for example, that a culture that values directness will tend to communicate directly online. As we stated at the outset, we do not put aside our values and judgements, our habits of thought and language, when we seat ourselves before a computer screen. The equation is, however, complicated by several factors.

Firstly, cultures are internally diverse, not only in terms of people but also in terms of practices. Most obviously, individuals of a given cultural background are not uniformly indirect/status-conscious/polychronic, but, equally, particular cultural practices and contexts vary in the directness, power distance, time orientation and so on that is required or considered appropriate. The studies by Hofstede (1980) and Hall (1976), although ground-breaking in their identification of dimensions of difference, involved a certain amount of stereotyping. But while Hall makes blanket generalizations about French/German/Japanese patterns of high- and low-context communication, these concepts can be used in more nuanced fashion. Gallois and Callan (1997), for example, do not take entire national cultures to be high or low context, instead holding that specific cultural practices tend towards one or the other (pp. 44–50).[6] Thus higher- or lower-context communication strategies will be called for in different situations in a given culture (such as a family dinner, school classroom, medical consultation, business negotiation, news interview). Similarly, individualism will not be equally evident in all pursuits in a highly individualistic culture. And even Hall (1976, p. 19) suggests that there are pockets of polychronicity (inherent in jobs such as newspaper editor) in otherwise monochronic cultures.

Clearly not all regularities in cultural practice are variable to the same extent: cultural values (such as respect for age) can be quite pervasive, while certain conventions (such as salutations) can appear relatively arbitrary. Nonetheless, not even the most entrenched value is a factor to the same extent and intensity in all situations. Thus culture is not a calculable force exerting uniform pressure on communication in predictable ways across contexts.

If we relate this argument to our topic of investigation, we see that online cultural practices will similarly show variation in cultural conventions. Wikipedia authoring, business emails and online dating, for example, are unlikely to manifest the same degree or form of collectivism, directness and self-disclosure, and their participation patterns and politeness rituals are unlikely to coincide. And although some of these online practices may be predictable from their offline counterparts, others are specific to CMC: for example, corporate websites, personal home pages, personal blogs, email discussion lists, Internet forums, email language exchanges (tandem learning), instant messaging, and web-based audio- and video-conferencing. That is to say, they are not simply pre-existing practices that have been transferred online. Equally, however, they are not completely alien to existing forms of communication. How, then, do cultural conventions (regarding, for example, directness, explicitness, power distance, uncertainty avoidance, rhetorical patterns) arise in these online genres? If we accept that cultures comprise diverse practices with different sets of conventions, how can we predict *which* cultural patterns will be salient in a given computer-mediated environment?

Further complicating the dynamic, we find a variety of local pressures (institutional, personal, economic, material) specific to a given interaction and impinging on the way it plays out. This brings us to explorations of a further hypothesis we identify in the research into cultural differences online.

Online cultural conventions result from the complex interaction of multiple factors

A relatively small number of writers problematize the interface between culture and technology. Zorn asks, 'In which areas does the provided technology interfere with users' culturally diverse expectations and communication styles?' (2005, p. 10). Ulijn and Lincke (2004) flesh out this question in relation to negotiating practices:

> How do CMC and FTF contribute to a win-win strategy in negotiation? How do CMC and FTF affect the participants' ability to empathize with each other? Are the negotiation strategies of Anglo, Nordic, and Latin negotiators affected differently depending on the medium? Is the ability of Anglo, Nordic, and Latin negotiators to empathize with each other affected differently depending on the medium?
>
> (p. 111)

This is a considerably more complex set of questions than those assuming that CMC can be extrapolated from communication in other contexts. The study compares negotiation simulations by students exchanging messages via a negotiation support system with those carried out FTF. Rather than finding that CMC has a consistent effect on negotiating styles (for example, more or less empathetic), it shows that the negotiating styles of cultural groups are affected differently by the online environment (p. 130). Specifically, it identifies greater use in CMC negotiations of 'we' and of cooperative speech acts (admit, confirm, show goodwill) among the 'Anglo' participants; of 'you' and of general speech acts (explain, request, suggest) among the 'Nordic' participants; and of 'I' and non-cooperative speech acts (criticize, object) among the 'Latin' participants.

On the one hand, the authors attribute the differences between CMC and FTF negotiations to the need to compensate for the 'lack of audio and visual channels' (p. 116) in CMC. On the other hand, the compensation strategies are seen to be different for each cultural group. Thus CMC does not affect negotiation styles in a uniform manner; it does not simply increase or decrease expressions of cooperativeness or empathy.

These findings demonstrate the complexity of the combined effects of culture and technology on negotiating strategies, and the resulting unpredictability. Using Hofstede's (1980) scores, Ulijn and Lincke at first hypothesize that participants from the more collectivist Latin cultures may show more cooperative strategies online than the Anglo/Nordic ones (p. 116); however, their results indicate the contrary. They interpret these results as correlating with Hofstede's categories of 'masculine' (competitive) and 'feminine' (affiliating) cultures, and not determined by individualism and collectivism as anticipated.

The important point here is that while cultural differences play a determining role online, it is not clear *which* cultural tendencies will be salient in a given computer-mediated environment; thus we can expect the results to differ when the medium varies. Ulijn and Lincke's article shows that while there are connections between cultural conventions in FTF and CMC behaviour, these are not straightforward, and the latter is not simply predictable from the former.

Again indicating that cultural values do not necessarily map neatly onto CMC, Ulijn, O'Hair, Weggeman, Ledlow and Hall (2000) ponder whether text-based Internet communication automatically privileges low-context (explicit) communication, as is often suggested, or whether indeed it may equally well support high-context communicative strategies, for example in allowing one time to think before writing and reading, as Nishiguchi (1997) argues (Ulijn et al., 2000, p. 305). Similarly open to the notion of a more complex interplay between culture and communicative medium are Setlock, Fussell and Neuwirth (2004) in their investigations of perceptions of 'quality' in negotiations via instant messaging.

In both the articles cited above, Ulijn and his colleagues take their cue from an early paper by Ma (1996), which, although it rehearses some of the hypotheses developed above, has been taken up by others in ways that problematize the idea of any simple correspondence between CMC and FTF communication.

Ma analyses interviews with US and East Asian (principally Chinese, Korean and Taiwanese) students about their experiences of intercultural Internet relay chat. Both the Asian and the American students felt that they had revealed more of themselves online than they were accustomed to and adopted a more direct and explicit style because of the medium. The American students, however, still felt that their Asian interlocutors had communicated indirectly and avoided talking about themselves (pp. 182–183). We can conclude that their communication style was more direct than usual but still not as direct as that of the US students.

Ma suggests three reasons for increased directness of communication among participants of both cultural groups. Firstly (and echoing the hypothesis that cultural conventions are filtered by CMC), the low-context text-based environment, with its absence of non-verbal channels, is said to reduce the possibilities for nuancing propositions. Secondly (again invoking the idea of a diminished social dimension in CMC), there is said to be less risk to face in CMC, because geographically separated participants 'usually do not share a common social network' (p. 178). This results in less pressure to protect face by expressing oneself indirectly. Thirdly (and echoing the hypothesis whereby CMC liberates us from cultural constraints), the lack of non-verbal cues is said to lead to more uninhibited behaviour in CMC. These factors work together to block cultural pressures to communicate indirectly, but apparently succeed only partially in doing so. Cultural rules are weakened, but not erased. Despite the increased directness of both the US and the East Asian students, there remains a noticeable cultural difference in approach between the two groups.

Ma's research can be read as an elaborate version of the 'filter' hypothesis, whereby one of the factors that is filtered is the pressure to conform to cultural rules. Although Ma draws the conclusion that 'Intercultural communication via computer networks [...] seems to have modified, if not drastically changed, some previously identified characteristics of FTF intercultural communication' (p. 173), the modification is essentially quantitative. Other researchers, on the other hand, have pursued Ma's reasoning to argue that CMC offers an opportunity to disregard cultural rules, at least to some extent, and thus that the online behaviour of the students involves less a filtering of cultural conventions than a flouting of them. The difference is subtle, but nonetheless consequential: the technology, rather than constraining the expression of a cultural convention, is seen to have provided an opportunity to reject it. Yum and Hara (2005) cite Ma's article as evidence that the Internet provides an opportunity for 'interactants [to] break the rules typically governing self-disclosure'.[7] Bloch (2004) takes a similar line, arguing that weakening of the usual social constraints 'may allow writers to use rhetorical strategies on the Internet they do not feel comfortable with in other contexts' (p. 67).[8] From this perspective, the way cultural values play out in CMC becomes considerably less predictable. While these authors provide evidence of cultural patterns in CMC, these do not necessarily mirror patterns identified elsewhere in a given culture, and may even contradict them.

The articles quoted in this section have moved away from the assumption that culture is a constant that will be more or less obvious in different contexts. Taking this a step further, and drawing on the work of Bolter and Grusin (1999) on new media, Murray (2000b) and Thatcher (2005) hold that CMC is not merely shaped by cultural and technological factors, but in turn shapes cultural practices and uses of technology. Thus email is changing the way people write, and television newscasts are starting to resemble websites in their screen design and use of graphics (Thatcher, 2005, p. 282).

Similarly working against the assumption of cultural constancy, but from another angle, is the work of Belz (2001, 2002), Hewling (2004) and O'Dowd (2006) on the impact of local imperatives and institutional contexts (educational culture, purpose of communication, task and assessment design, timetabling, computer access), which can override cultural pressures in shaping online communication.

The question remains of how to theorize the complex interplay of broad cultural values, specific cultural practices, technological/material constraints and local contexts, in order to understand why particular cultural patterns may emerge in one online environment but not in another.

Genre and the evolution of cultural practices

Rejecting the assumption of seamless cultural patterns across equally seamless modes of CMC, Thatcher (2005) writes,

> Because communication technologies restrain and reinforce certain communication possibilities and corresponding rhetorical and cultural patterns, they do not relate to or fit each cultural and rhetorical tradition the same way. Rather, communication technologies develop complexly different relations to each cultural and/or rhetorical tradition across the globe. Consequently, each rhetorical tradition uses each communication technology with a distinct sense of purpose, audience–author relations, information needs, and organizational patterns.
>
> (p. 279)

This 'distinct sense of purpose, audience–author relations, information needs, and organizational patterns' that evolves in each case can be understood in terms of genre theory. The approach we take in the chapters that follow (first outlined in Hanna & de Nooy, 2003, 2004) draws on Freadman and Macdonald's (1992, cf. Freadman, 1998) theorization of genre, and parallels the approach of Kramsch and Thorne (2002) in considering genre as a pivotal concept in understanding the way in which communicative practices using new technologies evolve from existing cultural forms.

The concept of genre is a way of accounting for the differences – large and small – between various kinds of cultural practices, from detective novels to business emails to weather reports, from blind dates to dinner parties to wakes. It is used to distinguish interaction in different spheres, involving different purposes, participants, audiences and media, and entailing different conventions. It thus provides a way of understanding the heterogeneity to be found not only between but also within cultures.

Freadman and Macdonald (1992) propose a pragmatic notion of genre in their detailed exposition of the concept and its uses. They explain that a genre is not a set of features, but an active interpretation of a cultural practice that shapes and regulates that practice. That is to say, genre functions as a kind of template on which the practice is modelled and through which it is understood. A genre takes form not as a fixed set of rules but as a 'structure of conventions regulating a practice of interaction' (p. 7). A given instance of the practice in question may conform to a greater or lesser degree to its template, and deviations may in turn lead to revision of the template itself. There may indeed be competing templates for certain activities. The conventions of a genre, its 'regularities of practice', are thus subject to contestation and change, despite the inertia of sometimes ingrained habit (p. 9). They are thus 'modifiable sets of constraints rather than immutable sets of instructions' (p. 25).[9]

A culture, then, comprises diverse genres of activity, and the conventions associated with these activities are renegotiated with each instance of their practice. It is particularly useful to examine what happens when a new space for cultural practices opens up, such as occurs with the emergence of a new means of communication (and we can reflect on the arrival of radio, the telephone, television, well before email and text messaging). Much rides on the ways in which members of a culture engage with the technology. The direction a new genre will take is shaped by the ways in which participants interpret their own practice – and that of others – in relation to existing genres. Here 'the very choice of models has to be constituted', and 'the stake lies in vying for conventional respect for that precarious choice' (Freadman & Macdonald, 1992, p. 21). Users will tend to model their practice on an existing genre; the question is, which one? The introduction of email as a business tool, for example, offered multiple possibilities: would it mould itself on the template of the business letter, the fax, the memo, the scribbled note, the telephone conversation, the answer-phone message, or indeed some combination of these? Would the personal home page adopt and adapt the conventions of the photo album, the diary, the curriculum vitae, the school project, the bedroom wall or the notebook? Traces of these competing genres remain in the sets of conventions for various business email uses and types of personal website that have evolved.

What is important from a cross-cultural perspective is this: not only may cultural differences in, for example, letter writing be carried over into a new genre, but a quite different genre altogether (casual conversation, for example) may emerge as the primary model for practice in the new medium. Cultural differences in CMC can, then, arise in at least three ways. Firstly, different cultures may select different models for a new cultural practice (as we shall see in the next chapter with the case of the public discussion forum). Secondly, even when the same model is selected (for example, 'positions vacant' advertisements in print being the template for online job offers) the conventions for that model may not coincide in different cultures. Thirdly, the subsequent evolution of the template may be driven by different purposes and thus take a different direction in different cultures (the business email, for example, becoming more personal or more impersonal in its style and uses).[10] For these reasons, online cultural practices in a given culture are not simply predictable from a knowledge of cultural patterns in other forms of interaction.

Drawing on genre theory, Kramsch and Thorne (2002) discuss a case study of a French/US email exchange where university students using the same technology ostensibly for the same purpose – language learning – nonetheless model their messages on quite different genres of communication: academic discourse for the French and personal conversation for the Americans. The problems are exacerbated by the fact that the students write in the language of the other and so, for the recipients, the distancing effect of the foreign language is removed: the French students' texts look less like a piece of French academic prose than an unfriendly impersonal reply in English, while the 'ingratiating personal discourse' of the American students, expressed in French, is not perceived as building trust, but as 'lacking scientific rigor' (p. 95). The miscommunication is analysed by Kramsch and Thorne as a clash between 'two local genres engaged in global confrontation' (2002, p. 99).[11] The factors impinging on the choice of genre – how the exchange was set up, its status as a learning experience, students' personal goals, the fact that the US students posted from their own machines, outside class, whereas the French students submitted their contributions to the teacher who transmitted them – are complex.

The example is a clear demonstration that cultural others do not necessarily construe a given activity in the same way. The diagnosis by Kramsch and Thorne of these students' problems in terms of irreconcilable differences in genre corresponds with our own findings regarding the importance of genre as a means of understanding interactions between culture and technology. While they deduce different models as a way of explaining this intercultural breakdown, in the following chapter we undertake a cross-cultural comparison of another mode of CMC – the Internet discussion forum for the general public – to demonstrate, on a wider scale, different cultures using different generic templates as a basis for participation. At the same time, our study illustrates the complexity of the interface between existing cultural conventions and the cultural uptake of new communications technologies.

Conclusion

The wealth of findings turned up by recent research shows conclusively that culture plays a role in shaping online communication. Far from erasing cultural differences, the Internet has provided new opportunities for cultural differences to manifest themselves. Equally, however, the variety of research findings indicates that culture shapes Internet communication differently in different contexts, and that the dynamics are more complicated than a simple transfer of broad cultural values onto online interaction.

Having sifted through a number of hypotheses regarding the role culture plays in CMC, we can see that many of them, while not entirely false, give only a partial picture of the dynamics in play. Yes, the anonymity of online communication can liberate us from certain social constraints, but not uniformly across CMC contexts. Yes, the Internet favours speed, which might make for efficiency, but not so forcefully that these pressures cannot be resisted or avoided. Yes, offline cultural preferences reappear in cyberspace, but only certain ones and only in certain kinds of interaction. Yes, some cultural differences are diminished online, but then again others are exaggerated. Yes, cultural norms are transformed to fit the constraints of online communication, but this transformation can take a variety of creative paths. Technological constraints interact both with cultural pressures and with local, contextual imperatives to shape the various forms of online communication. Thus a knowledge of widely held values or of Hofstede's scores for particular countries is not sufficient to predict how interaction in a particular genre of CMC will pan out. What happens in one online context may not happen in another.

For these reasons, we need to look not at CMC as a whole but at particular online practices. Equally we need to understand culture not as a set of constant values but as a set of variable practices. And the concept of genre is the pivot that will enable us to link online and offline conventions for communication, and elucidate the ways in which cultural patterns evolve in new CMC environments.

In Chapters 3 and 4, we follow this process closely, and illustrate these arguments with a detailed examination of varying cultural conventions in one particular form of CMC: the public Internet discussion forum on a mass-media website. At a time when the phenomenon was still relatively new, we see the evolution of cultural practices in action, as contributors provide explicit commentary on the way they model their participation. And in the complex interaction between cultural, technical and contextual constraints, we see new, culturally specific ways of communicating emerge from more established genres.

Table 2.1 Cultural difference in CMC: Major research themes

Broad areas of cultural difference	Specific aspects analysed	Examples
approaches to communications technologies	preferences for one communication technology over another	Straub (1994), Japanese preference for fax over email
		Heaton (1998), Japanese/Scandinavian business: relative importance of video-mediated communication
		Heaton (2001), Japanese interest in pen-based computing, speech synthesis, Virtual Reality
		St Amant (2003), Ukrainian preference for cell phone over email in business communication
		Thorne (2003), US students: generational shift in communication tool preference from email to instant messaging
		Dinev, Goo, Hu, and Nam (2006), US/Korean attitudes towards anti-virus and other protective technologies
	purposes for which particular technologies are used	Dragona and Handa (2000), whether ICTs are seen as obvious sources for information/entertainment
		Thorne (2003), 'cultures-of-use' of communication tools
		Zorn (2005), 'technology scripts': assumptions about uses of technology
		Miller and Slater (2000), Trinidad: diversity of culturally inflected purposes of Internet use (relational, economic, cultural, religious)
		Gottlieb (2003), Japanese Burakumin: empowerment of marginalized groups

	Gottlieb (2003) and Zickmund (2000), recruitment to racist organizations
	Morris and Meadows (2004), Australian indigenous traditions for transmission of knowledge used as framework for modern indigenous communication
	Ess, Kawabata and Kurosaki (2007) and Kawabata and Tamura (2007), uptake of online technologies by different religious groups
	Chiou and Lee (2008), content of forum discussion (US/Japan/Taiwan) about popular TV programmes
wider cultural values influencing CMC	
attitudes to time	St Amant (2003), availability of business correspondents
	Ware (2005), time students devote to communication
dimensions identified by Hofstede (1980)	Tan, Wei, Watson and Walczuch (1998), Singapore/US: effect of status (power distance) on group CMC
– individualism/ collectivism	Kim and Papacharissi (2003), manifestations of individualism/ collectivism in US and Korean home pages
– uncertainty avoidance	Gunawardena et al. (2001), Mexico/US: Hofstede's dimensions in online group process
– power distance	Uljin and Lincke (2004), use of competitive and cooperative negotiation strategies online
– achievement-oriented/ relation-oriented ('masculinity/femininity')	Callahan (2005), correlations between Hofstede's dimensions and website design features

Table 2.1 (Continued)

Broad areas of cultural difference	Specific aspects analysed	Examples
		Würtz (2005), individualism/collectivism and website imagery
		Pfeil, Zaphiris and Ang (2006), cultural patterns in collaborative authoring of Wikipedia
		Gorman (2006), masculinity/femininity in website design
		Kim and Lee (2006) power distance and Korean/US consumer reaction to website design
		Osman and Herring (2007), power distance, collectivism and behaviour of Azerbaijani distance education students in synchronous chat
	low context/high context (LC/HC) (Hall, 1976) – explicit/implicit – direct/indirect – importance of face	Chen (1998), email debate requiring LC skills
		Morse (2003), LC/HC perceptions of asynchronous online learning
		Koeszegi et al. (2004), correlation between number of messages exchanged in computer-mediated negotiations, use of analytical support tools, and HC/LC
		Würtz (2005), LC/HC manifested in website visuals (images of people, consistency of layout)
		Thatcher (2005), Ecuadorian students frustrated by lack of emotional and other contextual cues in email (HC, collectivist)

discursive strategies	direct/indirect	
		Ko, Roberts and Cho (2006), US/Korean reactions to marketing websites align with LC/HC
		Zhu and St Amant (2007), US/Chinese perceptions of the need to provide information on Chinese-created websites
		Ma (1996), US/East Asian text-based relay chat
		Kim et al. (1999), Korean/Australian businesspeople: number of email exchanges necessary to obtain information
		Chase et al. (2002), web discussion: tolerance of criticism
		Shih and Cifuentes (2003), Taiwanese students/US tutors: criticism in email feedback
		Belz (2003), Ware and Kramsch (2005), German/US student email exchange: performance of critique; use of linguistic softening devices
		Ware and Kramsch (2005), German/US student email exchange: tolerance of didacticism
		O'Dowd (2006), German/ Irish students; Liao (1999), Taiwanese/Anglophone students: ways of eliciting information in emails
		Kim, Yu, and Sussex (2006), Korean/Australian email requests and complaints

Table 2.1 (Continued)

Broad areas of cultural difference	Specific aspects analysed	Examples
	rhetorical conventions, forms of argumentation	Yang, Olesova, and Richardson (2008), European-based and Asian-based Russian students: directness in online discussion
		Chen (1998), Danish, French, German, Hong Kong, Turkish and US students: thinking patterns, expression styles, familiarity with form and practice of debate
		Kim et al. (1999), Korea/Australian businesspeople: intuitive vs logical sequencing
		Liao (1999), Taiwanese/Anglophone student emails: number of questions asked/answered; reciprocation of questions
		Kramsch and Thorne (2002), French/US students: genre (essay/conversation, formal/informal, factual/personal)
		Thorne (2003), French/US students: combative debate or amicable conversation in email exchange
		Hanna and de Nooy (2003, 2004) and Hanna (2002), French/British conventions for discussion (see Chapters 3 and 6 in this book)
		Atifi (2003) and Atifi and Marcoccia (2006), French/Moroccan discussion forums: openings and closings, greetings, themes, politeness rituals, length of messages, codeswitching
		Bloch (2004), use of Chinese rhetorical patterns in English language Internet discussion

	von Münchow and Rakotonoelina (2006), French/US Usenet forums: use of questions, reported speech, rhetorical coherence, forms of argumentation
	Zhu and St Amant (2007), impact of rhetorical style (indirect and inductive patterns) in Chinese-created websites on US readers.
language differences – vocabulary problems – connotations, stylistic turns – language as discourse (culture embedded in language) – forms of politeness	Liao (1999), problem of literal translations
	Kramsch and Thorne (2002), Ware and Kramsch (2005), Belz (2003), Toyoda and Harrison (2002), understanding of connotations
	Toyoda and Harrison (2002), miscommunication at the word, sentence, and discourse levels
	Shih and Cifuentes (2003), formal and informal greetings, expectations regarding expressions of gratitude, compliments
	Belz (2003), taboo topics
	Ulijn and Lincke (2004), use of personal pronouns in business negotiation as indicators of empathy
	Ware and Kramsch (2005), language as discourse
	Ware (2005), use of second-person pronouns and of questions as indication of relationship building
	O'Dowd and Ritter (2006), German/Spanish students: misinterpretations of tone, of humour

Table 2.1 (Continued)

Broad areas of cultural difference	Specific aspects analysed	Examples
	online participation patterns	Murphy and Levy (2006), politeness in Australian and Korean emails
		Biesenbach-Lucas (2007), forms of politeness in emails
		Kim et al. (1999), Korean/Australian emails: length of message, speed of reply
		Liang and McQueen (1999), Asian/Western students' interactive learning preferences: tutor-oriented/peer-oriented
		Shih and Cifuentes (2003), expectations regarding moderator
		Reeder et al. (2004), Canadian students of diverse origins: number and frequency of messages, postings to other participants or to facilitators, turn-taking
		Smith, Coldwell, Smith, and Murphy (2005), Chinese heritage/Australian students: length and topic of message, continue or start new thread, organizational or content messages
		O'Dowd (2006), German/US students: length of message
	online conventions	Kim et al. (1999), Korean/Australian greetings and signoffs
		Sugimoto and Levin (2000), Japanese/US use of titles, names, signatures, subject lines, message openings
		Cakir, Bichelmeyer, and Cagiltay (2002), use of emoticons

relationships, self and other		Koda (2007), differences among Asian countries in avatars' facial expressions and gestures
	formality/informality	Kim et al. (1999), Korean/Australian business emails: effect of status
		Gerritsen and Verckens (2006), Flemish/Dutch business student emails; O'Dowd (2006), German/US student emails
	public/private, importance of face	Ho (2000), Singapore students; Shih and Cifuentes (2003), Taiwanese students: attitudes towards making communication public (individual email vs group discussion)
	online representation of identity	Miller and Slater (2000), self-representation in terms of national identity in Trinidadian home pages
		Reeder et al. (2004) and Chase et al. (2002), content, length, style of self-introductions, degree of self-revelation in student discussion postings
		Kim, Yu, and Sussex (2006), personal information in self-presentation in Korean/Australian emails
	understanding of online relationships – attitudes towards self-disclosure – task-oriented/relationship-oriented – what constitutes friendly behaviour	Miller and Slater (2000), Trinidad: ways of distinguishing between serious and casual online relationships
		Shih and Cifuentes (2003), self-disclosure by Taiwanese and US students in web discussion and email
		Yum and Hara (2005), Korean/Japanese/US self-disclosure in personal online relationships

Table 2.1 (Continued)

Broad areas of cultural difference	Specific aspects analysed	Examples
		Thorne (2003) and Kramsch and Thorne (2002), French/US students: relationship based on intellectual exchange or personal disclosure
		Belz (2002, 2003), Ware (2005) and O'Dowd (2006), German/US students: expectation of task-oriented or relationship-based email exchange; consequent disclosure of personal info
		Zorn (2004), focus on task or on relationship
		Belz (2005), German/US students: role of questions in online relationship building
	collaborative behaviours	Heaton (1998), Japanese need for spatial and hierarchy cues in computer-mediated cooperative work (vs Scandinavian)
		Kim and Bonk (2002), Korean students socially and contextually driven; Finnish students group-focused, reflective and theoretically driven; US students more action-oriented in online conferencing
		Ulijn and Lincke (2004), Anglo/Latin/Nordic: use of cooperative speech acts
		Setlock, Fussell, and Neuwirth (2004), US/Chinese collaboration via Instant Messaging

	Convertino, Zhang, Asti, Rosson, and Mohammed (2007), US/Chinese uses of CMC tools in remote collaboration
stereotypes and preconceptions of the other	Ware and Kramsch (2005), German/US students; O'Dowd and Ritter (2006), Spanish/US students
impact of local factors	institutional context	Belz (2001) and Basharina (2007), educational cultures (method and purpose of learning)
		Belz (2002), Belz and Müller-Hartmann (2003) and O'Dowd (2006), academic calendars and accreditation systems
		Shachaf, Meho, and Hara (2007), cultural differences in expectations of library services' impact on use of virtual reference desks
	computer access	Belz (2001, 2002), German/US students; Basharina (2007), Russian/Mexican/Japanese students: access shapes length and frequency of messages
		Ware (2005), German/US students: experience with norms of Internet etiquette
	individual and subcultural differences	Chase et al. (2002), cultural gaps between individuals
		Belz (2002), individual agency
		Ware (2005), individual motivation

3
Debate or Conversation? French and British Public Internet Discussion

Having explored beliefs about culture's manifestations online let us pursue the question of cultural and generic convention and their interactions with each other and with technology through the particular example of the mass-media public discussion forums introduced in Chapter 1. We present two snapshots of the forums, at particular points in their evolution to show, firstly, variation across cultures (this chapter) and variation over time, which does not, however, result in the erasure of cross-cultural difference (the following chapter).

The rise of discussion forums on media websites

Discussion forums attached to the websites of prominent French and British media organizations (daily newspapers, a news magazine, a radio and television site) provide the data for this chapter's cross-cultural comparison of CMC practices. The data were collected from the websites between 2000 and 2002, a time when the forums were no longer entirely new, and forum participation was settling down into recognizable patterns that persist today. However, particularly in 2000, large numbers of new participants from the general public, unused to electronic discussion, were still joining regularly, prompting recurrent commentary inducting them into the conventions for each site.

Prior to the mid-1990s, online discussion was the province of bulletin boards, newsgroups and email discussion lists. These tended to attract highly computer-literate participants, often affiliated with universities or the computer sector, seeking discussion on specialized topics of interest with which they identified closely (cf. Adams, 1996, np; Herring, 2002, pp. 115–116). Around the mid-1990s, however, newspaper websites started to proliferate, first in the US and quickly following elsewhere. At first, these websites tended merely to reproduce their hard copy online, but they soon began to incorporate a range of interactive features, including discussion forums. And this development brought Internet discussion to a much wider, less specialized public than previously.

Early opportunities for reader participation on media websites were often modelled on the 'Letters to the Editor' format (as opposed to communication with other readers), such that many contributions were never published or were extensively edited and opportunities for interactive discussion between contributors were severely limited.[1] Light and Rogers (1999) give the example of the BBC's 'Talking Point' when it was launched in late 1997, and of CNN's message board of the same period, which, although it published all postings, discouraged through its format exchanges between contributors. Rapidly, however, media websites started to provide fully fledged discussion forums, allowing posted messages to appear immediately (inappropriate ones being removed *post hoc*), and facilitating interaction between soon booming numbers of participants.

In 1999, Williams and Nicholas were able to report that '[v]irtually all UK and US newspapers and the vast majority of regional and even local titles are now represented on the web' (p. 122). While Schultz's 1999 study of 100 US newspaper websites showed that only a minority of these (33 per cent overall) offered online forums, this proportion doubled (68 per cent) for the category of larger newspapers (1999, np),[2] and within a couple of years, forums had become standard features of the websites of national media organizations. Thus by 2000 *The Times* stood alone among the British broadsheets in not providing an Internet discussion forum (Cowen, 2001, p. 194), and forums featured on the websites of all the French national dailies except *Le Figaro*.

Mass-media websites quickly became among the most recognized and most visited online sites in their respective countries and – for prominent newspapers and broadcasters such as *The New York Times*, the BBC, *Le Monde* – internationally.[3] As a result, the current affairs and general interest forums they provided attracted large-scale participation by a wider cross-section of the population than had been the case with the more specialized bulletin boards and newsgroups of earlier days. Media website discussion forums quickly became forums for the general public, attracting many people new to the concept. Light and Rogers (1999) reported that a third of their sample of participants in *The Guardian*'s 1997 election forum had no previous experience of electronic discussion and that since the study the proportion of newcomers to forums was continuing to rise (np).[4]

Such high traffic meant that participation in these forums was unlikely simply to replicate the practices of the Listserv discussion lists or Usenet newsgroups with their academic, professional and aficionado orientation and population. 'Online forums are not newsgroups' comments one of Light and Rogers' (1999) respondents (np), while another elaborates the distinction with the opinion that 'ordinary mortals wouldn't visit [the newsgroup] uk.politics' (np).

How, then, has the generalist public discussion forum evolved, given the influx of non-specialist users? And has this evolution taken the same path in different cultures? By 2002, some clear patterns had emerged in British and French media website forums, and these patterns were sufficiently different from each other to suggest culturally specific ways of engaging with this new genre of communication.

The case study

Our findings are based on a close study of Internet discussion sites attached to four prominent media websites: those of the British Broadcasting Corporation, two high-circulation 'quality' daily newspapers, the UK's *The Guardian* and France's *Le Monde*, and the French news weekly *Le Nouvel Observateur*.[5] Our study of the forums covers the period 2000–2002, with access to the archives of *Le Monde* dating back to 1999.

By this time, these four general interest websites are all well established, already in their second or third version, and with a high volume of traffic. *BBC Online* exists since 1997, when it already had a function for users to post comment (Light & Rogers, 1999, np). A major site redesign in 2001 foregrounds its 'message boards', comprising over 75 interactive forums on a wide range of topics (Graf, 2004, p. 26). *The Guardian*'s web presence was launched in 1996 and becomes *Guardian Unlimited* in January 1999 with prominent and extensive 'talkboards' (Cowen, 2001, p. 190). The BBC website is far and away the largest and most visited news website in the UK and one of the most visited worldwide, with *The Guardian* at second place among news websites in the UK (McCarthy, 2003).[6]

The French sites chosen are similarly prominent. First among the French press in attracting visitors to its website in 2002 is *Le Monde*, and while *Le Nouvel Observateur* ranks sixth, those ranking higher in visitor numbers are either specialized (*Les Echos, L'Equipe, Télérama*) or do not offer forums at this time (*Le Figaro*). [7] *Le Monde* developed its first website in late 1995. It was relaunched with forums as *'Le Monde Interactif'* in 1998, and reaches its third incarnation – *'Le Monde.fr'* – in 2000 with *Forums le Monde* a highlighted feature (cf. Friceau, 2000, pp. 41–44). The year 1999 marked the launch of *Le Nouvel Observateur au quotidien*, [8] and forums (*'débats'*) appear with its remodelling as *Le Journal Perm@nent* in 2000–2001.

The four sites chosen are comparable in that all address an educated public with an interest in current affairs. They each offer general interest and current affairs forums, subject to similar sets of rules prohibiting offensive messages, and with similar mechanics of posting. They are all moderated: although messages are posted directly to the site, they may subsequently be removed or edited by a moderator if they are deemed to infringe the Code of Conduct.[9] All accommodate informality and can cope – to varying degrees – with non-standard grammar and spelling. Finally, all four aim to facilitate discussion *between* participants.

Differences between the four sites are not simply binary (French vs British). Indeed the most obvious differences between exchanges on these sites reflect subcultural differences between reading/listening populations: political leanings to the left or right, degrees of staidness or trendiness, of censorship or libertarianism, of tolerance of offensive language distinguish the sites in ways predictable from the media organizations concerned. However, despite this heterogeneity, and despite participation on all sites from native and non-native speakers from a variety of cultural backgrounds, there are marked differences in communicative strategies between the British and the French sites, to the point where we can make some generalizations about Anglophone and Francophone Internet discussion practices in such contexts.

Notions of discussion

Since all four sites aim to facilitate discussion, and lay claim to high intellectual standards, we shall start by comparing the ways in which 'discussion' is defined and interpreted. Firstly, the labels given to the discussion facilities are revealing:

Le Nouvel Observateur: *Débats*
Le Monde: *Forums*
BBC: Message boards
The Guardian: Talk

The *débats* proposed by *Le Nouvel Observateur* are debates in a quite precise sense: discussion starters supplied by the magazine invite polemical stances. In the overwhelming majority they are provocative, calculated to polarize viewpoints and indeed raise tempers as far as possible:

- '*Trouvez-vous normal, ou pas, de limiter les libertés publiques au nom de la lutte contre le terrorisme?*' [Do you think it reasonable or not to restrict public freedom in the name of the fight against terrorism?]
- '*L'IVG – Vous êtes pour ou contre?*' [Abortion – are you for or against?]
- '*Oussama ben Laden, terroriste ou héros?*' [Osama Bin Laden, terrorist or hero?].

In this context, even questions that do not require a yes/no answer and appear less incendiary (such as '*Que représente Walt Disney à vos yeux?*' [What does Walt Disney represent for you?]) invite similar polarization (in this instance, between pro- and anti-American sentiments). Discussion on the *Nouvel Observateur* site, unlike that on the other three, can occur only within the confines of the debates proposed.[10]

Discussion at *Le Monde* takes place within the context of *forums*. These are defined by themes for discussion (such as 'Environment' or 'Politics'), the list being rounded out with '*Autres sujets*' [Other topics]), later '*Tous sujets*' [All topics].[11] The use of 'forum' suggests that, despite the absence of the word 'debate', these spaces are for the exchange of opinions, and self-reflexive commentary posted by participants explicitly distinguishes the notion of 'forum' from that of chat. Although the seemingly indeterminate '*Autres sujets*' appears far removed from the construction of opposition on the *Nouvel Observateur* site, it is striking how many times life on this forum too is described in terms of confrontation, from the tennis match to the pitched battle, by way of the friendly punch-up said by one participant to characterize the French *modus operandi*.[12] It is only in 2001 that this forum – and this one alone – is opened up to include '*le chat*' and '*le small talk*', a move we shall discuss later in the chapter. Previously, sustained interaction could only take the form of debate, as we show in Chapter 6 when we study the case of two ill-fated English girls who attempt to use the forum as a penpal pool.

In sharp contrast to this unsuccessful gambit, learners of English who follow the BBC's signposts to their very own message board will find that a simple 'write to me' message can unleash 12 pages of postings on hobbies, pets and ambitions (as is the experience of Anna, K., who posts a short self-introduction to the 'Welcome to our Message Board' topic of the 'Learning English' section, 23 February 2002). This may be an extreme example, but the interpretation of discussion as conversation characterizes interaction on the BBC site. Unlike 'debates' and 'forum', the label 'Message board' gives no promise of an exchange of contrasting ideas and opinions.

While the 'house rules' define the purpose of the message boards as 'providing an atmosphere in which constructive and mature dialogue takes place', such constructive maturity finds its voice in conversation. On the home page, the tagline to the label 'message boards' reads 'Daily conversations in the UK's largest community', the 'Welcome' message starts with the imperative to 'Get Talking!' and the topics menu is headed by

300 + CONVERSATIONS, HAPPENING NOW!
WHAT DO YOU WANT TO TALK ABOUT?

(BBC, 2002a)

This emphasis on conversation is reflected in the organization and selection of topics offered. Like *Le Monde*, the BBC makes room for discussion of an extremely wide range of topics (from World News to TV soaps to cooking to local weather), but unlike either of the French sites studied, discussion as debate is far from prioritized, although it does figure in a section entitled 'The Great Debate'.

'Talk' is the title of *The Guardian*'s discussion site, and the 'Talk Policy' is revelatory:

We want The Talk to be the place on the net where you will always find lively, entertaining and, above all, intelligent discussions. The last thing the net needs is yet another site where any attempt at conversation is drowned out by a few people hurling mindless abuse at each other.

(*The Guardian*, 2002)

Once again, participation in such 'intelligent discussion' is construed as an 'attempt at conversation'. The ever-proliferating discussions proposed by participants canvass such issues as 'vacuous celebrity chitchat', the comparative ugliness of Yorkshire villagers, funny Freudian slips, sad singletons or, indeed, 'Anything':

Anything on Anything
The arts – 1/7/02 03:26am
(*The Guardian*, Latest Discussions list, 1 July 1 2002)

Other sections are provided for seeking information or advice, but unlike the BBC, there is no specified area for debate.

Our evidence here supports some notion of cultural determination of the form that discussion will take: of our apparently comparable sites, the French display a tendency to view discussion as an opportunity for debate, whilst on the British ones discussion means first and foremost the chance for a chat.[13]

Debate

This is not to say that debate is excluded from the British sites. Is it then possible to move from *Le Nouvel Observateur* or *Le Monde* forums to discussions on the *Guardian* or the BBC sites identified specifically as debate (as opposed to discussion) and find uniformity within a precise genre of online debate? Apparently not. It seems that the overriding characterization of Internet discussion in terms of debate or conversation has consequences for all interaction on these sites.

Postings to the debates of *Le Nouvel Observateur* offer a large number of clear definitions of what contributors expect of interaction. Contributors frequently state that the forum is there for people to *express opinions* and to discuss them *seriously*. You are expected to formulate your ideas, make a point, develop an argument and discuss points made by others. Comments must be *pertinent* and *address the topic*, and personal attacks should be avoided. Apart from this last, which is constantly infringed, these rules of engagement are clearly shared by most participants and invoked regularly to criticize postings by opponents. Thus Frederic asks Lariflette exactly what his point is and suggests his contribution needs to be more relevant.

Vous n'avez ni argumente ni rien apporte au debat.
Si vous voulez participer au debat, il vous suffit de reprendre les points developpes par d'autres et les discuter.[14]

[You have neither argued a point nor contributed anything to the debate. If you want to participate in the debate, all you need to do is take up the points developed by others and discuss them.]

(Frederic, *Les quotidiens gratuits* [Free daily newspapers],
25 February 2002)

At *Le Monde*, these same rules hold, confirming the status of the forums as spaces for debate. Eschewing low-grade insult swapping, factual and linguistic inaccuracy, participants describe themselves as there to debate, that is, to formulate an argument, to set out and defend their ideas.[15]

> – *On veut convaincre les autres de ses idées.*
> – *On veut participer à un débat collectif et, à son niveau, même si on n'est pas journaliste, polémiste, homme politique, avoir quand même sa part des échanges et son mot à dire sur les grans et petits sujets de société.*
> [– We want to convince others of our ideas.
> – We want to participate in a collective debate, and, at our own level, even if we aren't journalists, polemicists or politicians, we nonetheless want to play a part in exchanges and have our say on social issues great and small.]
>
> (V. Graslin, Pourquoi des forums? [Why forums?],
10 February 2000)

The BBC's 'The Great Debate' can eventually be found under 'News & Sport', where it is divided into four sections ('topics'): 'World Views', 'The Front Page', 'It's Your Parliament' and 'Virtual Soapbox'. Again demonstrating that debate is not the central concern of the BBC site, 'The Great Debate' boasts few topics compared to other sub-headings of the News and Sport category: compare Football (5 topics), Five Live (other sports, 9 topics), Weather (5 topics, including notably the popular 'Talk about the weather'). Moreover, the subtitle to 'The Great Debate' is (yet again) 'Conversation for the Nation', with readers encouraged to 'come and join our conversations or start your own'. Far from being emphasized, there are only two reprises of the word 'debate' within the 'Great Debate' section, occurring where the function of the topic 'World Views' is defined and clarified:

> This is the place to debate world events. Let us know your opinions on the stories behind the headlines.
>
> This discussion is for high quality, non-inflammatory debate [...].
>
> (BBC, 2002b)

With 'debate', like discussion, being glossed as conversation, there is very little to distinguish the BBC Great Debate boards from message boards that make no claim to hosting debate. In both cases, postings tend to be informal and brief (some consisting of simple interjections), and relevance to the topic is optional. In fact, it is quite difficult to find a discussion that a *Nouvel Observateur* contributor would recognize as a debate. 'Debate' seems to be best understood as a thematic label – conversation about current affairs.

As mentioned above, Guardian Talk does not set aside a particular place for debate, yet it is not uncommon for participants to refer to their discussion as debate, particularly under the International topics and in more professionally oriented 'talkboards' such as 'Education Talk'. Participant reference to 'debate' frequently coincides with efforts to monitor interaction, whether in reasserting the topic or in enunciating techniques of argumentation (citing sources, getting the facts straight). Such exchanges, however, are not separate from short chatty postings but alternate with them in the same discussion. It is not, then, that *The Guardian* readers do not know what debate is, nor how it might be enacted: it is just not the dominant model for Guardian Talk, and takes place within conversations. Thus in the History folder of Guardian Talk (a reliable source of sustained argument), we find in a discussion of 'The Indo European Homeland Question' the following quick succession of postings:

> Mornin' folks (-:
> check this out:
> http://news.bbc.co.uk/1/hi/sci/tech/2174437.stm
> > (Velikovsky, 9 August 2002, 8:36 AM)
>
> Morning Vel – give me a moment and I'll get stuck into that!
> > (dru2107, 9 August 2002, 8:41 AM)

This is followed 11 minutes later by the latter's point-by-point rebuttal of the article referred to. If debate excludes conversation on the French sites, the two coexist comfortably on the *Guardian* and BBC sites.[16] It seems that the overarching construal of participation as conversation is the primary determinant of interaction on the British sites. This becomes even clearer when we compare the range of tolerance of digression on the various sites.

Tolerance of digression

At *Le Nouvel Observateur*, when discussion of punishment of crimes by foreigners drifts from 'delinquent foreigners' to foreigners in general, William capitalizes his exhortation *'REVENONS AU SUJET'* [Back to the topic] (WILLIAM, *'La double peine'* [Double penalty], 25 January 2002). Strict relevance is demanded. On the same site, Tommy's response to

Xtophe, while it addresses the topic (Jean-Paul II's papacy), also criticizes sanctimonious hypocrisy. Tommy therefore feels it necessary to apologize for reacting *'en dehors du débat'* [off topic], assuring participants his conclusion won't be *'si décalé que cela avec le sujet'* [as irrelevant as all that] (14 November 2001). Even such minimal digression is apparently cause for concern.

This is a far cry from conventions at the BBC, where there is no sense that sticking to the topic is essential or even desirable. This is clearly illustrated by the wave of discussion that swept the site following the introduction of a new format in the first week of May 2002. In *every* section of *every* message board affected the change was extensively discussed. There was no sense that this topic should be treated separately (under 'Technical Terrors', for instance – which would of course have marginalized the discussion). In contrast, on *Forums Le Monde* discussion of changes in format or registration is carefully pigeon-holed in *'Les forums – Vos questions'* [Forums – Your Questions]. This example also fits with a wider pattern of behaviour on the BBC and *Guardian* sites in which topics define not so much the subject matter under discussion, as the community to which a contributor belongs. Thus, the topics discussed under 'World Views', 'The Front Page', 'Virtual Soapbox' and 'It's Your Parliament' overlap enormously at the same time as they evolve in unforeseeable directions. Once you have joined a community with a basic interest in world or British affairs, it seems, you can talk about almost anything.

The introduction of the new format is of further interest to our study in that the very changes it brought about, and their reception, relate precisely to the issue of relevance to the original topic. Under the new format, the various threads within (for example) 'World Views' no longer all appeared intertwined as they had previously. They now had to be clicked on separately to be read. This was interpreted as 'encourag[ing] people to post on topic' (Bruce Robertson, Outta here, 8 May 2002). Previously posters were all part of one very large discussion branching off in various directions ('everyone talking at the same time', Outta here, Eamon O Ceallaigh, 8 May 2002), whereas the new format aimed to separate discussions by topic. Protest indicates that this segregation was seen by many as restrictive and undesirable:

[The new format] does mess the flow of our posts unbelievably [...].
(Delia Jones, Outta here, 8 May 2002)

> i want to freeflow between discussions [...]. i don't understand the
> production team's obsession with keeping topics together. the people
> who post don't seem to have any problem following threads.
>
> (tripti paarthi, Outta here, 8 May 2002)

The latter contributor felt that as a woman she was 'capable of following more than one conversation at a time' (Outta here, 8 May 2002,
17:54 PM), and, typically, the flow of discussion then went to women
in power, to Margaret Thatcher and her minimal sleep requirements, to
studies of optimal sleep times.

Similarly on Guardian Talk, it is not unusual for a thread to drift from
theme to theme. Moreover, a personal chat between regulars can surface
as part of any discussion (for example an exchange between shelagh53
and dreamsn about how the former spent Saturday night bubbles up in
discussion of the relative merits of Asterix and Tintin [17 February 2002,
1:31–01:45 AM]). Occasional comments about being 'off topic' are rarely
complaints, but show awareness of detours:

> This thread will have to settle down into being about something if it
> is to go anywhere.
>
> (Henry94, Time for another Reformation in the UK,
> 5 June 2002)

Thus, on the BBC and *Guardian* sites, there is no sense that digression is
a problem or that any postings after the first one need to relate to the
original topic. Topics do not define the discussion, and the point of these
conversations, unlike debate, is not to arrive at an answer or, failing that,
a stand-off in which all parties have laid out their arguments. Rather,
topics are conversation starters and the game is to keep the ball rolling,
or indeed passing over the net in a succession of entertaining volleys,
rather than delivering the winning, unanswerable smash. Hence we find
the *Guardian* thread 'Killing off a thread' about conversation stoppers,
initiated as follows:[17]

> Does anyone else feel odd if their post is the last in the thread, i.e. no
> one posts any more? I don't know whether to feel satisfied that I've
> had the last word, or to be embarrassed that I've killed the discussion.
> Also, starting a thread that no one subsequently contributes to is
> mortifying. (hint, hint!)
>
> (patrick 1971, 18 September 2001)

Some 11 months later it boasts *12,000* postings, including such phatic offerings as

> ... erm ...
>
> (mijj, 12 August 2002)

and

> go thread go.
>
> (BuddhaPest, 9 August 2002)

Although this is an extreme case, threads on the *Guardian* site are far longer than those on the other sites studied and are typically peppered with chatty digression, there being little to add in the way of new perspectives on a topic after the first thousand messages. At the other extreme, and again demonstrating the importance of topic-driven exchange over conversation on this site, *Le Monde* discussions are closed and archived as read-only folders after about 50 messages, which the moderators consider sufficient to explore a topic thoroughly.

With the vagueness of the topic *'Autres sujets'*, it might have been expected that this *Le Monde* forum could take the same meandering form as the British sites, yet the commitment to debate described earlier produces a general understanding that discussion is to be topic-driven. 'What is the subject matter of *Autres sujets*?' asks Godlewski (*'Nom de la section....'* [name of the section...], 2 August 2000), opening the discussion thread and questioning why 'sport' is the only suggestion. And when Eleanor, an English student, ventures on to this forum in order to practise her French, she is advised to take a topic – any topic – and talk about it:[18]

> *[S]i vous désirez parler de n'importe quel sujet, la vache folle, l'évolution de la monarchie dans votre pays ou la construction européenne, n'hésitez pas!*
>
> [If you want to talk about any topic whatsoever, mad cows, the changing role of the monarchy in your country or the construction of Europe, don't hesitate!]
>
> (Lambda, *'Welcome chez les grenouilles'* [Welcome to frog-land], 24 February 2000)

The role of *'Autres sujets'*, then, is to cover topics for debate that haven't been foreseen in the listed categories. Certainly, other kinds of messages find their way on to *'Autres sujets'*, but the occasional requests for penpals or various kinds of information are clearly treated as aberrant: even in a discussion called *'Autres sujets'* it is possible to write off-topic. 'Off-topic' postings of another, more acceptable, kind are the *'exercices de style'* [stylistic exercises] occasionally posted by regulars: the appeal of these messages to notions of cultivated wit, and their authors' status as regulars, earned by participation in debate, ensures that such pieces – be the subject matter so slight as bathroom tiling – are tolerated.

As mentioned earlier, the arrangement of *Forums Le Monde* changed somewhat in late 2000: *'Tous sujets'* [All topics] replaced *'Autres sujets'* and explicitly made a place for conversation, previously excluded:

> *Soulevez ici les thèmes qui ne rentrent pas, à votre avis, dans les catégories ci-dessus.*
> *Le 'chat', le 'small talk' sont aussi admis. Mais seulement ici!*
>
> [Raise issues here that in your opinion do not fit in the categories above. 'Chat' and 'small talk' are also allowed. But only here!]
>
> (*Le Monde*, 2002)

Although the word 'chat' (with the sense of chitchat) has some currency in French, the use of English terms in the definition of this forum is not simply another example of English vocabulary creeping into French. Rather, it is an indication that 'chat' and 'small talk' do not really belong to French discussion, the quotation marks drawing attention to their foreignness. Chat is not being accepted and assimilated into the forums of *Le Monde* but set apart and contained in a single space. The injunction 'But only here!', with its exclamation mark, emphasizes the attempt to quarantine debates from this foreign interloper.

In practice, although less weighty threads such as *'Noeud pap blanc'* [white bow ties] flourish within *'Tous sujets'*, postings nonetheless stick to the topic, however flippant, in a way that does not happen on the *Guardian* and BBC sites. And discussion is not unrestrained in its choice of topic in this section. Despite its deceptively inclusive name, *'Tous sujets'* does not in fact seem to be for all topics. Indeed, we find instances of threads being removed by moderators from this section and placed elsewhere. As a contributor points out when a thread on Zola is shifted in this way, this practice is surely inconsistent with the definition of

'*Tous sujets*' as issues that 'in your opinion' lie outside the other categories (pascom, '*Redéfinir TS?*' [Redefining 'All topics'?], 12 October 2002). The moderator, Michel Tatu, defends the relocation:

> *Il le fallait ! Le fil dont il est question devait aller en littérature. Sinon, à quoi bon créer des sections ?*
>
> [It had to be done! The thread in question had to go into Literature. Otherwise, why bother making sections?]
>
> (Modérateur, 13 October 2002)

And he responds by removing '*à votre avis*' [in your opinion] from the definition. With moderators and various participants enforcing a strict interpretation of and adherence to the forum categories, there seems little chance of chat and small talk breaking out of their containment in this one forum and becoming generalized phenomena on the forums of *Le Monde*.

Le Monde is alone amongst our four sites in providing a miscellaneous 'Other Topics' section, but the reasons for its absence elsewhere are not identical. Whereas *Le Nouvel Observateur* simply excludes off-topic discussion, in contrast, on the British sites, there is no need for a designated area: you can put your ramblings – or your entertaining attempts at keeping the conversational ball in the air – just about anywhere.

We see that despite the similarities in technology, in declared aims of the sites, in means of participation, significant contrasts differentiate the French and British sites. Whereas the French sites are treated as places to develop and exchange arguments on stipulated issues, the English sites are seen as sites for conversation, and any discussion is likely to freewheel from topic to topic with serious debate carried along in the flow of small talk and chitchat.

Cultural models and online behaviour

Let us return to the wider issue driving this section of the book, and reflect on the role of culture in online communication. To what extent does our analysis support a simple correlation between online behaviour and cultural behaviour in other modes of interaction? Clearly, the two opposing tendencies discerned in our data (debate vs conversation) can be linked with sets of more or less hackneyed generalizations regarding the cultures concerned: French passion, British reserve, seriousness of

French engagement with forms of intellectual debate, British avoidance of social conflict. And what could the chattering classes, represented *par excellence* by the *Guardian* and BBC publics do but chat? Yet we contend that, without the benefit of actually monitoring the sites concerned, one could join up the dots in a completely different way. The *Nouvel Observateur* discussion starters in translation might well evoke the English tradition of team debating, and in the light of this cultural practice one might expect – accumulating stereotypes – sportingly serious debate, rather than the insistence on chattiness on the British sites. Conversely, *The Guardian*'s one-liners could be associated with the *'badinage'* [wit and repartee] of French dinner-party discussions. In other words, whilst the online patterns parallel some norms of cultural behaviour, they do not reflect others: they hold up not a general mirror to the communicative practices of a culture, but a highly selective one.

Online behaviour, then, is linked to other culturally determined modes of behaviour, but not in predictable ways. In order to explain the ways in which the patterns we have presented articulate with other cultural practices, we need to return to the question of genre outlined at the end of Chapter 2. The discussion forum posting is a recent genre in a relatively recent medium (CMC), and when a new genre presents itself, the conventions that arise in that genre will depend on the ways in which a culture engages with it. Freadman and Macdonald (1992), in their detailed exposition of the concept and uses of genre, explain that when we see ourselves as participating in a genre, we are not simply following a set of rules, but engaging in an act of interpretation that determines our practice:

> [L]abelling does not simply tag a given text for the convenience of knowing where to store it, but shapes it in the manner of a template for the purposes of a reading.
>
> (p. 24)

That is to say, the labelling of a textual genre, rather than being dictated by the shared elements of a group of texts, actually shapes the production of such texts. Equally important is the role of commentary. According to Freadman and Macdonald, commentary – statements descriptive of practice – may function to entrench conventions or, on occasion, to modulate them. Through the use of metaphors or allusions to existing forms, commentary interprets and moulds a practice in terms of a particular model or template (1992, pp. 95–106). This function can only gain in importance in a situation where habits are not ingrained, as in the case of a relative newcomer such as electronic discussion on media websites at the time of our study. Conventions of participation can be dictated from above to only a very limited extent: they cannot be decided unilaterally by the newspaper editors or website designers, and the direction the genre will take relies greatly on the conventions participants establish through the interpretation of their own practice and that of others.

So how do our forum contributors interpret what they do? We turn our attention to the templates, metaphors and labelling statements that appear in postings. Note that we are not concerned here with judging whether contributions actually resemble in fine detail other genres taken as models. As Freadman and Macdonald note, '[o]ne genre, taken as a component for another is transformed according to a function it must serve' (1992, p. 25). Rather, our interest is in the force of these comparisons and metaphors in shaping both understanding and practice. Let us also remind ourselves that such modelling is not immutable but subject to change, that for a nascent genre it is a 'precarious choice' (p. 21), and indeed we have already seen transformations such as the small-scale introduction of chat on the *Le Monde* site.

Written and oral templates

Despite the 'message board' metaphor, interaction on the BBC site is modelled on verbal exchanges, particularly informal verbal exchanges. The same holds for Guardian Unlimited Talk, which dumps the comparison with writing altogether and styles itself a 'talkboard'. Participants frequently refer to what they are doing as nattering and ranting, listening and overhearing. The abundance of conversational metaphors is perfectly coherent with the manifestation on these sites of traits – such as the importance of community-building over topic – found in informal spoken interaction. And when they are not involved in chat, the models are still oral. An extended voicing of opinion on a subject is referred to as 'getting on a soapbox' and, in its Great Debate section, the BBC offers a 'Virtual Soapbox' where you can 'speak passionately [...] and tell us why we should listen'. A posting to *The Guardian*'s 'Politics Talk' abundantly illustrates this modelling:

Tom

If you would like to get off your *soapbox* for a moment, I was not *talking* about whether Bush is legitimate or not. Frankly I dont care,

I have been bored to bloody tears on this site *listening* to you lot argue about it. People should move on.

I was just *talking* about the actual process of the elction. It's OK I will have the discussion with someone who can hold a rational *conversation*.

(twicken, Why do people *rant* on about the
US election supposedly being stolen?,
4 April 2002 [our emphasis])

In contrast, on a *Le Monde* 'Autres sujets' thread discussing why people participate in online forums, various contributors clearly position Internet discussion as a form, not of spoken debate, but of *writing*:

Ce que les forums de discussions permettent par-dessus tout c'est de renouer avec l'écriture comme moyen de communication. Les occasions d'écrire étaient devenues rares depuis l'apparition du téléphone, presque qu'anecdotiques en fait, mis à part une réclamation d'assurance ou une liste d'épicerie les opportunités de pratiquer sa prose, et de se faire lire surtout, étaient pratiquement inexistantes.

[What discussion forums allow above all is to revive writing as a means of communication. Opportunities to write had become rare since the appearance of the telephone, almost the stuff of anecdotes, in fact, apart from the odd insurance claim or grocery list. The possibility of practising one's prose, and especially of being read, was practically non-existent.]

(Joho, *'Pourquoi des forums?'* [Why forums?] 13 April 2000)

This is far from an isolated example on the French sites. In the same discussion, V. Graslin writes,

– *On veut briller par la qualité de sa prose [. . .];*
– *On veut participer à un tout nouveau mode d'expression, avec la même griserie que les premiers émules de Gutenberg se sont mis à imprimer ou à lire des livres il y a quelque cinq cents ans;*
[– We want to shine through the quality of our prose.
– We want to participate in a brand new means of expression, with the same intoxication as Gutenberg's imitators as they set to printing or reading books some five hundred years ago.]

(10 February 2000)

And Antoine Syrt adds,

Les forums sont un extraordinaire moyen de réfléchir, et en plus ils obligent à exprimer, par écrit, ses idées.

[The forums are an extraordinary means of reflection and moreover they force us to express, in written form, our ideas.]

(13 April 2000)

Far away from the evident writerly care of these messages, in a *Nouvel Observateur* debate in which sideswipes are taken at participants' linguistic abilities we find this:

J'ecris au vol et j'ai pas le temps de m'appliquer comme certains ou certaines, je n'utilise pas les accents et je ne verifie pas ce que j'ecris.le principal c'est que mon messages passe,le reste n'a pas d'importance.

[I write on the run and I don't have time to apply myself like some, I don't use accents and I don't check what I write, the main thing is that my message gets through, the rest doesn't matter.]

(Kurupt, *'La double peine'* [Double penalty], 11 January 2002)

Even here, where the quasi-literary delight of the *Le Monde* contributors is absent, there is still the insistence on participation as *writing*.

Neither tendency is absolute. The use of the dead metaphors 'say'/*'dire'* and 'talk'/*'parler'* to refer to the content of postings (as in 'your message said [...]') is widespread on all sites. The BBC site carries a few messages clearly patterned on letters, perhaps for comic effect. *The Guardian* readers collaborate to produce limericks/poems. And both *Le Monde* and *Le Nouvel Observateur* participants compare what they are doing to discussion at the bar of a café – the site of discussion of current affairs amongst equals. Yet it is only comparison: the web is like, but not identical to, discussion over a drink, because whereas oral discussion is ephemeral, interventions on forums – according to one *Nouvel Observateur* contributor –

restent inscits dans le cyberespace. Nos conneries accèdent à l'immortalité et à la posterité sans passer par l'académie.

[remain inscribed in cyberspace. Our rubbish attains immortality and reaches posterity without having to go through the academy.]

(Keemun, *'La libre expression sur Internet'* [Free speech on the Internet], 14 April 2001)

It is, that is, written.

Tellingly, what suggests that these contrasting models (written communication for the French sites, spoken for the English) are not just products of the particular sites studied is the fact that when the *Le Monde* forums are referred to as places for conversation, as is from time to time the case, it is most often by an Anglophone contributor. Examples include the following:

> The Internet is a wonderful thing. Now we can read your newspapers and participate in your conversations, if you will permit it.
>
> > (David Dalton, '*Combattre le modèle américain*' [Fight the American model], 30 August 1999)

> Parlant un francais minimal (ou affreux), [...] puis-je joindre un 'chat room'. [Speaking minimal (or appalling) French, [...] may I join a 'chat room.']
>
> > (Laura, '*les etrangers, sont-ils bienvenus?*' [are foreigners welcome?], 20 July 1999)

This patterning of discussion on written or oral communication accounts for further differences between the French and the British sites, in conventions of length and turn-taking for instance.

Length and turn-taking

On all four sites, messages from registered participants appear when they are posted. On the British sites the potential for quasi-synchronous discussion is exploited such that they often function like chatrooms, with a fast turnaround between messages and lots of one-liners, or indeed simple exclamation marks or other forms of interjection by punctuation/emoticon:

> Aha.
>
> > (finnegansawake, Thread for extremist right-wing adolescents of any age (part 2), *The Guardian*, 30 April 2002)

> ^|^|^|^|^|^|^|^|^|^| *mijj hides behind fence*
> ^|^|^|^|^|^|^|^|
>
> > (mijj, Spanking brand new ((((HUGS)))) thread, *The Guardian*, 4 June 2002)

Endless numbers of short messages such as 'Yes you are right' (Net Nut, B.*.P., BBC, 7 May 2002), 'Bravo!' (Andrew Stone, Anti American Hysteria, BBC, 26 August 2002), 'Twaddle. Complete and utter twaddle' (TomRoss73, Widespread mispronunciations, *The Guardian*, 14 May 2002) and 'Yep, I would....' (Lutece, There's a hell of a lot of hidden racism on the left, *The Guardian*, 4 June 2002) pass without comment. The presence of such short postings, often only seconds apart in an online BBC or *Guardian* conversation, helps to explain the vast number of postings in some threads.

Long messages, on the other hand, are viewed as soliloquies (fine for the soapbox but an aberration in conversation) or oddities. They invite comment, censure and even censorship. When veteran BBC poster Mick Anderson01 provides a 700-word exposé comparing religions (Anti-semitism. Why?, 7 May 2002), it is evidently something of an event and in the ensuing discussion, the author keeps referring back to his post and defending it. This length of argument is apparently considered worthy of particular notice. Similarly, a 300-word posting to Guardian Education Talk provokes this ironic reply: 'Much amusing stuff to dissect here, which I'll do later when I've finished writing 1700 words of weak generalizations, padded with non sequiters and plain error [...]' (James, 1. F, Sign the Guestbook (please!), 13 May 2002). And although a cursory glance through the *Guardian* threads might suggest that lengthy messages do occur, in most cases they prove to be cut-and-paste jobs from other websites – perhaps the online equivalent to reading aloud bits of the morning newspaper – as opposed to sustained exposition on the part of the person posting the message.

Meanwhile, at the BBC, moderators can actually remove messages for no other reason than that they are too long. One message was culled at 575 words (Stewart Knight, Free Speech at the BBC?, 5 May 2002) and discussion amongst contributors shows that this was no isolated case. Brevity, it seems, is the soul of quality.

In marked contrast to the fast turn-taking on the UK sites, we have the *Le Monde* contributor who worries that he/she posts too frequently, which might amount to chat:

> *je m'abstiens souvent de répondre de peur de monopoliser les fils ... donc dans quelle limite peut-on écrire des messages ? car à trop faire de messages, ce forum deviendrait un 'chat', ce qui n'était pas la vocation première je suppose.* [I often refrain from responding for fear of monopolizing the threads ... so how often can one write? Because if there were too

many messages, this forum would become a 'chatroom', which was not its prime objective, I imagine.]

(miaou, '*Nom de la section ...*' [name of the section ...],
2 August 2000)

If the format offers the potential for synchronous dialogue, it also allows for asynchronous interactions, and it is this aspect that is exploited on the French sites: in contrast with FTF confrontation, with its immediate, even hasty responses, the Internet discussion forum allows you the time to think before replying. And if the emphasis is on taking one's time, there is an expectation that messages will be more substantial.

Contrast the constraints on length at the BBC with the anxious contributor to a *Le Monde* forum who finds the software unable to cope with the size of his messages and, when advised by the moderator to cut them after every 500 words or so, frets at characteristic length. The unity of his text will be spoiled; it may even be interrupted by other postings from those who reply to his first paragraphs without waiting for their continuation (Brunner, '*Cas particulier des messages longs*' [The question of long messages], 12 January 2000, and ensuing discussion). The technical and generic constraints are here in conflict. Meanwhile, in another discussion of the forums, expatriote expresses the annoyance he experiences when he opens discussion messages '*pour ne lire que quatre ou cinq mots totalement dénués d'intérêt!*' [to find only four or five words totally devoid of interest] (expatriote, '*Vos questions*' [Your questions], 10 February 2002).

A certain length is not just tolerated but *expected* in the *Nouvel Observateur* debates and hence, whilst we find neither complaint nor apology regarding long messages (and plenty of messages upwards of 500 words), the occasional very short messages seem to require some self-reflexive remark. In replying simply '*oui*' to the thread question 'Is the Constitutional Court impartial', '*pepin le bref*' uses both his pseudonym (Pippin the Short) and the subject line – '*en bref*' [in short] – to comment on his own contravention of convention (11 February 2002). Similarly, Zamil92 prefaces his three-line message with '*au risque d'être un peu court*' [at the risk of being too short] ('*La double peine*' [Double penalty], 4 February 2002). Short messages on both French sites rarely comprise fewer than four lines. We can see that taking oral or written genres as the model for Internet discussion has clear consequences for the development of cultural conventions for forum participation.

Implications

The evolution of a new genre

A good deal has been published about the hybrid nature of CMC, the fact that CMC incorporates characteristics associated with both oral and written communication (see notably Crystal, 2001; Herring, 2001b; Murray, 2000a). Researchers have also noted that this hybridity is not uniform across CMC genres, with synchronous CMC (such as chat) mimicking more of the structures of spoken discourse than asynchronous CMC (such as email) (cf. Herring, 2001b; Sotillo, 2000). What emerges from our case study, however, is that such hybridity is also not equally dosed across cultures, that a CMC genre – public Internet discussion in this case – may appropriate to a greater or lesser extent the norms of spoken or written discourse in different cultures.

The question remains as to how cultural differences such as those we have identified arise. We argue that they result not from some kind of blanket cultural preference for written or spoken discourse on the part of the French or the British, but from participation being modelled on different genres in each case. On the one hand, we see that online behaviour is not divorced from the rest of the culture: participants apply conventions derived from other forms of cultural interaction. On the other hand, the genres selected as the template for online discussion do not coincide on the French- and British-based forums, hence the references to written genres on the former, and oral on the latter. If, as Mangenot (2002) notes, 'any new genre is constructed on the basis of existing genres' (p. 4),[19] clearly it is not necessarily constructed on the basis of the same genre in different cultural contexts. We can conclude that the cultural conventions that evolve in a new CMC genre depend not only on technical constraints and shared values, but, to a large extent, on the way in which that new genre is understood in relation to existing genres. In our case study, we have seen models of debate and conversation shaping the purpose of the interaction and tolerance of digression. In addition, cultural variation in length and turn-taking can be shown to derive from the choice of spoken or written models. Furthermore, we have seen that the choice of models was not simply predictable from familiarity with the cultures in question.

This is clearly demonstrated by the fact that other models have been used in other contexts. In their study of Francophone and Anglophone UseNet discussions on environmental topics in 2001, von Münchow and Rakotonoelina (2006) show that the Francophone discussions were more conversational and digressive than the Anglophone ones. The

Anglophone participants in these forums (a narrower demographic in a more specialized mode of discussion with different origins) evidently did not model their practice in the same way as the Anglophone general public did in the discussion forums on the British mass-media websites.[20]

On the other hand, studies by Mangenot (2002) and Kramsch and Thorne (2002) of online communication in educational contexts show university students modelling their participation in ways similar to what we have seen in the discussion forums for the general public. Contributions to an online debate by Mangenot's students (future French-language teachers) averaged 1700 characters (approximately 300 words), with structuring typical of written discourse and a notable absence of features of chat (2002, p. 4). They were deemed to be 'closer to written than oral' genres of pedagogical production (p. 1). Meanwhile, Kramsch and Thorne's study of a French/US email exchange between university students showed the French students using 'factual, impersonal, dispassionate genres of writing' while the Americans used an oral style (2002, p. 98). Both these studies refer to the Francophone approaches as institutional forms of discourse, which raises the possibility that participation on French discussion forums for the general public, open to scrutiny, may also hark back to classroom genres.

But, one might protest, it's all very well to demonstrate these culturally aligned tendencies with data from the period when moderators and participants were finding their feet. Perhaps the Internet doesn't of itself eliminate cultural difference – but might it not offer the opportunity for difference to be elided? Perhaps over the intervening years, as cultures have had the opportunity to rub shoulders online, these contrasts might have been effaced? And as forum use has taken off as a genre in its own right perhaps the original oral and written models have been left behind? It is time to move on to look at the present day.

4
Plus ça change...: Are Online Cultural Differences Fading Over Time?

Cultural change

Cultures and the practices through which they manifest themselves are not static, but under constant renegotiation. Thus genres are not immutable; they continue to evolve. In the case of Internet discussion it could even be argued that, as a relatively new mode of interaction, it is somewhat more susceptible to change than more traditional forms of communication.

Our previous chapter demonstrated pronounced cultural differences between the norms of participation on French- and British-based Internet discussion forums using data from 2000–2002, when the forums were still a relatively new feature of media websites. But now that the novelty has passed, it is worth examining whether the contrast has remained strong. To what extent do our findings remain valid, and what conclusions can be drawn from the directions in which participation has already altered during these few short years? The question is particularly salient given the widespread notion that global communications technologies are leading cultures to converge. Is there, then, any evidence that French and British conventions of Internet discussion are becoming more similar? Are the cultural differences we have identified in the forums being attenuated or accentuated by the changes taking place? The question resonates with French debates about the defence of cultural identity in a world of global communication.

Widening our corpus to include discussion forums attached to a larger number of media websites, we check the extent to which the differences we identified continue to distinguish forums on French and British sites, and analyse the changes that have taken place.

Continuity of cultural differences?

Among the French press, the contrasting tones and political outlooks of *Le Monde*, *Libération*, *Le Figaro*, *L'Humanité*, *Le Nouvel Observateur* and *L'Express* attract markedly different readerships, as do the BBC, *The Guardian*, *The Times*, *The Telegraph* and *The Independent* among the British press. When comparing communication patterns in the forums on their websites, however, we find that in 2007–2008 some clear contrasts remain between the French sites, on the one hand, and the British sites, on the other, notwithstanding the deep ideological divisions between the news providers in each culture. Moreover, the two noticeable changes that have taken place – one on the British sites, one on the French – serve to emphasize the different cultural approaches to public Internet discussion.

Let us start with a quick survey of what has altered little since 2002. Despite the continuing rapid evolution of Internet technologies, the mechanics of discussion (threading of messages, opportunities to reply or start new threads, archiving, pre- or post-moderation) remain largely unchanged on the French sites studied. Clearly, the repeated overhauls of the forums prior to 2002 resulted in sustainable modes of interaction. However, while the French sites are thriving, and while enthusiasm remains high on the British sites, opportunities on the latter for the general public to pursue discussions in the way we have described are dwindling.

Digression

The extent of digression remains the clearest difference between French and British forums. French debate remains topic-driven: participants are disciplined in following the topic, and moderators in enforcing it if lapses occur. Although debate on a *Nouvel Observateur* topic such as '*Peine de mort*' [the death penalty] may degenerate at times into an exchange of insults, some three and a half thousand messages later, the thread is still on topic. Even on the forums of the popular television station M6, there is no off-topic chatter in current affairs threads. Chat is effectively quarantined into dedicated spaces, such as 'Coin détente' [Relaxation corner] at *Le Monde*, 'Le Salon' at *Le Figaro* (described as a forum for all topics, 'serious or not') or the separate Chat function at *Le Nouvel Observateur*.

No such discipline reigns on the forums of the British sites, as conversations move freely and endlessly from topic to topic, whether the subject is serious or trivial to begin with, and chat is endemic. And although contributors recognize that the forums are full of 'inane, off topic, chatter', as juniorswailing complains on a BBC Radio 2 message board (Big punch-up on BBC Radio 4 message boards, 17 November 2006), in general they remain unperturbed by it. Not so, the proprietors of these same quality news sites. This has led to some interesting measures being taken to curb digression, leading to an even starker contrast between the British and the French forums.

Curbing digression/chat on British forums

Clearly there are costs involved in hosting discussion forums, especially in moderating the discussions, but also in the server load. The potential return for proprietors lies partly in the possibility of selling advertising on the forum pages (exploited by most of the French sites), of encouraging subscription to the online edition (the path taken by *Le Monde*, where only subscribers can post messages to the forums), or, more widely, although less directly, through the connection established between discussion and the rest of the site. Lively forum discussion can be presumed to maintain audience/readership and foster interest in the news or entertainment that is the core business of the host media organization. On the other hand, discussion that routinely loses any connection with the media content may be seen as less profitable.

This seems to have been the case with *The Independent*'s 'Argument' forum, which was, in a sense, a victim of its own success. This forum hosted vast, animated, digressive discussions like those of the BBC and *The Guardian* until May 2004, when the resources needed for moderation were deemed too costly to sustain. In encouraging participants to migrate their discussions to the Delphi Forums platform, *The Independent*'s forum editor expressed his 'apologies to everyone who had been hoping for the 100,000th post in the idle chit-chat thread!' (daveyf, Independent Argument, 2004). His message includes the following invitation: 'We hope that those of you who have debated intelligently and with open minds will feel free to submit letters for publication to *The Independent*.' In other words, reader participation will be scaled back forthwith to 'Letters to the Editor'.

While *The Guardian* appears content to maintain its iconic and hugely popular 'Talk' site, with its mix of banter and discussion, the BBC has attempted to curb chatter, limit general discussions and connect its forums more closely to its radio and television programmes. Since late 2006, current affairs discussions can no longer be accessed thematically through the category 'News & Sport'. This category has disappeared from the front page of the discussions, and participants need to navigate via particular radio programmes – either Five Live's 'World News' or 'UK News' – in order to access current affairs message boards. (The current small number of news-related message boards – two – can be contrasted with the six pertaining to the radio serial *The Archers* and the four on gardening.) Moreover, the 'house rules' now explicitly limit digression, with moderators able to remove messages 'considered to be off-topic for the particular message board' (BBC, 2007).

The BBC's 'Today Programme' went even further with its changes on 16 November 2006, no longer allowing users to launch threads, but providing a single daily discussion starter on a topic discussed during the radio programme. The changes provoked outrage from users. 'Today' threads were hijacked to debate other topics that interested readers, and to complain about the changes, seen as a form of 'censorship'. The moderators struggled to enforce the new rules, and were mocked by users:

'Zzzzzzzzz'
Today's debate, determined to avoid the areas that people used to discuss on the old 'free for all' boards.
(skinningroveparker, 19 November 2006)

Substantial gaps appeared in threads, where the moderators removed large numbers of messages. Users deserted to other BBC message boards, and joined or created rival forums hosted on other sites. Over a year later, a significant proportion of the messages posted on the 'Today' message boards continued to criticize the moderators' choice of topics, complain about restrictions on free speech and introduce alternative discussion topics (such as 'Saudi oil supplies' to subvert a question on 'Yellow school buses'). The struggle persisted for 18 months until the *Today* message boards closed completely (31 May 2008). The only reader input envisaged on the new web page is that of sending an email to the editorial staff. However, a link does appear to *Have Your Say*, a new-look BBC forum where participants can post comment on a small number of BBC News stories (half a dozen topics are active per week). Clearly, opportunities for reader-initiated discussion have contracted markedly.

The approach of the 'Today Programme' resembles that of *The Times* and *The Telegraph*,[1] which eliminate chat and digression by limiting the extent to which contributors can respond to each other. Despite its title of 'Debate', the forum at *Times Online* only allows contributors to post a short response to a small number of stimulus questions, each linked to a print article. The 'debate' appears as a list of these comments, which are rarely interconnected. The 'Speaker's Corner' of *The Telegraph* functions in the same way: postings appear as a series of individual comments, with no dialogue taking place.[2] Certainly this format prevents the forum from being swamped by chat, but at the cost of any interaction between participants, of any genuine debate. Participation here is no more interactive than sending a 'Letter to the Editor'.[3]

We can see that opportunities for participation by the general public on British news sites now tend to take one of two forms. On the one hand, there are open forums like those of *The Guardian*, where participants propose topics and respond to each other. Highly interactive, they boast lengthy threads with lots of short, phatic messages, include personal conversations and may drift far from the original subject of discussion. Although they clearly represent the preferred model of participants on the British sites when left to their own devices, they are becoming fewer in number, as their hosts close them down. On the other hand, there are facilities like those of *The Times*, which allow contributors to post comment in response to questions posed by the editorial team. These are structured so as to avoid conversation taking place. Although they remain strictly on topic, these are not really discussion forums at all, in that participants reply to the editors, rather than to each other.

Neither of these forms, however, resembles the French current affairs forum, in which polemical discussion between participants is rarely interrupted by off-topic chatter, and which is, without exception, highly interactive. On the *Nouvel Observateur* site, interactivity occurs despite the forum design, which obliges users to respond to the topic question rather than directly to another participant. This constraint is simply circumvented by posting the name of the person to whom one is replying as the subject line, and in this way the forum functions just as interactively as the others.

Focused debate of this kind, where the point is to make a point and where chat is successfully relegated to designated spaces, must appear as an unattainable grail to hosts of British current affairs forums, on which sustained on-topic discussion is reliably achieved only through obtrusive moderation – seen as stifling free speech – or through limiting interaction between participants. The 'French' model of focused debate is clearly available to the wider British public, proffered by the website administrators, but is strenuously resisted.

Long messages

Long messages continue to be unremarkable on French sites, and actively discouraged on British sites. Messages upwards of 500 words are common on the forums of *Libération, L'Express, Le Nouvel Observateur*, especially as the first posting in a thread, which is expected to outline an argument and provide evidence to support it. Messages at *L'Humanité* are the longest with postings of over 1500 words in some cases, while messages at *Le Figaro* are somewhat shorter, tending not to exceed 400 words. Although *Le Monde* limits postings to 4000 characters (approximately 700 words) it invites longer messages in its user guide, explaining that this technical constraint can be overcome by splitting your message into two and posting the second half as a reply to the first. Messages on the British sites, on the other hand, rarely exceed 300 words. *The Times* limits postings to 1000 characters (around 170 words), while responses from other participants discourage long postings at the BBC: at 403 words, the first message in the 'Relationships' thread (DonG, 10 July 2005) received the immediate reply 'Reader's Digest?' (pincer_movement, 10 July 2005).

Short messages

A noticeable change since 2002 has taken place in the greater acceptability of short (one- and two-line) messages on French forums. Shorter turns lead to rapid-fire discussion, more conversational and informal in style than previously. This often occurs when a participant who has previously outlined an argument returns to comment on a reply. Nonetheless it is extremely rare to find a one-word answer on French sites (and they are excluded on, for example, the *Libération* forums, which are pre-moderated). Simple agreement requires elaboration. In any case, short messages on French sites never simply fulfil a phatic function; they are used to give a point of view, however succinct.

The rise in short messages is most evident in the forums of *Le Monde*, and points to an interesting development in relation to a neighbouring genre of Internet communication. For on these forums, it is now acceptable to open a new thread with a first message drawing attention to a news item or opinion piece available elsewhere and adding a brief comment and invitation to discuss the story. The linked item is more often than not an article from *Le Monde*, which means participants are spontaneously producing the kind of forum so clearly desired by the hosts of the BBC's 'Today Programme'. The links, however, may also point to blogs, and indeed to a blog on the *Le Monde* site maintained by the very same contributor.

Forums and blogs: Neighbouring genres?

Since our 2002 research, 'web logs' – commonly referred to as blogs – have become an increasingly mainstream genre of CMC. Blogs consist of commentaries, arranged in reverse chronological order, on which readers of the blog can usually post comment. At *Le Monde*, which allows subscribers to set up their own blogs within the site 'lemonde.fr', we can see that some earlier functions of forums have effectively been taken over by blogs, which may explain the greater frequency since 2002 of short messages on the forums of this site: those who wish to provide regular, extended comment on current affairs open blogs. And these bloggers have more control over the archiving and permanence of their musings than contributors of forum messages.

Thus, on the forums of *Le Monde*, and especially in the months following the launch of the blog facility (2005–2006), contributors could be found using the forums as a way of attracting visitors to their blogs: posting a short message linking to the blog, where a longer, more developed version of the argument appears. At *Le Monde*, then, the two genres are distinct but related. The proximity of the genres for French Internet users is also evident in the example of Eric J.-L. Breton, a regular contributor to the debates of *Le Nouvel Observateur*, who has since published his contributions to this forum as part of the archives to his blog (Breton, 2001–2002). A clear continuity appears between French forum postings and blog entries, a connection not apparent in British forum postings. Breton obviously saw his postings as journalistic writing worthy of conservation, which points to a possible explanation for this cultural contrast: the traces of the modelling of forum participation on written and oral genres, discussed in the previous chapter.

Modelling on written and oral genres

Although French forum participation includes more exchanges that are conversational in form (short replies, informal register) than previously, we still see traces of the modelling of forum participation on written genres. This is particularly evident in the emphasis on the quality of messages and in concerns expressed by participants about the ephemerality of their contributions.

Postings to French forums are automatically erased after a period of time (the length depends on the particular forum). *Le Monde*, however, archives debates perceived as worthy of preservation, making a large number of threads on momentous topics prominently available in a read-only section entitled *'Les grands débats des forums'* [Great debates from the forums]. And a number of contributors would like *Le Monde* to go further in rescuing messages from oblivion: suggestions have included compiling a 'best of' section,[4] where the choice would be based on quality of the message, rather than import of the debate, or rewarding valuable messages by placing them in the print version of the paper as 'Thought of the month from our forum'.[5] Quality is indeed rewarded in a similar way at *Le Figaro*, where a *'Message du jour'* [Message of the day] appears on the forum home page. Furthermore, *Le Figaro* readers rate messages on a scale of 1 to 10, a ranking that appears as a bar chart attracting other readers towards widely appreciated contributions. Similarly, *L'Express* devotes a column of its forum home page to *'Les plus lus'*, linking directly to the messages that have been read most often. Meanwhile, *Libération* goes so far as to publish selected contributions in the paper edition. On this site, the written nature of the genre remains clear, with moderators claiming the right to intervene to correct grammar, punctuation, spelling and paragraphing.

None of these features appears on those British forums that have retained an interactive format. The contrast between the ephemerality of exchanges on the BBC and *Guardian* sites and the concerns about the quality and preservation of messages on the French sites indicate that the original modelling of messages on oral and written genres on British and French forums respectively has continued to shape the way contributors understand their participation in forums.

An evolving genre: *Plus ça change . . .*

Internet discussion does not have a long history. However, our analysis of the changes that have already become evident in the way forum participation occurs on French and British media websites – efforts to curb digression on British sites; the limited introduction of chat, shorter messages and links to blogs on the French sites – attests to the strength of the old adage that the more things change, the more they remain the same. The French forums remain places to exchange pertinent points on a given issue, while on the British discussion threads debate, unless tightly controlled, is carried along in the flow of conversation. When possibilities for chat are introduced on the French sites, they remain separate from the forums proper. And French participants have shown how easily forum messages can be assimilated into the new, more obviously written genre of the blog.

This evidence runs counter to a prevalent discourse of globalization as the erosion of cultural difference, the idea that using identical communications technologies leads cultures to converge. Worldwide, those endowed with computer, Internet connection and the time – language students, for example! – can participate in electronic discussion forums: the tyranny of geographical distance is indeed diminished. But as our study of the French and British media forums has demonstrated, it is illusory to imagine that the widespread arrival of this technology has made possible some mode of social interaction which would be uniformly, universally performed. Internet discussion does not take the same form across cultures, and indeed also varies within cultures, and the evolution of these forms over time does not lead them in the direction of homogeneity.

Pedagogical implications

Now, as we saw in Chapter 2, many language and business communication teachers, among others, currently use Internet exchanges to teach cross-cultural skills, widely assuming that online interaction replicates offline FTF experiences. We have seen that although the online conventions identified in the French and British discussion forums are consistent with certain other practices in these cultures, they are not simply predictable from them. Nor can they be automatically extrapolated to the rest of the culture. Indeed they are not necessarily applicable even to other genres of CMC (emails, personal home pages, blogs).

What happens in one place may not happen elsewhere. Discussion techniques used online are just as likely to backfire FTF. Five-minute expositions, laced with insult, in the style of the *Nouvel Observateur* contributions will not be tolerated in dinner-party debate in France, any more than a personal chat about the weekend's activities in the middle of a televised debate would be acceptable in the British context. Here extrapolation from CMC is at best unhelpful, at worst misleading. Again, if one were to generalize from our sites to verbal communication one would think that French allows for very long conversational turns, without interruption, whilst English begs for interruption. This is in contradiction with the evidence that 'cooperative interruptions' are a feature of French oral discussion, expected as an indication of attentiveness and interest on the part of one's interlocutor (Béal, 1990, pp. 24–25; Liddicoat, 2000, p. 61). And if we were to extrapolate to written communication, we might incorrectly assume that English speakers can't keep to the topic or indeed concentrate long enough to construct a written argument, whereas Clyne (1987, p. 76, referring to Kaplan, 1972, p. 257) suggests that tolerance of digression in essays and dissertations is similar in British, American and French academic writing, with a tendency towards *more* digression in French writing. Clearly it is risky simply to assume continuity between the cultural conventions of different genres of communicative practice, whether they be FTF or online genres.

So what are the implications? Should the widespread educational practice of putting learners online be abandoned? Clearly no – but what does need to be rectified is the pervasive blind spot regarding the cultural and generic specificity of online communication practices. Our example of online discussion facilities is eloquent in this regard. Like any other sphere of public discussion (whether it be the pub, the letters page of the newspaper or the bus stop for that matter), the Internet discussion forum is culturally defined in terms of purpose and communicative conventions. While this might rightly be understood as curtailing its use in cross-cultural training, simultaneously it confirms its status as an invaluable tool in this context.

To understand what is learnt online as generalizable principles, to extrapolate incautiously from a culture's behaviour in an online forum to a culture as a whole is ill-founded and even dangerous. Internet discussion is not a teach-all. At the same time, since CMC – in its many forms – does not take place in a culture-free void, our results confirm that this medium provides spaces in which learners may experience cultural alterity, and this in forms which go far beyond simple encounters with facts about other cultures. Students logging on to discussions based in another culture *can* learn a great deal about cultural practices: teachers have the opportunity to sensitize them to differences in discourse patterns, explicitness, irony, allusions and so on, as well as different world views and values. And some of these practices will be useful elsewhere: the question is, 'which ones where?' To articulate the question is to start to understand both the potential and the limitations of teaching with genres of CMC. These parameters are our concern in Part II of this book.

Part II

Language Learners and Intercultural Internet Discussion

5
Public Discussion Forums as a Tool for Language Learning

Introduction

The communicative possibilities of the Internet have been eagerly seized upon by those who deal in the teaching of communication, including language teachers. As a result, there are currently vast numbers of language learners engaged in email exchanges with learners in other countries, while teachers from around the world organize discussion activities between their geographically distanced classes. As yet, however, comparatively little pedagogical use has been made of the learning opportunities offered by public Internet discussion.

In this chapter we consider the uptake of Internet-based technologies in foreign language education, and discuss the additional possibilities offered by public Internet discussion forums along with potential obstacles to their use. The chapter also functions as an introduction to the second part of this book, where we analyse several case studies of learner-participants on discussion forums. The opportunities and challenges described below in summary form will be explored in detail in these case studies.

Online language learning: An overview

For language learners and teachers today, the most salient aspect of CMC is the unprecedented opportunities it offers for contact with the cultural other whose language is being learnt. This interest in the potential for intercultural communication was, however, much less evident when computing facilities first became widely available in language departments. In the early days of CALL in the late 1970s and 1980s, attention was concentrated on human–computer interaction, with self-correcting language drills and interactive reading and writing activities. Computers were seen as instructional tools within classes considered as relatively monocultural. Widespread access to the Internet in the 1990s, however, rapidly changed the focus. Certainly, linguistic and cultural resources were suddenly available as never before, but the emphasis shifted to communication between learners, rather than between learners and machines. By 2000, CALL had become Network-Based Language Teaching (NBLT) (Warschauer & Kern, 2000), learners were emailing each other around the world, and intercultural contact came to the fore of teaching practices.

As NBLT first evolved, the manner in which intercultural communication played out online was rarely considered: the achievement of contact and communication itself was the all-engrossing concern. Quickly, however, attention came to focus on the intercultural dimension of the experience. This can be attributed in part to the growing acceptance of principles of intercultural education. It also derives from the lived experience of CMC exchanges where the educational goals are not reached, and realization of the falseness of the 'impression that as intercultural contact is now easier than ever, intercultural learning can also be achieved more easily' (O'Dowd, 2006, p. 65). Various studies (such as Fischer, 1998; Kern, 2000; Kinginger, Gourvès-Hayward & Simpson, 1999; Kramsch & Thorne, 2002; O'Dowd, 2001, 2003; O'Dowd & Ritter, 2006; Tella, 1996) record the lack of automatic progression to the useful demolition of stereotypes, affable exchanges of messages and intercultural understanding or even learning. Such cases of conflict and miscommunication point to the importance of two principles: firstly, that computer-mediated intercultural contact does not of itself produce successful intercultural communicators (a tenet that also holds for intercultural encounters of other kinds); and secondly, that cultural difference in engagement with technology produces difference in communication. The case studies of the present book provide further support for these principles.

One effect of the rise of Internet-mediated language exchanges since the 1990s has been a change of pedagogical focus from language proficiency to a much broader notion of communicative competence. Kern, Ware and Warschauer (2004) summarize the impact of the shift to long-distance collaborative projects as follows:

> First, it expands the focus beyond language learning to an emphasis on *culture* (i.e., intercultural competence, cultural learning, cultural

literacy). Second, it expands the notion of context beyond the social to include broad social discourses. Third it problematizes the notions of its own inquiry, namely, communication and intercultural competence.

(2004, p. 244)

Similarly, O'Dowd (2006, p. 73) notes burgeoning interest in 'intercultural approaches [...] which attempt to fully exploit the interactive features of information and communication technologies in order to provide rich opportunities for intercultural collaboration and ethnographic investigation'. Such statements suggest that a 'cultural turn' has taken place in the field of online language learning, and, as we shall see, public Internet forums provide an ideal site for pursuing this focus.

Current practice: Telecollaboration and tandem learning

Valuable forms of situated learning are provided by CMC's potential for spontaneous, purposeful written communicative exchange, for which the teacher is not the ostensible primary audience, even though he/she may have access to it. Currently, the two most widely used types of language learning activity using CMC are tandem learning and telecollaboration via email. Given impetus with projects funded by the European Union, tandem learning (learning exchanges involving two individuals) is particularly widespread in Europe, while telecollaboration (exchanges between two classes) has become more popular in the US. Email tandem learning is a pedagogically focused keypal partnership and is available to learners outside an institutional setting. While the emphasis in tandem learning is on autonomous work regulated by the two learners involved, telecollaboration incorporates greater input from teachers in terms of preparation, guidance and feedback. As Thorne (2006, p. 9) points out, however, the distinction between the two is less clear in practice, in that teachers may set up tandem exchanges within institutional settings.[1]

It is not that other possibilities for communicative language learning online do not exist, just that they are much less frequently used. To take an example of what is available, Opp-Beckman's (1999) overview of Internet activities that may connect learners with an authentic audience includes not only participation in discussion forums, MOOs/MUDs, chat sites and simulation games, but also the creation of web pages and electronic newspapers, the writing of electronic postcards, guest entries on sites such as that of the White House, and responses to surveys and opinion polls. However, tandem learning and telecollaborative class exchanges currently overshadow all other uses of the Internet in language learning. Various Internet sites offer services to match classes across the globe: Intercultural E-mail Classroom Connections reports that it has 7650 teachers signed up, in 82 countries (IECC, 2008), while the ePals network connects 'over 120,761 registered classrooms, 6.5 million students and educators in 191 countries for classroom-to-classroom penpal exchanges and cross-cultural learning projects' (ePals, 2007). As stated above, the use of keypals is not restricted to institutionalized language learning: the Tandem project, promising 'autonomous learning with a partner', provides a vast number of language pairings to interested individuals, in addition to class groups (Tandem, 2007), while at the time of writing the Mixxer lists 21,212 individuals looking for partners in addition to 390 requests from teachers seeking partner classes (Mixxer, 2008).[2]

At their best, both tandem learning and telecollaboration foster autonomy, provide an opportunity to develop a relationship with one or several native speakers, and as a result promote a personal investment in the learning exchange. Additionally, teachers have been attracted by the motivating novelty of CMC,[3] and by the opportunities for preserving the interactions and thus for later reflecting on form and content (see, for example, Kern et al., 2004, pp. 245–246). Thus O'Dowd's list of what might be learnt through such forms of online communication includes autonomy, language awareness, writing skills, grammatical correctness and higher-order thinking skills (2006, p. 89), and his own work emphasizes the possibility of developing intercultural understanding through telecollaboration.

The two models are, however, not without their drawbacks. Interaction is restricted to communication with other learners, a situation that is safe and reassuring for beginners and younger learners, but somewhat limiting for more advanced and adult learners, who need practice in venturing beyond the classroom. The institutional setting itself can be a source of difficulties in the case of telecollaboration: as O'Dowd (2006, p. 193) affirms, such exchanges require a high degree of coordination between teachers, and difficulties arise when assessment expectations, academic calendars or indeed academic cultures do not coincide, as further demonstrated by Belz (2001, 2002), Belz and Müller-Hartmann (2003) and O'Dowd (2006, pp. 136, 140).

Another issue which presents itself in the case of both tandem learning and telecollaboration is that of language choice. In a typical example, an individual/class learning English in France is paired with an individual/class studying French in the US. Both (sets of) participants are thus in a position to occupy the roles of learner (of the target language) and expert (in their home language and culture).[4] The question of which language to use when must be negotiated between partners or teachers, which usually results in a somewhat artificial language protocol, the choice ranging from each participant writing in the language of the country where he/she is based, to each participant writing in the language of the other, via various kinds of code switching (see O'Dowd, 2007, pp. 9–10; Thorne, 2006, p. 13).[5]

None of these scenarios is ideal when compared with a situation where learners can engage with native speakers who are actively looking for interaction entirely in the target language, and where interaction takes place in a context driven by a desire to communicate opinions and exchange ideas rather than by assessment or language learning goals. This brings us to an exploration of what Internet forums can offer language learners – for they remedy some of the shortcomings of the models discussed above – and a survey of the obstacles to participation.

Public Internet discussion: Pedagogical possibilities and constraints

As we have seen in our opening chapters, public Internet discussion is, for many populations, an accepted and vibrant cultural practice, attracting wide numbers of participants. Although the general interest sites we have surveyed do have their core of prolific members, participation is also open to those less dedicated (or with other pastimes). This possibility of immersion in an authentic practice of the target culture is arguably one of the most attractive aspects of discussion forums for the language learner, but certainly not the only one.

Below we summarize traits particular to Internet forum discussion which recommend its pedagogical use. The aim here is not to suggest that participation on Internet discussion boards is the only or the best way for learners to engage in CMC for purposes of language and culture acquisition.[6] Nor do we imply that forum participation is necessarily easy or automatically beneficial. Nonetheless, we do contend that such participation has a number of advantages that are being overlooked (see Tables 5.1 and 5.2), as part of the current wide neglect of this genre in the uptake of CMC in language learning.

Table 5.1 Merits shared by three forms of online exchange available to language learners

E-tandem, Telecollaboration, and Public Internet discussion all offer opportunities for

- authentic communication with native speakers
- extensive language practice
- intercultural learning
- development of learner autonomy
- integration of expert feedback (implicit and explicit)
- reflection on form and content

Table 5.2 Features specific to public Internet discussion

Aspects distinguishing Public Internet discussion from Telecollaboration/ e-tandem:

- logistics
  - immediate availability of interlocutors already engaged in the activity
  - no coordination necessary
  - no language protocol necessary
- beyond the virtual classroom
  - not restricted to communication between learners
  - need to negotiate goals beyond institutional ones
  - need to communicate on the terms of native speaker community
- not reliant on the development of a personal relationship

Distinguishing features

Availability of interlocutors

Immediately obvious in the public discussion forums of newspaper and television sites around the world is the large number of people from all walks of life eager to interact with others on topics of mutual interest. There is no difficulty in finding partners with whom to exchange ideas: hordes of willing and proficient speakers are available in a wide range of languages, and need no persuasion to engage in the activity, for they are already involved.

The existence of public discussion forums independent of any particular educational institution therefore presents considerable advantages for teachers. The time involved in setting up class-to-class collaborations has been pointed out by various authors (for example, Kern et al., 2004, p. 243; O'Dowd, 2006, p. 109; Thorne, 2006, p. 7). From a purely logistical point of view, public forum participation recommends itself in that the exigencies of locating partner classes and partner students, and the inevitable breakdowns of workgroups (through illness, incompatibility of partners, withdrawal of students from course and so on) are avoided. No investment of time is needed in coordinating class timetables or devising back-up plans lest a collaborative partnership should fall through: on active forums, discussion takes place every day of the year. Of course this lack of teacherly responsibility also brings with it lack of control and raises questions of how to engage students, what counts as successful involvement and performance and how to assess it. These questions will be taken up in Chapters 9 and 10, where we present specific ideas for teaching (for) forum use.

This availability of interlocutors already involved in discussion for its own sake also eliminates the problem of deciding on a language protocol: there is no need to swap between languages to give both parties an opportunity for language practice, as participants – whether native speakers or not – come with the expectation that discussion will take place in the language of the forum.[7]

Finally, on most forums, there is room for discussion on any number of themes: current affairs (national and international), social issues, culture (films, books, music, art), sport. Most of the kinds of topics selected by teachers for telecollaboration activities are already available and under discussion in these public forums. Sometimes, however, this will require some negotiation: unlike keypal conscripts, interlocutors on a discussion forum are not motivated to respond to a posting about a particular film/text/issue by the need to complete assessment, but rather because a message interests them or makes a contribution to the discussion at hand. Learners can certainly use forums for language practice, but to do so they need to engage with the goals of other participants, for otherwise they run the risk of receiving no response or an off-putting one.

Authenticity of learning situation

The motivation of participants brings us to the notion of authenticity of communication. NBLT has frequently been applauded for its potential to bring greater authenticity to language learning activities, as by Thorne:

> The use of Internet technologies to encourage dialogue between distributed individuals and partner classes proposes a compelling shift in second (L2) and foreign language (FL) education, one that ideally

moves learners from simulated classroom-based contexts toward actual interaction with expert speakers of the language they are studying.

(2006, p. 3)

Whilst telecollaborative exchanges certainly lead learners to interact with native speakers, it is less certain that they leave behind the 'simulated classroom-based context' to do so.[8] Sometimes, it is the activities proposed that ensure that the exchange remains a pedagogical exercise. But however imaginative the activity, learners know that they are communicating with other learners. Although this provides a reassuring environment for younger learners and beginners, it does not challenge more advanced and adult learners to cope in situations not specifically designed for their benefit. Students are still safely within the classroom, virtual though it might be, with scant opportunities to engage with the 'target culture' in roles other than that of learner.[9]

In contrast, on public Internet discussion forums learners have the opportunity to participate in activities not especially geared towards them, and not governed by the norms of classroom communication. As we shall see in the following chapters, however, this is not as simple as it sounds. It involves trying to communicate on the terms of the mostly native speaker forum community already in place or finding a way of negotiating those terms. Perhaps uncomfortable with a situation where others cannot be automatically expected to make allowances for them, some students continue to communicate as if in the classroom, reluctant to define themselves in ways other than 'learner' in the target language. As we shall show, teachers can play an important role in preparing these students to meet the challenges of such interactions.

It must be admitted, however, that once the forum interaction is linked to a formal learning situation, a stubborn student can always turn it back into a learners-only exercise, into pretence. Thus a member of an advanced French class (described in Chapter 9) could ask her teacher, 'So do we really have to post our message on the forum, or can we just email it to you when we've written it?' Even in the most authentic language learning activity, authenticity is never guaranteed. The apparently beguiling invitation outlined by Thorne above – to step away from 'simulated classroom-based contexts' – is sometimes strongly resisted.

Reduced reliance on development of personal relationships

The success of telecollaborative and e-tandem learning activities tends to rely on the quality of the relationship that develops between geographically separated participants. As its name suggests, the keypal partnership is modelled on the penpal relationship. And while the keyboard may have replaced the pen, the fundamental understanding of the genre remains largely unchanged: it is an exchange between a pair of individuals, already positioned as friends. In contrast, successful participation in public Internet discussion is largely independent of such relationships, although they do evolve in some cases. This has both advantages and disadvantages.

On the one hand, Intergroup Contact Theory provides evidence that friendships between people from different cultural backgrounds lead to more positive intergroup attitudes (see Dovidio, Gaertner, & Kawakami, 2003, for an overview of the research). Activities that promote the development of interpersonal relationships therefore offer strong potential for enhancing intercultural empathy. In their discussions of tandem and telecollaborative exchanges, Little and Brammerts (1996), Müller-Hartmann (2000), Belz (2005) and Thorne (2006) all emphasize the positive effects that developing a personal relationship can have on motivation and learning. These exchanges thus tend to take as their starting point the exchange of personal information. The case for such personal preludes to discussion is mounted by, for example, Müller-Hartmann (2000) and Thorne (2006), who argue that assertion of identity is crucial in that it allows for the creation of personal relationships of trust and a positive affective dimension which will support and facilitate successful interaction. In their projects, students therefore select their telecollaboration partners from self-presentations provided by their overseas peers. On the other hand, a personal relationship is far from guaranteed, and the literature is peppered with accounts of failed encounters of this kind and the cost of these to learning, motivation and intercultural understanding (Belz, 2002, 2003, 2005; Belz & Müller-Hartmann, 2003; Kramsch & Thorne, 2002; O'Dowd, 2003, 2006; O'Dowd & Ritter, 2006; Ware, 2005).

Unlike these exchanges, public Internet discussion is not predicated on personal knowledge of one's interlocutors, and not intended as a path to intimacy. Compared to telecollaboration and e-tandem, it is therefore much less likely to lead to intense friendships (and the motivational, linguistic and intercultural rewards thereof), but also less likely to lead to the kind of disappointment experienced by students where no personal relationship ensues (and the resulting discouragement and negative stereotyping of the other). Public Internet discussion does not demand an affective investment: that may make it not only less emotionally engaging than other forms of Internet exchange, but also less threatening, less risky. While individuals on the discussion forums may have different agenda, there is no danger of being locked into a partnership with someone whose unwritten codes and expectations are opposed to one's own.

This does not mean to say that public Internet discussion is devoid of human warmth. Cordial acquaintance with regular participants is common, and on many sites it is possible to pursue an exchange privately through an individual message to a participant. It is even possible for personal discussion to arise on some sites in keeping with the prevailing genre conventions: it is far more common on the British sites than on the French sites we have studied for the reasons outlined in Chapter 3. But even where personal messages are discouraged, precious relationships can nonetheless be generated. In other words, on discussion forums, personal relationships – whether of amity or enmity – initially grow out of participation in a joint activity, rather than vice versa.

A striking example of this is afforded by the language forums of Wordreference, a professionally oriented site for translators, students and language enthusiasts (explored in greater detail in Hanna, 2006). Although Wordreference includes possibilities for personalization (the use of icons and signatures), opportunities for the statement of the personal are restricted both in profiles and in discussion. Messages are removed and threads closed by moderators when it is deemed that they have strayed too close to the personal. Thus, when 'Coffee drinking habits' veers towards the particular from the culturally general (that is, when participants post accounts of their own caffeine consumption), a moderator intervenes, '[T]his thread falls outside the Cultura[l] guidelines, since it leads to large doses of chat and personal opinion' (Chaska Ñawi, Cultural Discussions, 'Coffee drinking habits', 25 August 2007). One would therefore expect the primary value of participation to lie in the quality of answers provided to the enquiries which fuel discussion. And yet this is not the case. A questionnaire launched to celebrate the millionth post concludes by asking participants, 'What is your favorite thing about [Wordreference]?'[10] Certainly, the responses do refer to instant answers, learning, cultural discussions, but overwhelmingly and completely outweighing other answers, what do people like about this determinedly non-social site? The camaraderie, friendship, politeness, company, the helpful and congenial people, the respect, the cordiality, the community, the fact that it's a second family and that it shows that the global village is a reality. Despite the apparently arid terrain of non-social interaction, personal engagement flourishes. Or, to quote one of the moderators, 'The friendly interchanges you will see here, amidst the serious conversations, come from shared work, rather than social activity' ('Introduction area', Cuchuflete, 22 October 2006).

The example of Wordreference shows personal engagement growing out of collaboration and stands in contradistinction to the assumption of many telecollaboration projects, namely that successful work can be founded only on pre-existent interpersonal relationships. It also shows that the motivating element of personal engagement is not necessarily excluded when discussion moves away from exchanges between individuals. As the relationship produced is with a community, rather than an individual, one kind of richness may indeed not be available, but other forms are. One person ceases to represent a whole culture, either positively or negatively. While perhaps intense positive affectivity is not produced – or at least is not possible within the code for behaviour on these and other issue-driven forums – neither is the negative affectivity which results from incompatible pairings of individuals or creation of dysfunctional online study groups.

We can see, then, that participation in public discussion forums is qualitatively different from communication with keypals and telecollaboration partners. The fact that it is less relationship-oriented means that public Internet discussion provides a useful space for developing competence in other kinds of exchanges. For although personal conversation is an indispensable genre, it can be a limiting one. As the first step in so many learning activities, it predisposes the student to launching conversations about the self that inevitably position him/her as the exotic little foreigner/the other. He/she may fail to learn strategies for opening and maintaining communication of other kinds. Similarly, personal relationships, while motivating, are not a universal basis for communication. A large number and variety of communicative situations, and notably casual and professional exchanges, are not predicated on personal knowledge of one's interlocutor or even on the assumption of a sympathetic ear. The techniques of being personable, rather than personal, of managing to create positive affectivity through participation in an activity rather than detailed personal presentations are, in many cultures, characteristic of relationships between professional adults and worth developing. This competence is a useful addition to a learner's expanding repertoire, and the chapters that follow will examine specific aspects of task design and preparatory activities that promote it. As we shall see in Chapters 6 and 8, students are sometimes at a loss as to where to begin in an interaction where the exchange of personal information is not the starting point. Public Internet discussion provides opportunities for learning in this area, and practice in approaching interlocutors in ways other than as potential buddies.

Opportunities for learning: Language, culture and identity

Communities of practice

Thorne (2006) stresses the advantages of age-peer interaction in telecollaborative partnerships. However, learners can also benefit from a more diverse range of interlocutors, speakers of the target language who are not necessarily of the same age and occupation. This is particularly true for university students and other adult learners. Furthermore, in a university-level group there may be a range of ages: ironically, the pursuit of cosiness in the form of the age-peer match will end up excluding someone (the older student in the class) from such a partnership.

Internet discussion forums are opportunities for immersion in diverse communities of practice. On general interest boards the online community covers a much wider population than the average telecollaboration class. Indeed they rely for their existence on differences in points of view and so we find variation by region (including expatriates), age, race, level of education, expertise, life experience and opinions. Thus the learner who reads the various debates is exposed to diversity of opinion within the target culture, rather than concluding that all the French hold the same views or that contrast with respect to the home culture is the only relevant form of difference. Perusal of the forums allows learners to plot the forms a debate takes in the target culture and how it is constructed and fought out.

Plunged into a set of exchanges with pre-existing rules, written and unwritten, the learner experiences cultural alterity in ways close to those undergone when one arrives in-country, in a foreign firm or educational establishment. The learners are not the makers of the rules (as they can be in a telecollaborative partnership) and at the same time the work of deducing them is facilitated by having extensive models available in the form of the previous postings.

Public discussion forums, then, would seem to be an ideal site for situated intercultural learning. Of course, despite the efforts of moderators, forum life can be messy, and learners will need to spend time seeking out debates which interest them and to which they can contribute, reading through many messages to which they will not respond individually. However, this is all part of the practice.

Moderation and feedback

Usefully for teachers and learners, it is common to find a certain amount of explicit and implicit instruction given on discussion forums: in addition to user guides, codes of conduct, and frequently asked questions, responses to messages often incorporate feedback. A discussion forum potentially brings together participants with divergent expectations of what appropriate behaviour in a site of public discussion might be, and so, in order to ensure the continued functioning of the group, mechanisms exist for dealing with such differences, which may be cultural or subcultural. The most visible of these is intervention by a moderator, who arbitrates on the suitability of messages, moving or removing those deemed incompatible with the forum guidelines. The official moderator is, however, not alone in monitoring the list: moderators rely on users to signal problematic messages, and so other participants – self-appointed and unofficial moderators – take it upon themselves to comment on both cultural and linguistic aspects of contributions.

Through both these forms of intervention – official and unofficial – questions regarding suitability of messages are raised and dealt with at regular intervals, and justifications are offered for treating contributions as acceptable or otherwise. Commentary on messages involves not only policing of behaviour, but also judgements of quality. Whether through readers rating messages on a scale of 1 to 10 (as on the forums of *Le Figaro*) or through replies praising or criticizing particular contributions, attention is drawn to messages that are considered models for others to follow – whether it be for their ideas, arguments, wit or language use – or to avoid. In a forum where the evaluation of messages is carried out with a minimum of congeniality, it can function effectively as a kind of informal teaching of the conventions for discussion.

Language learners on a public discussion forum can, of course, expect far less linguistic feedback than participants in an e-tandem exchange specifically designed for this purpose. Nonetheless, contributors do offer feedback on language use, as the examples in our case studies show. Occasionally there are direct comments asking for clarification. More often, however, feedback is indirect. It can, for example, take the form of a little joke or wordplay on an inappropriate expression used; quotation marks are sometimes used to highlight the unusual nature of the words, or their incorrect formation. Less obviously, native speaker participants will reformulate an idea or a sentence in more colloquial terms, and learners need to be encouraged to look out for these subtle forms of linguistic feedback. Few contributors will comment on spelling and typographical errors unless comprehension is impeded. Indeed such inaccuracies are not uncommon among native speakers on discussion sites, and so, useful as forums are in providing authentic language input, learners certainly also need exposure to other, more carefully edited models of language use. Nonetheless, the kinds of moderation and commentary described above (and illustrated through-out the following chapters) mean that public Internet discussion offers a potentially privileged site for students to obtain individual feedback on their performance from people other than the teacher and indeed from outside the institutional framework. An important issue is how to optimize this potential, for, as we shall see, feedback is not necessarily noticed or heeded by learners (see Chapter 9). Part of the answer lies in developing learner autonomy.

Autonomy

As argued above, the public discussion forum offers learners the oppor-tunity to move beyond the relative shelter of activities designed specif-ically for them. Participation is open both to independent language enthusiasts honing their skills outside an institutional framework and to students working under teacher guidance. Public discussion forums thus provide opportunities not only for those who are already autonomous, but also for teachers to foster autonomous learning habits among their students, habits which will support their institutionalized learning and allow them to continue learning from further contact with the target cultures. This approach to learner autonomy does not involve simply pushing students out of the classroom, but rather equipping them to survive and learn in a less scaffolded environment. For autonomy is not an innate capacity but a skill to be acquired: to paraphrase Beauvoir, *'on ne naît pas autonome, on le devient'* [One is not born autonomous, one becomes so].[11] Tasks (such as those outlined in Chapter 9) requiring students to look out for indirect or subtle feedback, to pay attention to aspects of self-positioning, to notice genre conventions can all be part of this process of learning to learn from interaction and decreasing one's dependence on explicit instruction.

Cultural knowledge and intercultural awareness

The integration of issues of language and culture is especially evident on Internet discussion forums. Already, in order to participate effectively, some cultural knowledge is essential (see Chapters 6 and 9): a newcomer to a current affairs forum will not only need to find out about a given issue in order to have something to say about it, but will find messages laden with an abundance of local references. This provides an excel-lent opportunity for the purposeful study of newspapers and magazine articles, with an immediate pay-off evident in being able to communi-cate with other forum participants. This background knowledge is often simultaneously available by piecing together clues from the allusions in the forum messages. The forums thus provide both access to cultural knowledge and a reason to access it. The cultural information that can be gleaned from forum messages is situated; it is inseparable from particular ways of seeing and points of view. Thus, with some guidance, learners are able to discover that debates in different countries, even about apparently transnational issues such as the environment or euthanasia, do not simply coincide (see also O'Dowd, 2006). Different cultures do not even always share belief in the same 'facts' (for example, about the environmental merits of this or that source of energy).

In terms of intercultural learning, then, student participants have the opportunity to relativize the repertoires of hot social issues and stances on them which are available in their own cultures. They will need to consider whether and how their cultural outsider status should be used, or how to speak as a member of a community (of discussants) whose cultural identity does not coincide with that of the majority. Furthermore, as the students whose experiences are reported in Chapter 9 discover through forum discussion, intercultural communication is not just about managing the presentation of one's own culture and one's perceptions of the target culture; it is also about being aware of the other culture's perceptions and the way in which one will already be positioned in debate by virtue of one's (disclosed or supposed) cultural origins.

Asynchronous communication

For language educators, one of the attractions of online exchanges via email or message boards is their asynchronous nature. Unlike FTF communication, no instantaneous reply is required. Time can be taken between turns, which favours opportunities for preparation, participation and reflection. Depending on the pedagogical set-up, it may also allow for teacher intervention or advice at critical moments. Public Internet discussion shares these merits, and additionally, its format provides an accessible record of exchanges which can be consulted for information about (for example) communicational gambits, the structure of the interaction and the evolution of arguments. This record can then be the starting point for in-class discussion with students.

Perhaps the most significant aspect of asynchronous online communication is the opportunity for all to take the floor. Echoing other discourses about the democratization of access to and production of knowledge through the Internet, teachers have pointed to the potential for 'equal levels of participation' (O'Dowd, 2006, p. 79). Of course, this argument is only valid in situations where all students have access to the technology; otherwise participation is limited by socio-economic factors. Where the technology is available to students, however, it can indeed facilitate interaction for those whose voice is less often heard in the classroom. Removed from the ingrained dynamics of classroom interaction, all students – be they shy, inarticulate, unpopular, culturally discouraged from speaking publicly or victims of active discrimination, which militates against them sharing their views – can have their say. Furthermore, the learner whose equal participation in fast-moving FTF conversation is hampered by lack of spontaneity in the language and the consultation of reference books may find that the slower pace and invisibility of Internet discussion forums favour production in a foreign language. Asynchronicity also allows time for reflection, whether on accuracy, form, content or cultural difference (Lamy and Hampel, 2007, p. 41; O'Dowd, 2007, p. 31; O'Rourke, 2007, p. 53), and is reported to promote thoughtful attention to the contributions of others in online discussion, leading to more coherent interaction (Weasenforth, Biesenbach-Lucas, & Meloni, 2002) and to learning from others (Kreef-Peyton, 1999, p.19; O'Dowd, 2006, p. 77).

Given our study of differences in behaviour between and across French and British sites (see Chapter 3), however, we cannot assume that the asynchronous mode is the preferred option of native users. While we saw a clear preference for asynchronous, reflective discussion on the French sites studied, we noted that several British sites prefer a relatively fast turnaround between messages. Thus the time taken by a beginning learner of English to reflect on previous entries, compose, recompose, correct and send a message corresponds to much water under the bridges of *Guardian Unlimited*. On the other hand, the marginally asynchronous nature of these more conversational forums will still give the advanced learner time to self-monitor.

These benefits are not without their problematic counterparts. Lamy and Hampel remind us that online writing can have both 'facilitative and inhibitory effects' (2007, p. 76) on learners: some students may experience increased anxiety caused by the permanent record of their interactions, by the necessary reliance on written communication, and indeed by the use of technology itself (pp. 76–82). If we are to reap the benefits of online learning, we need to find ways of reducing these stresses.

A second-language identity

The vast majority of participants in public Internet discussion use pseudonyms. This means that anonymity can be preserved amongst class members if they so choose. But even when this is not their choice, if classmates are spread across large enough discussion boards, they have the opportunity to play social roles different from those they usually assume with respect to each other, as we have seen above, and also to play roles other than that of language learner. That is to say, discussion forums offer opportunities to try out various speaking positions and, in so doing, to develop a viable identity through which to communicate in the foreign language.[12] This possibility, however, raises significant challenges, discussed below.

Challenges and obstacles

The many potential benefits of public Internet discussion for language learners, outlined above, are not intended to suggest that public Internet discussion provides a necessarily happy and unproblematic space for intercultural contact, any more than other modes of online exchange. The benefits are not automatic, for, as we shall see, certain skills and awareness are required for optimum language and intercultural learning to take place. As O'Dowd remarks, 'the skills of interaction and analysis which are necessary for the success of intercultural telecollaboration do not come naturally to students' (2006, p. 222), who often need 'explicit guidance and training' (2006, p. 222). The observation is equally applicable to Internet discussion forums, and we could add autonomous learning skills and awareness of genre to the competencies O'Dowd mentions.

Participation in intercultural Internet discussion is, then, not without its pitfalls. Let us briefly survey some of the obstacles to participation by cultural/linguistic outsiders (such as language learners) in public discussion of this kind. And clearly there are obstacles, because despite its easy access and despite the popular belief that the Internet brings cultures together, instances of sustained intercultural discussion on public sites are relatively rare (see Chapter 8).

While authenticity in language learning activities is largely seen as laudable, it can also be intimidating. One reason for the neglect of public Internet discussion among language teachers and learners seems to be the somewhat scary realness of it all. If we unpack this a little, we find apprehensiveness regarding questions of language, culture and identity.

Language proficiency is often perceived as a greater barrier to interaction with native speakers than it actually is. Frequently, lack of language proficiency is blamed when in fact intercultural issues are responsible for misunderstandings. Our case studies show repeatedly that successful interaction is less dependent on linguistic competence than on other factors. A French participant with the pseudonym Sickofrosbif uses a very approximate version of English on the forums of *The Independent* (Chapter 8), and David, a North American, abandons the attempt to use French altogether in his contributions to *Le Monde* (Chapter 6). Despite these difficulties, however, both manage to garner considered responses and pursue productive exchanges, because they engage more or less appropriately in the cultural practice of discussion.[13]

This brings us to the question of culture and the need to understand the cultural norms of the specific genre at hand. In Chapters 3 and 4, we focused on differences in cultural practices on public discussion sites, which represent a stumbling block for unsuspecting visitors to the discussion sites of another culture. And in the case study in Chapter 6 we show how the success or otherwise of exchanges between Anglophones and Francophones on the forums of *Le Monde* is dependent on an understanding of the prevailing cultural and generic conventions. For example, in many cultures, the purpose of debate is not to reach agreement, but to engage in a frank confrontation of differing viewpoints. Furthermore, not all discussion on Internet forums takes the congenial and cooperative tone usually enforced in a classroom situation. Such debates, beyond the shelter of the classroom, certainly provide a training ground for developing very useful argumentation skills but may not be experienced as supportive, and are probably unsuitable for younger learners (see Chapters 9 and 10). Although moderation shields users from the worst excesses of intolerance, public displays of hostility or even generically appropriate criticism may discourage participation by those less confident. And so we find learners preferring the cultural comfort zone of other learners on dedicated learner sites (Chapter 8).

But it is not only the assumed sympathetic audience of peers which is the attraction of these learner sites. While we have indicated the potential of forums in developing second-language identities we must also acknowledge a certain unpreparedness on the part of many learners to assume any role other than that of learner. Although theorists of online behaviour in fields such as cultural studies, social science or sociology speak of the possibility of reinventing oneself online, students and instructors, for all they are keen to shed the shackles of the Shy Learner, the Non-Participatory Learner, are not so ready to see the identity of Learner itself disappear. This is of course understandable and indeed this identity sometimes needs to be preserved to maintain the intellectual content of telecollaboration projects. Yet it is also a restrictive identity. If students continue to position themselves in this way in public Internet discussion, despite the limitations this identity places on them, it is perhaps because they cannot see any other way of asserting themselves in the foreign language. Self-positioning is, then, an aspect of interaction with native speakers that students often need to work on. And we shall see in the following chapters that discussion forums offer particular pedagogical opportunities for developing skills in this area: for reflecting on and experimenting with different modes of self-presentation, different ways of establishing a footing in the exchange.

Public forums: A neglected genre of online language exchange

To sum up then, participation in Internet forums provides valuable opportunities for development of language and intercultural skills through involvement in an authentic cultural practice that moves away from teacher–student or student–student dynamics. Although they present challenges, the forums also offer significant opportunities for developing learner autonomy and transferable skills. Furthermore, the forums abound in cultural information of various kinds: language learners can find not only factual information, but also how that information is deployed by natives, and what the conventions for interaction are, thus creating opportunities for developing intercultural understanding. These benefits mean that public Internet discussion deserves greater prominence as a means of facilitating interaction between language learners and native speakers and should be included alongside e-tandem and telecollaborative partnerships as a valuable tool for language learning.

Although public discussion forums are not designed with language learners in mind, it is certainly possible to integrate their use into a language class. In this case, however, task design is crucial, and, while there will be language/culture learning goals, these must be compatible with the goals of other users of the forum. This means bearing in mind the features that distinguish public Internet discussion from other kinds of electronic exchanges, and considering their impact on the kinds of tasks appropriate for its use.

The following chapters analyse stories of success and failure in engaging intercultural discussion on public Internet forums, discussing the difficulties that arise and suggesting how, with preparation and support, these problems may be minimized. In this way, the considerable potential for learning offered by participation in these forums can be realized.

6

A Funny Thing Happened on the Way to the Forum: Learners' Participation Strategies

An introductory tale (with apologies to Beatrix Potter)

Once upon a time there were four learners of French and their names were Fleurie, Laura, Eleanor and David. They hopped onto the Internet from Britain and the US and clicked their way across *Le Monde* (more precisely its online discussion pages). Fleurie and Eleanor, who were good little students, looked for penpals in order to improve their French, whilst Laura and David were much more concerned by vigorous debates about racism and cultural imperialism. In fact, David didn't even manage to write in French. Yet of the four, Laura and David were those who were warmly welcomed to stay and contribute, whilst Fleurie and Eleanor left, apparently discouraged.

As teachers of French, concerned to encourage use of that language, this looks at first glance to be the kind of tale we would *not* want students to be reading. Our recalcitrant English-using protagonist is neither reprimanded nor (linguistically) reformed while diligence goes unrewarded – hardly an edifying moral to our story. Why does it end this way and what can be learnt from it? To answer these questions, and to propose a properly improving conclusion to the tale, we analyse the strategies and practices of the four message writers. This chapter heads a series which looks at online discussion with a view to prompting suggestions for effective pedagogical practice in guiding student participation in public Internet discussion forums.

Our first case study, that of these four learners on the *Le Monde* forum, is particularly helpful in underscoring the crucial role of genre in intercultural communication. It also reveals the rich affordances of the discussion forum: the instruction provided by moderator and participants in initiating newcomers to the forum; the encounter with cultural differences; the exposure to cultural knowledge (including allusions to texts available for pastiche, such as Beatrix Potter's tale of 'good little rabbits' above) as part of a cultural practice. And finally, it alerts us to the question of appropriate speaking positions for participants.

The case study

Background

Our data come from *Forums Le Monde*, which have been described in Chapters 3 and 4. The bulk of the data was collected during 2000, with access to archives dating back to 1999, and whilst the site was over-hauled in late 2000, the changes which came into force do not effect our conclusions. In terms of using the forums for teaching purposes, however, it should be noted that contributing is now a privilege of subscribers.[1]

The list of forums available in 2000 concludes with the catch-all *'Autres sujets'* [Other topics],[2] and it is to this apparently open forum that our four learners are attracted. As seen earlier, *'Autres sujets'* provides participants with an opportunity to discuss any issue not covered by a list of topics including the Clinton–Lewinski affair, French law reform, agri-culture and racism, with *Sport* the only actual example of what an *autre sujet* might be: in practice it is used to canvas – with varying degrees of whimsy and passion – issues ranging from the minutiae of participants' lives to revisionist history.[3] *'Coin détente'* ['Relaxation corner'], the later venue for chat and small talk, does not yet exist, which means that these sometimes crop up in *'Autres sujets'*.

Our data therefore come from an *'Autres sujets'* forum where you might want to talk about sport (but generally don't), with a modera-tor, Michel Tatu, who regularly intervenes in discussion. According to official policy, the forum is open to contributions in both French and English, although, to quote the moderator, *'tout le monde ici est sup-posé *lire* le français'* [Everyone here is presumed able to *read* French] (1 September 1999). Given the non-specialized nature of the forum, the wide range of participants and the frequency of postings, on multiple topics, it would seem the ideal site where students of French might 'practise'.

Novelty

Strikingly prevalent in the forum is a discourse of novelty. Contributors repeatedly refer to the newness of the technology, and are unsure of the conventions of exchange: these are taken to be under negotiation, rather than predetermined. Questions are thus asked and answers offered as to the appropriate length of messages, the best means of posting them, the frequency with which one should contribute, which buttons should be clicked and so on. But however malleable or even uncertain expectations are with regard to genre, clearly participants still do have expectations. These are what allow them to feel competent to comment on the appropriateness of others' contributions, and to make predictions regarding the experience of the forum. This provision of commentary is particularly evident when a contributor signals the marginality of his/her participant status. One such marginal status (although not the only one) is that of the learner of French.

Genre, then, is not seen as rigidly predetermined and the same could be said of culture: contributors are well aware that although the forum supposes an interest in French culture and debate, since the medium is not geographically limited, many of their number are not French nor based in France.

Since neither culture nor genre is seen as firmly entrenched, both must be continually and explicitly negotiated in this forum. As Freadman and Macdonald (1992) have shown, such negotiating and restatement of cultural and generic rules turn up in a variety of places, such as the televised interviews and tennis commentary that are the objects of their analyses. We contend, however, that this regulatory work is intensified and presented with particular emphasis as part of a discourse of novelty, that this discourse and the negotiation it entails are absolutely integrated into the practice of the genre of Internet forum discussion in its early stages.

Now, it might be supposed that the novelty would wear off – and with it the need for continual reiteration and accommodation of norms – as Internet discussion becomes banal. Two aspects of forum participation, however, work to the contrary effect. Firstly, there is the fact that each discussion group constitutes a subcultural community, with its own standards of tolerance of digression and language errors and so on, specific to that forum. And secondly, there is the instability of membership, particularly in a wide-ranging forum with a high turnover of participants such as the one we are studying. Together these circumstances mean that there are constantly new participants needing induction into the forum community, although in 2008 this induction may be less about the buttons to press and more about forum-specific conventions.[4]

The negotiation of cultural and generic rules and guidelines takes place on the forum through moderation. To explore the way in which

it operates, we will look at the exchanges involving the four characters with whom we introduced this chapter: two Americans and two
English. All four sets of exchanges can be described as intercultural, in
that the main protagonists position themselves as linguistic outsiders
and in each case the subject of their message is intercultural exchange
of one form or another.

Four exchanges

According to their messages, David, Laura, Eleanor and Fleurie are all
learners of French. Their contributions to the forum appear between
July 1999 and April 2000.[5] Although their attempts to engage with other
participants present some parallels, more striking are the differences in
their strategies, in the responses they receive and in the overall success
of their contributions.

In each case, the opening gambit is explicit self-positioning as a
learner of French (and indeed, none of the openings is entirely error-
free), but this is done to varying effect:

David: *'Pardonnez-moi de ecrire en anglais. J'apprends toujours le
français.'* [Excuse me for writing in English. I'm still learning French.]
(30 August 1999)

Laura: *'Bonjour a tous, C'est evident que je ne suis pas francais. Je ne
suis qu'etudiante de francais a l'Alliance Francaise.'* [Hello everyone.
It's obvious that I'm not French. I'm just a student of French at the
Alliance Française.]

(19 July 1999)

Eleanor: *'Sault, je suis anglaise et j'aime la France. Pourriez-vous m'ecrire
pour m'aider a ameliorer me francias SVP. Merci!'* [Hello, I'm English and
I love France. Could you write to me to help me improve my French
please. Thanks!]

(20 February 2000)

Fleurie: *'Je suis Anglaise et je voudrais parler avec quelq'un pour amerliorer
mon Français.'* [I'm English and I would like to speak with someone
to improve my French.]

(9 April 2000)

The sense of this strategy is not the same in each case. For the two
Englishwomen, Eleanor and Fleurie, the self-positioning as English

students of French is not merely an opening move but is itself the message: the few lines quoted constitute the entirety of the contribution in each case. For Americans David and Laura, on the other hand, while the opening forms part of an apology for linguistic errors – Laura's message continues with '*Alors, je vous prie d'accepter votre propre langue dans un etat dechire. Je n'ai pas un truc sur l'ordinateur pour ecrire les accents*' [So I beg you to accept your own language in mutilated form. I don't have a thing on the computer to write accents] – it is also, significantly, a way of presenting their speaking positions as Anglophones. And unlike Eleanor and Fleurie, they will go on to speak.

It is in fact not quite accurate to call these first words of the messages the opening lines, for they are preceded by the reference or subject lines. Compare the following:

David: Réf: '*Combattre le modèle américain*' [Fight the American model]
Laura: ref. '*Steven*'
Eleanor: '*Les Anglais*' [The English]
Fleurie: '*Une fille anglaise*' [An English girl]

What stands out here is that whereas David and Laura's contributions appear as responses to other messages (David's replying to French criticism of the United States, Laura's to anti-immigrant sentiment), Eleanor and Fleurie each initiate a subject – themselves.

Innocents abroad?

Let's look at Eleanor and Fleurie's short, simple and rather naïve contributions first, and the ways in which they are taken up. Here we see the kinds of regulating work done by forum members: participants clearly consider it fitting that they provide explanations of why certain kinds of conduct and content are appropriate or not.

We have noted the preference for longer messages at *Le Monde*, yet while Eleanor's request is brief, the first response, from Grossefatigue, a regular contributor of banter, is even briefer: 'Why don't you write first?' (23 February 2000). In fact its title [*Tirez les premiers, messieurs les...*], clearly not addressed to Eleanor but to fellow (male) forum members, is longer.[6]

Grossefatigue's reply asserts the failure of Eleanor's contribution on both generic and linguistic grounds: the invitation to 'write first' implies that her request not only didn't qualify as a contribution, but didn't qualify as writing at all. And replying in English implies, perhaps unfairly, that her French is inadequate to the task. Any such perception is probably more to do with Eleanor's failure to grasp the conventions of engagement than with the accumulation of linguistic errors. On the other hand, Grossefatigue's subject line, with its historical allusion, serves to raise his reply from the merely insulting to the culturally knowing, and ensures that his message does count.

Eleanor's only other answer, from Lambda, is far more gracious, apologizes for Grossefatigue, thereby indirectly reproaching him for his lack of courtesy, but the burden of the message is the same: if Eleanor wants to practise her French – and what an admirable idea that is – then why doesn't she? He concludes,

> *'[S]i vous désirez parler de n'importe quel sujet, la vache folle, l'évolution de la monarchie dans votre pays ou la construction européenne, n'hésitez pas !'* [If you want to talk about any topic whatsoever, mad cows, the changing role of the monarchy in your country or the construction of Europe, don't hesitate!]

> (24 February 2000)

A few months later, Fleurie makes her attempt, under the perhaps more enticing title *'Une fille anglaise'* [An English girl]. She has slightly better luck in that someone seeking English practice suggests a language exchange (no details are given). But she also receives

- indirect feedback on linguistic accuracy in the form of a whimsical exposition on the derivation of her verb 'amerliorer' (which will have been understood by any reader who actually noticed it as a mild spelling or typographical error for *'améliorer'* [to improve])
- invitations to practise her French by *debate.*

The first of these invitations to debate points her to the 11 forums of *Le Monde* with *'des dizaines et des dizaines d'occasions de discuter sur tous les sujets que vous voulez'* [scores of opportunities to debate any subject you want] (Th. Paz, 9 April 2000), and the second suggests as subjects *'[l]a vache folle,' 'Mme Thatcher (aucun rapport avec le sujet précédent)', '[l]es Spice Girls'*, and *'[l]es oreilles du prince Charles'* [mad cows, Mrs Thatcher (no connection with the previous topic), the Spice Girls and Prince Charles' ears] (Lambda, 15 April 2000). This list, annotated with a smiley, concludes *'si ces idées ne vous ont pas fâché, je vous dis à bientôt sur ce*

Forum' [if these suggestions haven't annoyed you, I'll see you soon on the forum]. In other words, if Fleurie can take a bit of fun and respond to the badinage, then she is most welcome to join in. Finally, this correspondent requests the address of an equivalent website attached to an English newspaper.

Evidently, members are here attempting to instruct Fleurie and Eleanor in some of the ways of the forum – the rules of the game – specifically, those concerning subject matter and the purpose of participation. We suggest that the most useful way to understand what kind of a game it is is the notion of genre, with genre being understood as encompassing all aspects of a cultural practice: its linguistic and non-linguistic manifestations, and including in particular its cultural purpose (Freadman, 1998, pp. 21–22; Swales, 1990, pp. 45–46).

As stated earlier, the negotiation of genre is notable in this forum, and the rules that we have just seen communicated to Fleurie and Eleanor have been the subject of explicit debate. 'What is the subject matter of *Autres sujets?*' asks Godlewski (2 August 2000), opening the discussion thread and questioning why '*sport*' is the only suggestion. The responses to the two English girls give a nice list of what *Autres sujets* might be. In another example of generic awareness, the issue 'Why forums?' has also been debated (Graslin, 10 February 2000 and thread). Answers included, perhaps predictably, the advancement of knowledge through debate and discussion. Yet Fleurie's and Eleanor's preoccupation with the purely linguistic is not entirely out of place. For in the same discussion there is also evident delight in the playfulness of exchanges, frequent reference to the pleasure of writing and therefore to the production of written text as an end in itself (see the examples from *Forums Le Monde* quoted in the section 'Written and oral templates' in Chapter 3). Furthermore, no one denies the merits of linguistic practice, for native and non-native alike. The second, more kindly, answer to Eleanor reads in part,

'*Vous souhaitez pratiquer le français pour améliorer vos connaissances, c'est une bonne idée. Dommage que beaucoup de français n'aient pas la même! Leur façon de pratiquer la langue de Molière pourrait faire croire qu'ils ont dormi à l'école au lieu d'écouter :-)*' [You wish to practise your French in order to improve your knowledge, that's a great idea. A pity that many French people don't do likewise! The way they use the language of Molière makes you wonder whether they slept at school instead of listening :-)]

(Lambda, 24 February 2000)

A site of public performance in French, a site to practise French, yes, but no one is suggesting that the forum is the place for *gratuitous* linguistic exchange, nor (naturally enough) that its primary function is that of helping foreigners improve their French. Therefore, if non-native speakers such as Fleurie and Eleanor are to use the forum in order to develop their language skills, they still have to participate on its terms: that is, through taking a topic and talking about it. In other words, using the genre to their own ends entails understanding how to engage in it productively, or, to quote Anne Freadman, who is here applying the principles of Lyotard (1983): 'Any particular genre is defined primarily by the stake for which its participants engage in it. We have to learn how to practice a genre, we have to learn its ways and means, in order to use it to our advantage' (1998, p. 28). If Fleurie, Eleanor and their peers can learn the genre of forum participation, becoming aware not only of the form but of the stakes of discussion, they may find a way of making their purpose (improving their French) compatible with that of other contributors and thereby continue to participate.

But how can one learn a genre? We have suggested that moderation might provide a kind of informal instruction for students. In the replies exhorting them to 'write first' and suggesting topics, Eleanor and Fleurie are receiving initiation into French culture framed in terms of lessons in genre. And their lay-teachers are performing a job remarkably similar to that suggested for language teachers by Freadman in the same essay, that is teaching the cultural context of language use through an understanding of genre, ensuring that students learn the social purpose and the appropriateness principles of cultural practices.

However, Eleanor and Fleurie seem unable to take up their lessons. Both disappear without a trace.[7]

The Americans

David Dalton and Laura engage rather more productively with the forum. As stated above, their success doesn't seem to be predicated on proficiency in French. It doesn't seem to matter that David's message is mostly in English. With his nine words in French, he still manages to contribute more effectively and elicit more substantial responses than Eleanor with her eighteen. Eleanor's extras ('*Salut*', '*j'aime la France*', '*SVP*', '*Merci!*' [Hi, I love France, Please, Thank you!]) – however polite and connotative of the kind of goodwill which might found a personal relationship – are of virtually no help in achieving her aims. Neither friendliness nor linguistic accuracy is the measure of intercultural competence here.

Perhaps the first reason for David and Laura's comparative successes is that each responds to another message: unlike Fleurie and Eleanor, they enter, debating. In this way, they position themselves from the outset in discussion with others, thus satisfying one of the criteria for generic appropriateness highlighted by forum members. In contrast with Eleanor and Fleurie's search for penfriends, theirs is a task-centred approach: they learn by participating in the cultural practice rather than asking for experiences focusing on themselves. Interestingly, their messages about racism and cultural imperialism lead them to a point where questions of French culture and Frenchness (about which they are presumably curious) are explicitly addressed in the responses they provoke.

Let's look at their other strategies. Laura and David both apologize for their French. Why choose this gambit? Certainly the body of David's message is entirely in English, but it is not really necessary for Laura, whose French is quite adequate: had she not made a point of her foreignness, it would not have been as obvious as she claims. However, the apology allows Laura to give an outsider's view of France: this is not merely politeness, but a means to asserting a particular speaking position, from which better to engage in the debate. In other words, her opening enhances her capacity to participate in the genre. Like Muriel (8 November 1999), who locates herself culturally and geographically before replying to David (discussion below), she reinstates certain cultural borders, making them palpable on the otherwise apparently borderless web. And this facilitates the process of cultural self-definition of the forum, giving rise to explicit statements about culture.

A third point in common: having apologized for their linguistic inadequacies, and rebutted the arguments of previous messages, both Laura and David (almost incidentally) enquire regarding their eligibility to participate on the forum. Here we see another way in which they position themselves in order to speak. And in doing so they make the appropriateness of their messages an issue, thus inviting feedback on their participation in this cultural practice – without ever resorting to pleas to 'improve my French'.

Laura's enquiry about eligibility appears in her second message. This appears as a kind of afterthought to the first, in which she has taken another participant to task for railing against illegal immigrants. Like her first, the second message is prefaced by references to her outsider status and lack of French. Indeed, the second message expands on this issue:

'*Parlant un francais minimal (ou affreux), venant d'un pays plus ou moins deteste (les etats-unis, comme tout le monde a deja devine), [...]*' [Speaking minimal (or appalling) French, coming from a country that is more or less hated (the United States, as everyone has already guessed)]

(20 July 1999)

Unsure of her welcome, she asks for confirmation of her right to write both in the subject line (*'les etrangers, sont-ils bienvenus?'* [Are foreigners welcome?]) and in a direct question followed by a softening explanation:

> *'Au fond, c'est overt ou ferme, ce forum? Est-ce qu'on s'interesse aux grandes et mauvaises americaines*[8] *qui sont en train d'apprendre le francais, qui lisent (avec un petit robert, bien sur) les commentaires precedents avec interet.'* [In fact, is this forum open or closed? Is anyone interested in big bad Americans who are learning French, who read (using a dictionary, of course) the previous comments with interest?]

Michel Tatu, the forum moderator, is the first to respond:

> *'Bonjour Laura !*
>
> *Oui, vous êtes tout à fait la bienvenue – y compris et en particulier pour votre réponse à «Steve».*
>
> *Le forum est ouvert à tous, il admet même des gens qui parlent le français beaucoup moins bien que vous:-)'*
>
> [Hello Laura!
> Yes you are absolutely welcome, in particular because of your reply to 'Steve'. The forum is open to all, it even accepts people who speak French much less well than you:-)]

(21 July 1999)

Note that according to Tatu, Laura's French is more than adequate, but what makes her especially welcome is her contribution to debate.

David, who reads but does not write French, and argues for cultural dialogue between France and the US, is similarly accepted. In an oblique way he too asks to be admitted, phrasing his question as part of the case he makes: 'The Internet is a wonderful thing. Now we can read your newspapers and participate in your conversations, if you will permit it.' The moderator welcomes him in English with another big smile: 'Certainly, David, you are welcome:-)' (30 August 1999).

Here we see the moderator's efforts to promote certain kinds of exchange and this through encouraging rather than battling participants: clearly he is not simply replying to requests for entry but is also helping to mould the forum by stamping certain contributions with his approval. The enthusiasm of his welcome correlates directly with the fact that Laura and David are participating in the discussion as opposed to just positioning themselves as outsiders who would like to learn more and to turn discussion towards themselves.

David and Laura are also reassured by other members, who, additionally, take it upon themselves to explain what to expect on the forum and why indeed the forum is the way that it is. Yet again we can note the informal teacherly function to which the forum lends itself. The explanation put forward for the way things are done on the forum is, in its simplest version, 'we're French'. That is to say, genre is explained in terms of culture.

For example, Muriel, a French expatriate living in Spain, explains French culture to David, with the forum cited as a means of experiencing it. However, the intervention also, or primarily, deals with a specific point of conflict that Muriel is attempting to moderate. David has reacted to what he has obviously seen as an incendiary piece of American-bashing. Muriel's explanation – in English – of how the French comport themselves includes commentary on this, explained as 'provocation'. (Whether this in fact works as a satisfactory explanation for David, whether 'provocation' can count as a benign rhetorical ploy for him, is of course another matter.) Of the forum, Muriel writes,

> one thing which I liked particularly was to get reacquainted with French culture, and I mean by this the unmistakable way of being sarcastic, but also the kind of issues the French get all excited about... (like Roquefort, Napoleon, hormones beef, the Concorde, etc.)
>
> (8 November 1999)

In response to Laura's hesitation on the threshold of the forum, Baguette performs a very similar routine to Muriel, with the difference that he/she is rather more (ironically?) self-deprecating about the French. Baguette warns Laura of 'les querelles' [the quarrels] that she will find and recycles various myths of Frenchness, as was perhaps predictable from the pseudonym:

> '*on espère que vous participerez à nos petites castagnes amicales (chez les Gaulois, les querelles pour un oui ou pour un non font partie du caractère national, au même titre que le saucisson, le beaujolais, le roquefort et Descartes [...])*' [We hope that you will participate in our friendly little

punch-ups (for us Gauls, quarrelling at the drop of a hat is as much a part of the national character as sausage, beaujolais, roquefort and Descartes)]

(21 July 1999)

Culture and genre

The responses to Eleanor, Fleurie, David and Laura indicate ways in which the intercultural is handled in the apparent borderlessness of the Internet: boundaries are reasserted, in the form of rules for acceptable behaviour. The official and self-appointed moderators of the *Le Monde* subculture deal with other cultures by asking them to conform. The kind of conformity required and the ways in which it is justified are perhaps unexpected to outsiders.

The feedback on successful forum engagement given to David and Laura on the one hand, and to Eleanor and Fleurie on the other, comes down to the same thing – we are here to debate – yet those instructions are justified differently. The remarks to Eleanor and Fleurie seem grounded in an appeal to genre: we're in a forum, ladies, so let's do what we're here for. David and Laura, on the other hand, are asked to make allowances for the French love of polemic, that is a cultural trait, which means that interaction on the forum will take the form of debate. They are being tutored in how discussion might be culturally inflected.[9] In other words, genre and culture are being used to explain and justify each other, are mutually defining, which seems to us an important lesson to be learned.

The interdependence of these two notions, the idea that culture might be apprehended and best described in terms of genre appears, then, not only in academic papers such as Freadman's (1998). Our case study demonstrates the way in which this interrelationship is present in the discourse of forum practitioners. If this is how language users conceive of and explain their practices, it makes sense for language teachers to pay attention.

How to practise your French without really trying

A funny thing happened on the way to the forum. Laura and David got distracted from their French language studies but ended up receiving lessons in French culture, whilst the dutiful Fleurie and Eleanor were apparently unable to pursue the laudable agenda of improving their French.

So is the story a useful one for language students and teachers? Yes, if recounted as a cautionary tale, for the respective successes and failures of David and Laura, Fleurie and Eleanor show us that the Internet forum can indeed be the site of invaluable learning, but that such learning is not guaranteed. In the case of the Fleuries and Eleanors of our classes, the danger is that they are so bereft of useful strategies in this context – in terms of both performance and analysis – that they will only interpret lack of success as personal rebuff. And to them we would want to say 'it's not all about you'. Or, in other terms, trade in that 'self'-centred approach for a task-based approach. Then you may be able to turn things to your advantage. Get the genre right and the linguistic opportunity opens. And getting the genre right is an important part of culture learning. Being culturally competent means assuming a speaking position appropriate to the genre in which one is participating. From this perspective, 'practising French' is not a helpful way of framing an online discussion task for students. Rather, what is required is recasting 'practising French' as practising Frenchness: performing it *through participation in a cultural practice*.

This is a general principle, but we submit that Internet forums provide a particularly useful opportunity for its application. To start with, as argued in the preceding chapter, there is the undeniable fact that this is a genre in which students can participate, despite the triple tyrannies of distance, isolation and dictionary dependence. But if issues of generic and cultural specificity pass under students' (and teachers') radars, if attempted interaction on discussion forums replicates classroom practice rather than engaging with the norms and conventions of the other, then a remarkable opportunity is missed for allowing students to participate in a cultural practice with and on the same terms as native speakers.

Furthermore, if the particular forum draws in a wide enough membership, it is a genre of which commentary is an integral part, and this commentary can provide essential lessons, either through self-reflexive discussion as to the nature of the forum or through targeted moderation of postings by other participants. With a little guidance, students can be brought to understand the importance of cultural and generic appropriateness, which they may otherwise have considered to be abstract notions.

However, in order to arrive at these outcomes, teacherly attention must be given to the kinds of forums recommended to students as well as to the way in which the Internet forums are presented and treated in class. Exposure to helpful moderation would seem to be facilitated by choice of a forum where wide participation, a reasonable turnover of members and an active moderator mean that giving feedback to fellow participants is all part of the usual interaction, integrated into the business of the site. While the choice of such a forum doesn't exclude the possibility of learners being shot down by hostile forum participants, if the general atmosphere is supportive, chances are that the student may also receive encouragement from other forum members (as was the case for Eleanor).

Successful teaching of forum debate as genre involves getting the students to attend to it as such, that is, not just as a site in which non-natives may freely partake in linguistic practice. It seems advisable therefore to preface any student involvement with an investigation of what successful participation would mean for a particular forum. The objective of such a treatment would obviously go well beyond the eventual involvement of students in that forum (students only able to argue on the *Le Monde* website would have rather limited cultural skills); rather the point would be to sensitize them to the usefulness of such preparatory work and its application in other genres.

In the case of Internet discussion forums, then, we have found that understanding the stakes of the genre (debate on topics of general interest in the French forum) is critical to participation. This, alone, is, however, not enough to guarantee the ability to participate in the genre, and we conclude with a final lesson to be learned from the stories of our four outsiders. Teachers and researchers have repeatedly encountered the problem that 'when e-mail discussion lists are established, learners and instructors may not know what to communicate about' (Leeman, 1999), and in Chapter 8 we will see a further example of this, with the lame proposition of the weather as a subject for debate. The solution, however, has to be more than the suggestion of topics, which failed so completely to engage Fleurie and Eleanor. Firstly – and this may have been the problem for the Englishwomen – lists of topics do not of themselves persuade students to attend to forum participation as a genre of communicative behaviour (that is, as more than language practice). The second point is closely related: in order to enter into the quick of debate, to make the link between your language skills and the real world of your fellow participants, you need to understand the terms of the discussion and be able to make a contribution. Our uptake of the term 'cultural knowledge' has thus far been limited to the realm of the performative, that of cultural skills as opposed to knowledge about a culture. However, if the fundamental purpose of a forum is to provide opportunity for debate, participants must have something to say. 'Cultural knowledge' in a more traditional sense should therefore not be opposed to 'cultural skills' but re-emerges as a skill itself necessary to successful performance. And while some students may have the general knowledge requisite for at least entering a debate on a foreign language website, they will still need to acquaint themselves with the points of reference, the critical events and players in the debate for that other culture. Again, this has implications for teaching: preparatory work on a forum – if on a designated topic such as the environment – could well include isolating and fleshing out the references (who is this Cohn-Bendit? why the references to Larzac? what is the European parliament? what are the greatest concerns about climate change in France?). This doesn't mean forsaking one set of cultural references for another, but rather adding them to one's repertoire: amongst the encouraging lessons from our case study, we have seen, both in the lists proposed to Fleurie and Eleanor and in the arguments advanced by David and Laura, that the outsider's view constitutes an accepted speaking position on the *Le Monde* site. However, as we will see in subsequent chapters, the outsider's view is not the only one available to students, and it is one that needs to be negotiated with fellow participants.

Through techniques such as those sketched above and illustrated in more detail in Chapter 9, teachers may instil a reflective process whereby one's performance – successful or otherwise – is analysed, and the analysis applied to further performance. Students may then – unlike Fleurie and Eleanor – engage with the rules of the game sufficiently to return to the forum, learn some more and even contribute to some interesting discussion along the way.

7
Face Off: Identity in Online Debate

Introduction: From genre to identity

Our preceding discussion of genre raises the question of the identities that language learners are able to assert in online discussion. For some learners, adopting a speaking position appropriate to the genre may involve investing oneself in an L2 identity – an identity in the second/foreign language – that is unfamiliar, uncomfortable, or indeed unimaginable.

Prevailing myths of the Internet as a space where 'You can be whoever you want to be' (Turkle, 1995, p. 184) suggest that such reinventions of identity should be easily accomplished. Indeed, when the pedagogical use of the Internet discussion forum first came to our attention, one of its most appealing aspects was the potential for students to recreate themselves as speakers of another language. They could thus be freed from the role of language learner, that role in which one is typecast by interlocutors who, hearing a non-standard accent and seeing non-verbal signs of unease, apportion one the limited conversational share of the outsider, only up to answering questions about oneself, home and, just possibly, the trip so far. And for those students who typecast themselves in that role, who can only ever imagine speaking French 'not badly for an Australian/Norwegian/Singaporean', we saw Internet discussion forums as an opportunity to stretch their competence and invite them to adopt speaking positions where being the pet foreigner would not work.

As the previous chapter already suggests, however, taking up these speaking positions is not as simple as it seems. It requires not only sensitivity to genre, but in many cases a significant shift in the way one sees oneself interacting in a second language.

In the following two chapters we pursue the question of online identity and its consequences for the use of Internet discussion in language learning. We start, in the present chapter, by questioning assumptions about the radical difference between online and offline identity. We examine accusations of deception that arise on the forums in order to reflect on the myth of the ease of imposture online and to understand the conditions under which identity becomes an issue in this genre. This enables us to see how identity is deployed in forum debate. The insights thus gained into the uses of identity have implications not only for language learners participating in online discussion. In Chapter 8, which analyses obstacles to and models for effective self-positioning online, we demonstrate the relevance of these insights for developing intercultural communicative competence more generally.

Facelessness and the power of the face

As soon as Internet communication is mentioned, discussion of identity seems inevitable. If the Internet makes it possible to communicate in ways previously denied us by our geographical and cultural context, so too does it seem to allow for the free and fraudulent creation of identity with an ease and on a scale which were previously impossible. Celebrated examples feeding anxiety on this topic range from the obviously unreliable 'Nigerian' money-laundering emails, through other routine attempts at phishing, to the use of chat and dating sites by sexual or homicidal predators to entrap their victims. While use of webcams is growing, in the current state of technological play, it is still less common to see our online interlocutors or to be seen by them – the self is projected textually. For many commentators, the defining characteristic of Internet communication is its facelessness, the fact that it allows for interaction without the putative guarantees provided by physical presence or at least a line of sight. This facelessness is seen by many to have spawned a mode of contact where onscreen, unseen interlocutors are fictional creations of human demiurges.

The surety assumed to be provided by the sight of the face underpins a long history of stories of identity fraud, where unreliable assumptions about identity are facilitated by bridal veils (Leah), failing eyesight (Jacob) or conveniently concealing vegetation (Cyrano de Bergerac) and architectural features (the Wizard of Oz). The word 'faceless' even denotes 'lack of identity'. This correlation between face and identity is not restricted to English: while French – the language of many examples in this chapter – has no cognate for 'faceless', there is nonetheless a cluster of everyday metaphors about arriving at the truth via the revelation of the face: we may note the words '*démasquer*' [unmask], '*dévoiler*' [unveil]. Face is seen as the guarantor of identity: without access to it, we apparently enter the domain of uncertainty, indeed deceit. Thus, echoing earlier cyber-utopians, Jauréguiberry proclaims,

> '*Ce relatif 'décollement' des internautes en regard des lieux, corps et statuts va permettre l'apparition d'un type d'action totalement inédit: celui de la manipulation identitaire à laquelle un individu va pouvoir se livrer en superposant une identité virtuelle à son identité réelle, une identité fantasmée à son identité sociale.*' [This comparative 'detachment' of Internet-users with respect to places, bodies and status will allow the emergence of an entirely new kind of activity, identity manipulation, to which individuals will be able to give themselves over, superimposing virtual identities on their real identities, fantasy identities on their social identities.]
>
> (2000, p. 136)

Referring specifically to identity in the Internet discussion forum, he says, '*L'individu manipule sa propre identité afin d'être réellement pris par ses interlocuteurs pour celui qu'il fantasme d'être*' [Individuals manipulate their own identities so that others take them to be the people they dream of being.] (2000, p. 137). To thine own self be true? Not any more.

But let us test the validity of these remarks. Despite the widespread anxiety which would seem to set up low expectations about sincerity online, in practice the public discussion forums which are our principal focus of attention are not riddled with challenges to identity and honesty.[1] Yet such moments can be found and are revealing both of the functioning and of the stakes of identity in this particular genre. Our first example, from a newspaper discussion forum, very pointedly destabilizes some of the claims about the brave new world of unseeable identity.

Questioning identity: The strange case of razzmattazz0

On 15 October 2002, the *New York Times* message board 'Gay Pride: the Fight for Civil Rights'[2] carries the breaking story of razzmatazz0's day. Razzmatazz0 (self-identified as a heterosexual male) has announced his intention to ask a co-worker if he is gay. But not all participants in discussion are convinced of razzmatazz0's sincerity. Is the story fact or fiction?

If you are even telling the truth at all, you need to be very careful. You are prying into matters that are none of your business.

(Bob_maddox, 15 October 2002)

Your posts have some traits to them that make me wonder if you are being truthful here about all this

(Bob_maddox, 15 October 2002)

His claim of questioning the coworker doesn't ring true anyway hon.

(Reverendbeth, 15 October 2002)

Is razzmatazz0, as he claims to be, a straight Christian office worker with an overwhelming (and for him inoffensive) urge to know his colleague's sexual preference? Is he truly someone who needs to know, won't approve, but won't let it interfere with work? Are the accusations of dishonesty well founded? Without access to non-verbal clues, no one can see razzmatazz0's shifty eyes, or manifestations of offended sincerity. (Nor, indeed, can anyone see whether he is a bored schoolgirl, a violent homophobe, an anti-Christian propagandist or a researcher of discrimination in the workplace.) The online world does indeed seem beset and beleaguered by uncertainties.

But what if this were a true story, as various contributors suppose? Opposing razzmattaz0's actions, Linguist asks, 'If he were Jewish, would you feel he was obligated to tell you?' (15 October 2002). Razzmattazz0 doesn't hesitate: 'That is easy to tell because the Jewish people in my office often take off for certain religious holidays' – that is, while he would like information on this point as well, it is available without proactive investigation on his part. Linguist has the perfect comeback: 'I don't. And my last name is not at all "Jewish" sounding. I don't particularly look Swedish, but few people think I am Jewish, even other Jews, unless I tell them' (15 October 2002).

This incident illustrates a number of pertinent points. Firstly, the varied reactions to razzmattaz0's postings show that participants on Internet forums *are* making truth valuations – they have not suspended that tendency, despite the impossibility of knowing who is who for certain. Secondly, both razzmatazz0's curiosity and the surprise of Linguist's acquaintances remind us that Internet interaction is not the only place where questions of identity can arise. Indeed, in both these cases, visual contact is available, without producing certainty: razzmatazz0 can't gauge his colleague's sexual preference just by looking and Linguist's appearance is explicitly stated *not* to be the clue to his/her Jewish identity. Judgements about identity, then, are generally based on a range of factors: appearance, yes, but also feasts observed, names, 'the ring of truth' and, significantly, verbal language (razzmatazz0 asks his colleague, Linguist tells acquaintances). It would seem then that the opposition between certainty and uncertainty does not neatly align itself with offline and online interaction or presence or absence of a visual channel. As Burkhalter says, of racial identity, 'Offline, of course, people do not present themselves with their lineage documentation or DNA analysis attached. Certainty of racial identity offline or online is always contingent – absolute proof is not available and rarely necessary' (Burkhalter, 1999, p. 162).

Why do we not display our DNA analyses or, indeed, why did razzmat-taz0's co-worker not tell all on day one at the office? Postings to the Gay Pride board tell razzmattaz0 that it is none of his business. More critical messages portray his colleague fearing the consequences of his outing and its detrimental effects on his professional future. Thus the episode reminds us also of the phenomenon of 'passing' in which one strives to be taken for a member of another group, as a means of finding acceptance, avoiding discrimination or sharing in the power of a dominant group.

Is it entirely unreasonable to extend the notion of passing to include the situation of the non-native speaker, who fears being disqualified from debate? The specifics of the razzmattazz0 story are particular to a particular contemporary US office culture and its adherence to the principle of don't ask don't tell, and we do not want to push the reading of the story as analogy too far, nor to suggest that the penalties for being revealed as gay (or Jewish) have not been infinitely more serious than those of being exposed as a cultural outsider on an Internet forum. Nor do we assert that razzmattaz0's colleague was necessarily faking straight-ness. But there are two lessons to take from the story: firstly, the ways in which we present ourselves may relate to power play; and secondly, there are many situations in which getting on with the job means not needing to know.

Identity on Internet discussion forums

These observations lead us towards a more critical understanding than that proposed by Jauréguiberry of how identity functions in Internet discussion. Burkhalter, discussing racial identity in African-American Usenet interaction, takes up Okamura's proposal of 'situational ethnic-ity', which 'pertains to the actor's subjective perception of the situation

in which he finds himself and to the salience he attributes to ethnicity as a relevant factor in that situation' (Burkhalter, 1999, p. 65,
citing Okamura, 1981, p. 454). Okamura's term derives from that of
'situational identity', a concept developed in symbolic interactionism
to describe the way in which various social identities and personal
attributes (ethnicity, gender, religious affiliation, sexuality, but also
political leanings, personal history, hobbies and – why not? – languages
spoken) will appear as more, less, or not at all salient according to their
relevance in a given situation. Here, identity is viewed as a discursive
practice: identities are constructed through interaction, formed as they
are performed (cf. Antaki & Widdicombe, 1998; Goffman, 1959); they
are not simply the expression of a pre-existing, stable, unified, authentic
self. Theorists in cultural studies have elaborated a parallel understanding of identity as an ongoing process, constituted through representation, and negotiated *in situ* (for example, Hall, 1990; Woodward, 1997).[3]

Let us then use the concept of situational identity to examine further the specific ways in which identity is used in discussion forums on
media websites. The widespread characterization of online interaction
as disjunct from the real world is intensely problematic with respect to
such forums. Discussion for the most part engages with current affairs,
politics and so on, denying any radical cleavage between real and virtual
worlds. More careful commentators[4] recognize that the extent to which
fantasy is expected in the construction of identity depends on the type
of CMC – Slater gives the example of online credit card transactions as
a domain where identity is subject to the same constraints online as
offline (2003, pp. 135–136) – and suggest that discussion forums work
with an expectation of verisimilitude, if not absolute honesty. How,
then, is identity presented and deployed within this genre, and under
what circumstances is it challenged?

Creating yourself online

Step one: Take one Internet connection

It could be assumed that the first essential ingredient for participation
in online discussion is an Internet account. In the following example
of an identity under challenge, from the early days of forum discussion, Kézako does not have one, using a patently false email address
(it translates as 'François has lied', the pronunciation of the 'at' sign
perfectly coinciding with that of the auxiliary verb). This brazen – or
indeed barefaced – 'dishonesty' has provoked some controversy on the
Le Monde website where he is posting, and his vigorous defence of his

privacy reminds us that rather than being seen as the catalyst for deceit, anonymity in the expression of opinion has often been understood as promoting honesty:

> '*Anonymat et démocratie sur le forum du Monde*
>
> *François@menti*
>
> *Plusieurs messages ayant «dénoncé» ma fausse adresse electronique, je me vois dans l'obligation de barber tout le monde avec mon cas personnel.*
>
> *Ah, le pleutre, le couard! Il s'avance masqué par honte de ses opinions! Volià ce que pourraient sous-entendre ces remarques.*
>
> *La vérité est beaucoup plus simple. Je n'en ai pas. Je squatte le PC d'un collègue qui a l'amabilité de ne pas s'offusquer de mes idées politiquement très incorrectes.*
>
> *Je pourrais bien sûr laisser mon no de tel, voire directement mon adresse personnelle pour éviter à mes contradicteurs d'utiliser le 36.17 code ANNU. [....]*
>
> *La démocratie passe aussi par l'anonymat. Le vote à bulletin secret est un grand progrès démocratique. En quoi mon absence d'adresse gêne-t-elle, si je cite poliment des faits précis pour étayer mes arguments?*'
>
> [Anonymity and democracy on the *Le Monde* forums
>
> François@menti
>
> Since many messages have 'denounced' my false email address, I find myself compelled to bore everyone with the specifics of my situation.
>
> Boo! The lily-livered coward! Ashamed of his opinions, he only ventures out with a mask. That's what the remarks could be understood to imply.
>
> The truth is much simpler. I don't have one. I'm a squatter on the PC of a colleague who is kind enough not to take umbrage at my very politically incorrect ideas.
>
> I could of course leave my phone number, or indeed my home address so that my opponents don't have to use the electronic phone book [...]
>
> Democracy is also achieved via anonymity. The secret ballot was a great step for democracy. Why should my lack of address be a problem if I politely cite precise facts to support my arguments?]
>
> (Kézako, '*Autres sujets*' [Other topics], 4 January 2000)

The exchange is indicative of the debate on online anonymity described by Donath:

> Anonymity (including pseudonymity) is very controversial in the online world. On one side, anonymity is touted as the savior of personal freedom, necessary to ensure liberty in an era of increasingly sophisticated surveillance. [...]. On the other hand, it is condemned as an invitation to anarchy, providing cover for criminals from tax-evaders to terrorists. The 'very purpose of anonymity', said Supreme Court Justice Scalia, is to 'facilitate wrong by eliminating accountability'.
>
> (Donath, 1999, p. 53, quoting Froomkin, 1995, par. 50)

Contrary to Scalia, we argue that the 'purpose of anonymity' is neither singular nor inevitably evil, but varies according to the purposes of the genre at hand. In the case of public Internet discussion, *'Démocranymat'* [Democranonymity], as Kézako calls it, soon came to be seen as a right to be respected, as witnessed by the subsequent organization of the sites to protect the privacy of email addresses.

Step two: Add one username

Nowadays, participants in Internet discussion forums are usually identified only by usernames or pseudonyms that do not reliably indicate age, gender or nationality. They do, however, (if prohibitions on the usurpation of names are respected) indicate the same user, identifiable from one posting to another on the same site, or at least within the same debate: the option of complete anonymity, in which there are no clues as to the authorship of each message, is incompatible with the functioning of the sites studied.[5] Often the pseudonyms are so clearly not 'real' names that describing them as deceitful is as illogical as decrying the disguises at a masked ball – and facelessness at the masked ball can be fun, as scores of witty pseudonyms remind us. Unlike the masked ball, however, there is no expectation that the masks will be removed at the end of the evening: the rule is *'Pas de spéculations ou révélations à propos de l'identité de tel ou tel participant'* [No speculation about or revelation of the identity of any participant] (*Le Monde*, 2007) – facelessness is not a danger but a right.

Even if we reject the determining role of visual contact in achieving positive identification, we must still allow that outside the content of the postings, clues to identity in online discussion are meagre: unlike newsgroup discussions, there are usually no email addresses;[6] many forums do not enable automatic signature tags, and some prohibit links to personal home pages. At the same time, despite the paucity of clues and the potential for deceit, there seems to be a generically defined sense that participants are individual, relatively truthful human beings. Classic assumptions are made – but how much are they insisted upon? Donath's allusion above to the courtroom provides an example of circumstances in which strict truthfulness is demanded.[7] When does such insistence occur on media-site discussion forums? When does identity matter to this extent?

Challenging identity

It is europeaneo's *national* identity that is first at issue in a 2003 *Le Monde* debate on the place of Poland in Europe. Addressing europeaneo, a certain kurukuru writes, *'mais comme je sais que vous n'etes pas un occidental et que vous voulez detruire l'europe culturelle, changé de pseudo !'* [but since I know that you aren't a Westerner and that you want to destroy European culture, change pseudonyms!] (5 May 2003). To this europeaneo replies, *'désolée je suis française et mon ami est italien... Tout les deux scientifiques...'* [Sorry, I'm a Frenchwoman and my boyfriend is Italian, both of us are scientists] (5 May 2003) before continuing the debate. This declaration regarding europeaneo's *professional* identity is further fuel for kurukuru's allegations of fakery. Now referring to europeaneo's previous statements regarding the US intervention in Iraq, kurukuru writes,

> *'Vous pretendez etre scientifique et vous nous sortez ça: [...]*
>
> *Vous etessupposé etre scientifique et vous ecrivez cela: [...]*
>
> *Je prefere rire de vos propos et douter de la réalité de ce que vous pretendez etre. En plus vous etes sourd, aveugle et de mauvaise foi ! [...]*
>
> *Vous m avez l air d'etre un quelqu'un de bien bizarre et de bien improbable. ...façon bien élevée de dire autre chose.'*
>
> [You claim to be a scientist and you give us: [...]
>
> You're supposed to be a scientist and you write the following [...]
>
> I prefer to laugh at your arguments and question the reality of what you're pretending to be. As well, you're deaf, blind, and insincere. [...]
>
> You seem like someone rather strange and quite improbable – which is a polite way of saying something else.]
>
> (kurukuru, *La Pologne veut-elle nous foutre dans la M?*
> [Does Poland want to drop us in the S---?], 5 May 2003)

Kurukuru presses home the attack in a later exchange, in which euro-peaneo seeks to distance fellow Europeans from North Americans. Europeaneo writes,

> '*Mais les européens ne veulent pas leur ressembler [...] nous nous sentons plus proches des peuples ayant une certaine sensibilité au monde qui nous entoure, plus proches des sud-américains, des indiens, orientaux, asiatique ou africains.*' [But Europeans don't want to be like them [...] we feel closer to people with some sensitivity to the world around us, closer to South Americans, Indians, Orientals, Asians or Africans.]

> (5 May 2003)

Kurukuru replies that Europeans and North Americans are all Westerners and discredits his opponent's European credentials in a way that affirms the myth of the face as reliable indicator of the truth:

> '*Vous commencez a vous devoiler. [...] le masque 'européen' est trop pra-tique pour cacher des pulsions inavouables ... d ailleurs pourriez vous nous dire qui etes vous ? 'Sud americain,indiens, oriental ....', car de toute evi-dence vous n'etes pas occidental et ce que vous revez au plus profond de vous c'est justement de vider l'Europe de toute sa personnalité et de tout son génie. [...]*' [You're starting to reveal [lit. unveil] yourself. [...] The 'European' mask is so handy for hiding impulses too shameful to mention.... By the way, could you tell us who you are? 'South American, Indian, Oriental...' for it is patently obvious that you aren't a Westerner and that what you desire in the very depths of your soul is nothing less than to empty Europe of her entire personality and genius.]

> (5 May 2003)

Clearly, kurukuru's intense interest in europeaneo's identity is no prod-uct of concern for a convivial sharing of the personal. Rather, the rhetorical value of these attacks has been to disable europeaneo's argu-ment: europeaneo is the cuckoo in the nest, the pseudo-European who seeks to destroy from within, the pseudo-scientist diffusing false facts. That is, these questions have much to do with winning the debate and little with discovering the true europeaneo. After all, if that were the issue at hand, wouldn't there be some other questions? Amongst the multiple non-standard usages in these postings is what one might have expected to be a puzzling movement between masculine and feminine forms. Europeaneo writes variously:

– '*Moi, citoyen européen, je ne comprends pas ces pays* [As a European citizen (masculine form) I don't understand these countries]';
– '*je me suis assez battu pour la cause italienne*' [I have fought long enough for the Italian cause] (masculine verb form);

but also

– '*je suis française*' [I am French (feminine form)]; and
– '*désolée*' [Sorry (feminine form)].

Europeaneo is the Orlando of the Polish debate, moving between genders, and no one seems perturbed. Unlike national identity and professional standing, his/her gender identification is irrelevant to the argument.[8]

The accusation levelled against europeaneo is the most common kind of identity-related challenge on the sites studied: someone is accused of mis-stating his/her true allegiances in order to advance an argument. (So few right-wing extremists, for example, think it politic to declare themselves such.) Jauréguiberry's explanation cited above as to why one might fake one's identity – to make others see the self we dream of being – seems remarkably narrow. The choice to deceive is not necessarily the outworking of a personal fantasy: the wolf in sheep's clothing does not really want to be a sheep.

This use of identity for reasons of rhetorical power rather than realization of fantasy is clearly illustrated by a BBC 'World News' discussion thread where the challenged online persona is presumed to be completely antithetical and indeed antipathetic to the offline identity. Here, gender *is* an issue, because it has a bearing on what becomes a heated exchange. What starts out as discussion of racism on the 2007 season of the UK's Celebrity Big Brother (Channel 4) is diverted from that topic at the second posting (perhaps unsurprisingly given our findings in Chapter 3) by a personal report of racial harassment experienced by a Muslim woman at the hands of a female 'Chav' (lout). The former, She-Naz, retaliated physically and an exchange of punches ensued. Although heavily censored by the moderators, the published thread still allows us to follow a litany of insults and challenges. She-Naz is accused of being neither Muslim nor a woman ('I imagine his y chromosomes came into being the first minute he realized how awful it sounded that he expressed pride in his hitting a woman and not a milisecond before' [SpeedRacerX, Celebrity Big Brother, 18 January 2007]). And the psychological explanation given is not about aspirational projection. SpeedRacerX makes the point in several posts; for example,

> As I said earlier, I dont believe you are a Muslim at all.
>
> I suspect that YOU have a deep hatred of Muslims and women and are pretending to be both to make them look bad.
>
> I truly believe that the reason they [Chavs] present their fictional Internet personas to be Muslim is because of their own internal xenophobia and feel the best way to express this is to present themselves as the group of people they dislike the most and to make said people appear to be lacking in moral compass.
>
> (18 January 2007)

If this is faking, then its purpose is the denigration of others rather than personal gratification or indeed personal safety. But whether or not they are justified, the accusations of fakery have the effect of disabling She-Naz's argument. While it could be argued that the nature of the interactions proves the point that anti-Asian racism exists in Britain, and while She-Naz does garner a few expressions of support, deploring the reported attack on her, any serious discussion is derailed by the dispute as to the veracity of her account. If it never happened, there's apparently no need to acknowledge the possibility of such incidents taking place between Britons. She-Naz posts,

> Righhhhhhhhhhhttttttttttt... if something happens to an asian person... they make it up!! Hmm... but if something happens to a white person its a big issue in this place? [...] Say for arguments sake I'm not lying then?
>
> (18 January 2007)

Significantly, the message containing this question seems to trigger the conclusion of the posts that pass the censor in this thread. She-Naz's challenge to check her identity by appealing to the Asian Life Board gets one post-able response, a 'Can't be bothered' message from rufflyknickers who is off to the pub. Who cares who She-Naz is? The argument is over for the day. It doesn't matter if this ennui regarding She-Naz results from wider uncertainty about her motivation and the identity she asserts on the BBC boards: here the doubt is used to foreclose any discussion of the particular question at issue.

So far our challengers have been reticent in justifying their diagnoses of fakery. The following set of examples cites linguistic evidence for the accusations. The source is the *Nouvel Observateur* debate on *la double peine*, the proposal that foreigners convicted of crimes in France should both serve their time and, subsequently, be deported. Kurupt objects on the grounds that this is discriminatory. Karniella, identifying herself as a foreigner, writes in support of the policy in a closely argued posting which, at over 400 words, cannot be quoted in its entirety. The extract below indicates the tone:

> '*Je suis 100% pour la double peine. Je suis en France depuis onze ans maintenant et je n'ai pas demandé la nationalité parce que je vis dans l'espoir qu'un jour je puisse retourner dans mon pays natal en Afrique qui d'ici là aura peut être change au niveau démocratie. En attendant, je suis en France, mes enfants ont la chance exceptionnelle de suivre une éducation scolaire et apprendre les valeurs de la liberté [...]*' [I'm 100% in favour of the double penalty. I have now been in France for 11 years and I haven't asked for French nationality because I live in the hope that I may one day return to my native land in Africa, which by that time will perhaps have changed where democracy is concerned. In the meantime, I am in France, and my children have the extraordinary good fortune to undertake school education and learn the values of freedom.]
>
> (Karniella – Gonesse, 11 January 2002)

Kurupt responds as follows:

> '*Toi etrangere vivant en France??? laisee moi rire...tu n'es qu'une menteuse.la facon de t'exprimer avoue intrinsequement que tu es francaise. [...] Tu utilise ce subterfuge pour donner plus de poids a tes idees mais je ne suis pas dupe.*' [You're a foreign woman living in France? Excuse my laughter – you're nothing but a liar. Your way of expressing yourself intrinsically reveals that you're French. You're using this subterfuge to give more weight to your ideas, but I'm no fool.]
>
> (Kurupt – Bruxelles, 11 January 2002)

Karniella writes too well to be foreign. Richmanporter, who is belligerently anti-French and claims to speak for the oppressed foreign worker, writes both too well and too badly, according to William:

> '*Richmanporter, je te soupçonne de faire de la provocation en faisant l'idiot. Tu sais écrire des mots difficiles et tu ajoutes des idioties. Si tes messages ne passent pas c'est peut-être que quelqu'un s'en est aperçu. Arrête de faire l'idiot et dis-moi si je me trompe.*' [Richmanporter, I think you're trying

to cause trouble by playing the fool. You know how to write difficult words and you add in nonsense. If your messages aren't being posted maybe it's because someone has noticed this. Stop being an idiot and tell me if I'm mistaken.]

(William – Paris, 16 January 2002)

Fake good foreigner, fake bad foreigner, both Karniella and Richmanporter serve the cause of the double penalty; Karniella by supporting it, Richmanporter by presenting the undesirable foreign element. If their accusers are correct, both online personae actually mask anti-immigrant agitators who represent an inverted model of passing, in that they are trying to pass as members of the marginalized group, in order to marginalize that group further.

If the accusations are right, these are failed exercises in fakery: the accusers have *seen through* the pretence. But we cannot be sure if that is what they are. What is, however, abundantly clear from the preceding examples is the rhetorical power of the identity challenge. Now, at a critical moment of a MUD role play, there is simply no point in expressing suspicions that one's opponent is not really a mauve goblin with telekinetic powers. But in an Internet forum, an identity challenge *is* a powerful weapon: this is bound up with the stakes of the genre, and these, particularly in the French forums, are about making a case.[9] If the point of the interaction is to participate in debate, the only reason worth faking identity is to gain the upper hand in that debate, and therefore the accusation of fakery, be it justified or not, works to undermine the power of the opponent's argument.

Identity, then, is as much a product of context, indeed genre, as of any fidelity to a pre-existent notion of self. The interactions studied in this chapter demonstrate that situational identity in the context of French discussion forums (and, when debate takes hold, on British and US forums) is the identity needed in order to make a persuasive argument. The freedom to make a case openly is the argument used in favour of anonymity; irrelevance to the debate is the explanation for the lack of attention to europeaneo's floating gender identification, accusations of fakery are placed in order to disable one's opponent and, equally, identity may be used in order to add weight to arguments.

Consequences for language learners

Now, if identity in Internet forums is about making (or faking) the point, this allows us to revisit that question of the identity students assert, and provokes reflection upon the range of options with which teachers equip them. The familiar repertoire in the early stages of learning is name, age, nationality and profession with the optional extras of address, family members, domestic animals, hobbies, likes and dislikes. These are our first steps in the foreign language and our first words in producing our identity in it. But the identity they produce can only take us so far in performing in French cultural practices.

Let us return then to the student who can see no role to play but that of fake French person or always already marginalized Anglophone (Hispanophone, Mandarin speaker and so on). The issues of the manipulation of identity online and the use of identity as it is bound up in generic stakes suggest a way through this dilemma. Identity becomes something you can use, as opposed to something you just are. You might use your identity to be socially pleasant – or you might use your identity to make a point. Identity is not something that is unmalleable with the only alternative being a false identity. Understanding identity as situational, as strategic, provides a means of refusing the role of *'la petite étrangère'* [the foreign lass]. It allows you to live your status as outsider as something potentially empowering, rather than restrictive, something that you might be able to use, but also something that you might choose not to use at all in a particular situation.

This chapter concludes with some examples of students using identity successfully, a foretaste of fuller discussion in Chapter 9. They come from online interactions in which second-year French students participated as part of a unit on argumentation.[10] Although our examination of online identity was not systematic, steps had been taken to avoid students approaching the forums in the spirit of penpal interaction: through contrast with examples from British sites, something of the generic and cultural particularity of French Internet forums was noted. When perusing forums, students were asked to collect examples of the verbal expressions used by participants to refer to themselves, and these self-descriptors (such as *'En tant que mère de famille, je trouve que'* [As a mother, I find that]) were on the whole useful for the production of arguments rather than life stories.

The messages posted by students show that the fact of living in Australia allows one to claim the right to post on such obvious topics as *'L'Australie, pays raciste'* [Australia: a racist country] and terrorism in Bali. But it can also be deployed in debates as diverse as smoking, road safety, language policy and wind power (the debate where, perhaps surprisingly, Australianness garnered the most enthusiastic response). Posting as a cultural other can give pertinence to one's arguments, far from detracting from them: here the outsider finds a place to be heard, in a French cultural practice, without playing the game of the Conversation With The Foreigner.

The frequency of postings where cultural identification is signalled is indicative of the (unsurprising) strength of students' identification as cultural outsiders. French is a foreign language – they are still allowing their foreignness to define them, although they are now using it productively. But there are so many other debates and other identities to be asserted, and students should be encouraged to think of different ways of introducing the self, according to the arguments in which they are taking part.

Kanduhn (Australie) manages to do this to some extent, presenting himself in three different ways in three *Nouvel Observateur* debates:

- In *'La violence terroriste'* [Terrorist violence] in response to a *'Kadich pour ceux de Bali'* [Kaddish for the Bali victims] he is simply an Australian grateful for the condolences offered by another forum member – but he also argues the undesirability of violent solutions.
- In the debate *'La cigarette et les moins de 16 ans'* [Cigarettes and the under 16s] he is a tobacco intolerant commuter.
- In *'Les transferts dans le football'* [Football transfers] he is a soccer fan with a friend in the English third division, who can therefore offer insights into rates of pay.

Each of these self-presentations allows him to make a point pertinent to the debate. But another thing to learn is that on French sites you might not even make an identity statement at all. On the kind of general forums we are looking at here, there is no point in presenting personal details that do not advance your argument and you do not have to play your identity as an entry card.

Encouraging students in this direction does not mean asking them to 'hide' their nationality or 'fake' the identity of a native speaker; rather, it means persuading them that nationality and speaker status may not be especially relevant to the issue of the day. If identity is to be strategic, then learners need to consider the full range of social identities and speaking positions available to them in order to stake their claim to participation. In the following chapter, however, which discusses the roles most readily available to outsiders, we shall see that, for many, asserting a wider range of identities in a second language requires a considerable imaginative leap.

8
Towards Intercultural Discussion: Getting Off on the Right Foot(ing)

Introduction

With the proliferation of discussion facilitated by Internet forums, one might imagine that, notwithstanding the problems encountered by some learners, intercultural communication now has fertile ground within which to flourish. Closer inspection, however, reveals that cordial intercultural exchanges are far from widespread in this genre. This suggests that, despite the apparent ease of contact, there remain significant obstacles to such exchanges.

This chapter explores one such obstacle: the speaking positions most readily available to cultural and linguistic outsiders. If we understand identity as constructed through interaction (cf. Antaki & Widdicombe, 1998; Goffman, 1959, see preceding chapter), then the position from which one speaks – the role one occupies within a discourse – is a major determinant of that construction. Now, some roles are ready-made and easy to slip into; they are obvious positions for people to take from the outset of a given interaction (doctor and patient, raconteur and audience, expert and novice, friend-in-crisis and sympathetic listener). For cultural and linguistic outsiders (such as language learners) venturing on public Internet forums, there are similarly a couple of obvious speaking positions ready to be occupied, such as the ones adopted by Fleurie and Eleanor. We shall see, however, that these are not necessarily conducive to fruitful participation, and can in fact be very limiting and/or discouraging in their effect.

Fortunately, however, there are other options, and the chapter goes on to focus on a case study that suggests an alternative to inhabiting one or other of these 'default' positions. The case study is a comparatively rare instance of sustained intercultural engagement on a discussion thread for the general public. Here we follow a core of Francophone and Anglophone participants as they negotiate their roles in order to pursue their communicative goals. For, as Davies and Harré remark in their explanation of positioning, discursive practices not only 'constitute the speakers and hearers in certain ways'; at the same time they constitute 'a resource through which speakers and hearers can negotiate new positions' (Davies & Harré, 1990, p. 62). In the case study we see participants using these resources to reposition themselves within an exchange. The interactional strategies we identify provide a model, not just for language learners wishing to participate productively in the genre of Internet forum discussion, but for successful intercultural communication more generally.

Border patrol in the 'borderless world'

Default position 1: Champion of one's culture

From the start of our project, we were suspicious of the myth of the Internet bringing cultures together in a 'borderless world'. Despite the ready accessibility of public Internet discussion forums from a technical perspective, we suspected that certain borders would reassert themselves in the form of the cultural conventions and values mobilized whenever communication occurs (and such cultural differences have been detailed in Chapters 2–4). To test this hypothesis, we set out to find examples of intercultural exchanges in public Internet discussion forums.

The monitoring of sites to collect data for this study supplied relatively few examples of sustained intercultural interaction. Although we had approached the myth of borderless communication with some scepticism, even we were surprised at the rarity with which participants from different language backgrounds conducted productive exchanges in the public genre of the Internet forum.[1]

Clearly, part of the equation is simple lack of curiosity, initiative or language skills, but, on the other hand, even where we found intercultural interaction on forums, often it did not take the form of discussion – that is, postings and responses constituting an exchange of views. Far more prominent on these sites is the incidence of 'flaming' and 'ranting' – insults and vitriolic diatribe.[2] Although 'verbal brawling' (Dery, 1994, p. 3) may erupt on any subject, such disputes are particularly present in exchanges referring to other cultures. A cursory consultation of any general interest public discussion site yields examples. The simple mention of France on a UK site can function as an invitation for French-bashing. US-bashing is even more widespread. Yet these are anodyne compared to discussion boards related to the Middle East, where ranting is at such a level that discussion invariably has to be pre-moderated (that is, postings have to be approved by a moderator before they can appear online).[3] Whilst French and US foreign policy and Middle Eastern politics are certainly contentious topics, this in itself does not explain the degree of ranting on public discussion sites. The material affordances of the genre itself also play a role.

As studies by Zickmund (2000), Gottlieb (2003), Dery (1994), Burkhalter (1999) and Nakamura (2002) show, with their analyses of cyberhate, flame wars and online racial identification, cyberspace is as much a space for spreading hatred as for fostering intercultural understanding. Whilst it can be harnessed to empower marginalized groups (Gottlieb, 2003), simultaneously it facilitates both dissemination of 'discriminatory propaganda' (Gottlieb, 2003, p. 200) and recruitment to racist organizations (Zickmund, 2000). Far from the utopia of the borderless world, the Internet offers easy opportunities for fortifying frontiers, for reinforcing stereotypes, for galvanizing racist hostility. This is particularly true of online discussion, which offers opportunities to stage intercultural battles. With its rapid, largely anonymous exchanges, its capacity for faceless interaction between strangers without means of redress (Sproull & Kiesler, 1986, 1991) and the dominance of an adversarial communication style in postings (Herring, 1996),[4] Internet discussion lends itself to volatile disputes, and never more so than when race and culture are in question. Burkhalter (1999) draws attention to the racial polarization in Usenet groups, showing how discussions are grounded in and serve to entrench preconceptions about ethnic groups. Zickmund (2000) focuses on 'linguistic warfare' – the 'pattern of insult and rebuke' (p. 249) – in right-wing newsgroups between white supremacist members and outsiders baiting them, which functions to reaffirm group cohesion through the exclusion of the other. The form (abuse and insult) and function (strengthening of in-group identity) of these clashes, however, are not restricted to neo-nazi bulletin boards, but are generalized phenomena on Internet discussion forums to the point where clashes commonly outnumber more measured encounters on questions of culture.

Whenever national identities are foregrounded in an intercultural interaction, participants invariably feel responsible for the way their country is represented. This has been noted among students involved in intercultural Internet exchanges: Schneider and von der Emde give the example from a German/US telecollaboration of a question posed by one of the German students as to whether most Americans have a gun at home. Conflict ensues from the enquiry as 'each side is unwittingly interpolated into representing their own national cultures' (2006, p. 188). And O'Dowd (2006) observes that students working online with foreign partners experience a heightened need 'to have themselves and their identity represented to the world as they perceive it' (p. 83). Indeed it is most often upon their status as representatives of their culture that the telecollaborative enterprise turns: it is for the meeting of cultural others.

This tendency, together with the polarized nature of Internet discussion, means that cultural/linguistic outsiders (such as language learners) who venture on public newspaper and media forums readily slip into the role of defensive representatives of their culture. This becomes the default position, a ready-made speaking position only too easily occupied. A defensive stance, in turn, increases the probability of intercultural conflict occurring.

Dedicated learner sites

Default position 2: Language learner

The degree of intercultural animosity on these generalist sites may lead motivated students to look elsewhere in cyberspace for opportunities to practise their language skills. An accessible alternative is public discussion sites for language learners. For example, the BBC operates two popular forums for learners of English: 'Ask a question' invites you to 'Ask your questions about the English language here and a teacher will try to answer them as soon as possible'; 'Communicate!' enables you to 'Share your experiences of learning English with people all over the world' (BBC Learning English Message Boards). Learners of other languages might turn to Unilang's 'Virtual School of Languages'. Run by learners for learners, it boasts forums relating to over 70 languages. On the French page, we find contributors of various backgrounds, identified by pseudonym, an icon, current location and the languages they speak or are learning. Like 'Communicate!', it is an active forum, friendly and enthusiastic, and attracts participants from a vast range of countries. These surely are examples of the borderless world.

And yet, these forums have very firm frontiers, frontiers replicating the classroom walls. While this might be expected in the case of the BBC's teacher-directed 'Ask a question' forum, the other forums too are highly restricted in their range and mode of discussion. This is not simply a consequence of strict moderation or of limited language skills (although these do play a role). Rather, a set of limitations is imposed by the way in which participants position themselves primarily as learners. This default identity for participants determines the topics and mode of discussion on these sites according to a small number of well-rehearsed patterns.

Encouraged by the forum's definition as a place to share learning experiences, postings to 'Communicate!' are most frequently on the keypal model – 'Hi, I'm Anna and I want to improve my English...' – such that messages consist largely of exchanges of greetings, and of information about age, location, local customs and hobbies. Whilst this is useful practice for the beginner, it is very limiting for language learners who have passed introductory level: discussion rarely moves beyond the central topic of the self. The only other speaking position that appears to be readily available to a more advanced learner is that of teacher, clearly produced in relation to the default position of learner. Thus Mrushko sets exercises for her fellow participants on phrasal verbs ('Don't let me down!', 22 February 2006), while LadyAutumn offers lessons on punctuation ('Practice Your English Here', 11 January 2006).

Similar conventions appear on the Unilang forums, with learners trading personal details. Here there is the added dimension of error correction (largely diverted into the 'Ask a Question' forum on the BBC site). Again, a version of the teacher role is readily adopted by other learners, who assiduously correct each error in the messages they read. Threads on Unilang's French forum typically start with participants writing a few lines introducing themselves and then asking other learners to correct their French, or writing a message in English and translating it underneath into French, or writing in English about wanting to practise their French. Thus much of the communication goes on in English (the default language on the Unilang site), about French. Due to both the formulaic nature of the self-presentations and the emphasis on error correction, there is very little uptake of the content of messages, and new threads often peter out once corrections to the initial message have been exhausted.

Giving information about one's pastimes and pets in order to initiate a discussion thread is quite alien to Internet forums addressing the general public. It is, however, ubiquitous on sites for learners. This form of self-presentation is modelled on practice in the language classroom. It corresponds to the description by Brown, Collins and Duguid of a formalistic 'classroom activity' that only superficially resembles an authentic cultural practice (1989, p. 34). The problem noted by these authors is that features of the classroom frame risk becoming integral to students' performance of the task (p. 34). This is what we see when students feel the need to reproduce the institutional setting in order to introduce themselves and communicate in a foreign language.[5]

The self-positioning as learner limits discussion primarily to oneself, one's immediate environment and one's language deficiencies. Learner identity on these sites is defined in terms of lack of competence. Indeed on the Unilang French site, where a seemingly more accessible *lingua franca* – English – is temptingly available, learner incompetence is assumed to the point where learners are not even expected to communicate in French. Thus, to launch a thread about French regional accents and dialects, JackFrost writes,

> I think I'll write this in English so everyone (including non-native speakers) can be part of this. But I don't mind if some of you want to speak French.
>
> (JackFrost, *'Ton Français'* [Your French], 14 June 2005)

Learner identity is not necessarily related to the level of French, but instead seems quite intransigent, as in the following example, where an advanced student seeks to continue learning through schoolbook strategies rather than venturing towards books published for a Francophone readership:

> *'Désolé si quelqu'un a déjà posé cette question, mais pouvez-vous me recommender un livre pour le vocabulaire français avancé? Merci!'* [Sorry if someone has already posted this question, but could you recommend a book for advanced French vocabulary? Thanks!]
>
> (Rob P, Discussion Group, 19 May 2005)

The learners' forum is a site where an exchange of views is simulated rather than stimulated, as the following proposal shows:

> *'Je crois que nous devons un sujet débattre ici pour améliorer notre français, pour l'utilise plus des temp.*

Est-ce que quelqu'uns avez un idée pour commencer?' [I think we should debate a subject here to improve our French, to use it more often. Does someone have an idea to start with?]

(Ryder22, Discussion Group, 21 November 2005)

The weather being the only suggestion (not an obvious choice for debate, although a standard of conversation practice), after four two-line responses on the day's snowfall and temperature, the thread reverts to the correction of grammatical errors. We can see how attractively safe it all is. There is no ranting, but then again there is very little discussion at all, other than differences of opinion on, for example, the use of *'on'* as opposed to *'l'on'* in French.

Just how hard it is to engage discussion can be seen when Parousia – whose level of French is more than equal to the task – tries to discuss student protests in France. Although her 600-word message is comparable in form and purpose to those posted on non-learner sites, the response is not. Her 20-word invitation to correct errors in the French is taken up at length in the first reply, while her ideas receive what amounts to a postscript. Parousia then launches another lengthy message, this time on the Rape of Nanking. Once again, JunMing fastidiously corrects the French, and only in a later message comments on the content, while the other five replies follow up language questions with no mention of the subject matter. Parousia's third attempt to elicit discussion is a posting about vegetarianism. This time, her efforts are entirely unrewarded: none of the five responses makes any reference at all to Parousia's views, instead focusing exclusively on questions of grammar and translation. Participant roles are polarized into those of teacher and pupil, as Parousia playfully points out to JunMing:

> *'J'espère que vous ne me recalez pas, Monsieur Le Prof de Français!'*
> [I hope you're not going to fail me, Mr French Teacher!]
> (*'A n'importe qui est là dans la vaste espace cybère'* [To anyone who's out there in the vastness of cyberspace], 24 April 2005)

Parousia outlines the choices available to her:

> *'Peut-être que je devrai aller sur un vrais forum français pour pratiquer cette langue même si les gens là seraient moins tolérants de mes fautes.'* [Maybe I should go on a real French forum to practise this language, even if the people there would be less tolerant of my errors.]
> (*'A n'importe qui est là dans la vaste espace cybère'* [To anyone who's out there in the vastness of cyberspace], 12 April 2005)

The contrast she makes between the learner forum and a 'real' forum suggests that Parousia regards communication in the learner forum as largely inauthentic. But she hesitates between abandoning this pretence and participating in a 'real' forum with its perceived, intimidating, lack of tolerance. Her dilemma is emblematic of the advanced language learner, caught between two options that do not lead one to the other. Between ranters and learners, it can be difficult to engage in discussion.

On the one hand, on the public Internet discussion site, no inbuilt allowance is made for linguistic/cultural outsiders and the frequently combative mode of interaction discourages the less confident. On the other hand, learner sites, although usually friendlier, are not a stepping stone towards enabling participation on more general sites. With their reliance on teacher substitutes, their focus on error correction, their lack of engagement with message content and their emphasis on personal information as a topic, they do not simply host discussion at a different level of language proficiency (from which one could progress towards discussion on the general sites); rather they host a different genre of exchange. Now, although the participants on these sites are taking responsibility for their own learning and making choices with regard to the method of learning (Benson & Voller, 1997), it is hard to see them as developing autonomy.[6] We see that adopting the learner identity most readily available on these sites is a way of remaining firmly within the virtual classroom and the cultural comfort zone of student–student interaction, rather than taking up the opportunity offered by the Internet to engage with the 'target culture' in roles other than that of pupil/teacher.

The question then becomes how to navigate between these two problematic poles of entrenched beginner status and verbal combat, how to bridge the gulf between learner sites and general sites and take advantage of the Internet's potential for broadening cultural and linguistic horizons. And happily there are examples of language enthusiasts taking up this challenge productively, and not only among the interculturally motivated visitors to the 'general discussion' forums of the Unilang site,[7] but even occasionally on discussion boards for the wider public. The following case study analyses one such example, and asks, what distinguishes the practice of these participants from that of those on learner sites? It teases out the conditions for successful discussion, focusing on the roles participants adopt, and the kinds of engagement and responses enabled by these speaking positions.

Case study: The 'Indy'

The 'Independent Argument forum' (the 'Indy') was a feature of the website of the British daily newspaper *The Independent* until May 2004, when the resources needed for moderation were deemed too costly to sustain. Existing discussions were, however, archived on Delphi Forums, and many of the active discussions migrated to that platform (with several thousand 'Indy' participants recreating the 'Idle Chit Chat' board, and others resuscitating the forum as 'Independent Argument – Redux'), so that the forum continues in a modified form.

Although there were ranters aplenty on the 'Indy', the forum nonetheless attracted geographically scattered and culturally diverse participants onto a number of threads. Hosted on the site of a British newspaper, 'Indy' discussion was nominally in English, but threads relating to France attracted a significant number of Francophones, keen to hone their English writing skills and engage in English-language discussion. Our case study is a thread in the 'World' folder entitled 'Are the French Awakening?' (Independent Argument, 2003–2004), in which discussion occurs in both English and French. Welsh also becomes a language of exchange on a smaller scale, and signoffs and greetings in other languages (Italian, German) commonly occur (although these do not necessarily denote proficiency in those languages). This thread is, then, an example of something approaching ongoing public intercultural discussion that does not replicate the classroom, something generally imagined to be commonplace in cyberspace, but in fact comparatively rare.

During the six-week period from 3 October until 14 November 2003, this thread attracted 401 postings from 43 contributors, whose cultural affiliation (gleaned through what they revealed in their postings) and language use defied geographical borders.[8] Participants included

- at least 10 Francophones writing in English and occasionally French (providing 11 of the first 17 messages, and thus outnumbering Anglophone participants at the outset);[9]
- two Anglophones writing extensively in French as well as English, several others using French in passing or learning French, still others with experience of living in France;
- a French–English bilingual and an Anglophone also communicating in Welsh.

Thus a significant proportion of contributors was functional in more than one language, and indeed this group contributed 194 (48.4 per cent) of the 401 postings. Most did not identify as current language students, but nevertheless identified as language enthusiasts or indeed lifelong learners. Cultural identity and intercultural experiences were often foregrounded in support of message content.

Examining the thread, we find that movement between languages is frequent. FDevraie (an Englishwoman living in France) and frogoff (a self-described 'Parisian cockney', French-born, English-educated), for example, oscillate between French and English as they negotiate which language will be the primary one for discussing their adaptation from British to French work practices (#129, #133, #135).[10] Welshman DaiSmallcoal's postings are just as likely to be in French as in English (or indeed, more often than not, a combination of both, for example #214). Issues of language and culture are a recurrent topic throughout the thread: the level of French spoken by immigrants in France; metaphors such as *'la gueule de bois'* [literally 'wooden mouth'] for a hangover; how and where participants had learnt English or French; the use of acronyms in French. Border crossing is thus both theme and mode of discussion.

The role adopted in many of the postings might be termed an 'interculturalist' one: the goal is intercultural exchange of ideas as much as second-language practice, and participants situate themselves at cultural intersections. The fact that a critical mass of plurilingual participants is active on this thread from its outset makes this position more readily available than usual to participants. However, the interculturalist position, where it is adopted, does not simply displace the other speaking positions outlined earlier, as we shall see.

Firstly, we see that the learner identity has not been abandoned or superseded. Rather, it is invoked temporarily when relevant: it is still available as an identity trait to be used. Integrated into the discussion is a certain amount of feedback on language use: surprise is expressed that frogoff and frenchval are really French (their English didn't suggest it); and language errors are corrected. In French, feedback on errors of gender, register, spelling and adjective agreement is offered and appreciated (#223, #230–234, #271, #300, #303), especially the correction of expletives. Correction of Welsh also occurs (#300, #302, #363). These corrections are just as detailed as those on the language learners' sites; the difference is that they have not become an end in themselves; rather they are interspersed with discussion. Participants are not only garnering useful linguistic feedback but having a genuine conversation. In addition, feedback on linguistic inaccuracy is often mutual and functions as a gesture of inclusion; having your language errors corrected becomes a mark of insider status.

Secondly, we find that this thread, which thus far might seem exemplary in its congenial cohabitation of languages and cultures, actually started with an invitation to rant, and still comprises a certain amount of ranting. An American with Cajun connections – fdday2 – starts the thread with some French-baiting:

> It seems there is a new willingness in France to look in the mirror & reevaluate what they see –
> http://www.iht.com/articles/112118.html
> Debate is interesting, but, will they change?
> (fdday2, 'Are the French Awakening?' #1, 3 October 2003)

The dig at the French means the thread could have quickly become polarized in the fashion of so many others. The reason it doesn't is that the initial exchanges are mostly between Francophones writing in English, doubtless attracted to the mention of 'the French' in the subject line. Half a dozen multilingual posters gradually become the kernel of message board activity. They position their identities as bicultural, correct each other's French and Welsh, and exchange views on moving country, home renovations and rugby. When fdday2 later attempts to pursue his anti-French agenda, he is excluded by this group as a 'dishonest debater' cum ranter (#316). However, in parallel with the intercultural discussion on this thread is an ongoing slanging match between American provocateur Sean1980 and anyone who will rise to her anti-French taunts, which at one point or another includes most of the bilingual group.

What at first seemed like borderless communication might more properly be understood as a realignment of borders. And in this revised geography, use of two languages becomes a mark of inclusion. The interculturalists, sympathetic to the use of French and English and seeking out cross-cultural contact, see themselves as engaging in 'reasoned discussion' (#216), and the line is drawn against Francophobes. Thus we find the explicit exclusion of fdday2 by four of the interculturalists (#345, #354–356, #362, #373), while fdday2 tries in vain to reassert ownership rights over the thread and asks the plurilingual contributors to move across to the Sports folder for their rugby talk (#359). In fact, this is not the first example of collective shunning by the group: AHM47, who attempts to ban the use of French, is also repeatedly excluded (#248–249, #263, #270). And in both these cases, the gesture of exclusion becomes a marker of one's own inclusion in the interculturalist group. We could even say that inclusion depends to some extent on exclusion, on defining limits to acceptability and designating what exceeds these borders.[11]

A form of unofficial moderation by participants thus occurs whereby the use of a foreign language regulates insider and outsider status. On the one hand, comprehension of French fosters complicity and conversation among the bilinguals; on the other, it implicitly excludes monolinguals when significant content of messages is in French (for example, #302). Furthermore, French is even used aggressively to expel Francophobes. AHM47's exhortation to 'Get lost.... There is no place in this forum for Fu....g frog language' (#246) is countered with expletives in French from the various bilinguals (#248, #249, #263, #270), including an elaborate tirade of colourful abuse (#263), destined for appreciation, not by AHM47, but by other readers of French.

> *'Ce qui est sympa quand on a affaire a des avortons intellectuels c'est qu'on peut les traiter d'enculé de leur mère suceurs de bite de chien malodorantes sans que le systeme censure le post ni que le pauvre cretin ne comprennes quoique ce que ce soit.'* [What's nice when you're dealing with intellectual midgets is that you can call them [intricate obscenities] without the system censoring the post and without the poor idiot understanding anything at all.]
>
> Y don't you agree ?
>
> that what you get when you are too mentally lazy to learn other people language.
>
> I enjoy English language, but my mental horizon is not limited to it.
>   (frenchval, 'Are the French Awakening?' #263, 8 November 2003)

It is noteworthy that the exclusion of ranters does not eliminate ranting; indeed the exclusion itself takes that very form, albeit elaborate ranting in French to bypass the automatic censor. And interestingly, these rants expelling anti-French participants give rise to further French lessons, with messages discussing the spelling of '*bite*' [vulgar term for penis], the adjectival agreement of '*malodorantes*' [foul-smelling], and whether '*chien*' [dog] should have been in the plural or not (#300 #303, cf. #271).

In this thread, then, we see that not only are the identities of interculturalist and ranter not clearly opposed or separate, but neither are those of discussant and learner, or indeed ranter and learner.

We find the same participants taking up an interculturalist position to engage with others, then invoking a learner or a teacher identity to comment on language issues, before taking on an aggressive role mirroring that of the ranter. Rather than predetermined by skills and mindsets, their positions are forged through ongoing participation, illustrating Burkhalter's argument that – online as elsewhere – 'Identity is interactionally negotiated' (Burkhalter, 1999, p. 66, cf. Antaki & Widdicombe, 1998).

Conditions for successful participation

The constant shifting between speaking positions in the 'Indy' discussion thread suggests that what distinguishes successful intercultural Internet discussion is more complex than participants adopting a particular role or attitude. Comparing the various discussion sites, one is initially tempted to wonder how language learners might be weaned from seeing themselves above all as learners in order to progress to seeing themselves as practitioners of a language, able to engage in discussion. And one might also ask how they might be encouraged away from ranting and towards an intercultural perspective. Analysis of the case study, however, suggests that these are in fact the wrong questions, that the various kinds of participation cannot be understood in terms of a linear progression, whereby unproductive speaking positions are supplanted by more effective ones. The active participation in multilingual discussion of the various 'Indy' contributors does not mean that they have ceased to see themselves as language learners. In fact they take advantage of any opportunity that presents itself for practising and improving their language skills: frenchval (who writes explicitly of this strategy) in English (#306), DaiSmallcoal in French (#222) and frogoff in Welsh (#265). And they are not above the finicky language corrections that preoccupy the learner boards: it's just that this interest does not exclude all others. Rather than progressing beyond the learner role, they move between the positions of learner and discussant: their identity as a learner flickers in and out of focus.[12]

Similarly, the path from ranter to 'interculturalist' is not a one-way journey of enlightenment, but a well-trodden track in both directions. Participants find that in order to pursue bilingual discussion, they need to draw the line and do a little ranting from time to time to assert their values. The structural similarity between ranting and the expulsion of ranters means that the same participants are engaged in both intercultural discussion and the exchange of insults, displaying both the best and the worst of intercultural communication: frogoff (#17), frenchval (#193), DaiSmallcoal (#270) and sarahg26 (#373) all lose patience and stoop to name-calling to ward off anti-French postings. Clearly we should not confuse cultural openness with 'niceness': displays of intolerance may be just as fundamental to elaborating and defending an interculturalist identity as displays of tolerance.[13] But even committed interculturalists themselves are not immune to the occasional xenophobic outburst: FDevraie's insights into the French mindset tip into a critical 'rant' about French hypocrisy (#41), as she herself recognizes (#45). And conversely, even confirmed ranter fdday2 is drawn into measured discussion with HijodePuta of the difficulties of living abroad (#120–127). This means that eradicating culture-bashing and abuse from civilized debate is not simply a question of excluding narrow-minded participants. Despite the overall impression, ranters and interculturalists are not stable identities, and are not separate groups of people.

Thus, successful intercultural Internet discussion depends not on participants progressing from one role or identity to a better one, but rather on their capacity to shift among a repertoire of positions, even contradictory positions. Here it is useful to adapt Goffman's concept of 'footing' in conversation (1981, p. 128) to the text-based genre of public Internet discussion: contributors establish a footing – a stance or an alignment – with other participants through their projection of a self in their message, and then need to shift footing to manage and to respond to the evolution of the exchange. Although shifts of footing are common in various 'forms of talk', the need for footing to be renegotiated is constant in public Internet discussion, due to the complexity of the participation framework, which is far greater than that of keypal exchanges and rivals that of the conversation in public discussed by Goffman. This is because, in Internet discussion, 'bystanders' (message board readers) can legitimately take the floor at any time and become 'ratified participants' (Goffman, 1981, p. 132) by contributing a message. Although one may direct one's message to a particular participant, the addressee is effectively multiple, ever-changing, and may indeed consist of 'anyone who's out there in the vastness of cyberspace', as Parousia puts it. The requirement to align oneself anew and manage disruptions is incessant.

We see from the case study that successful participants are adept at changes of footing. It is by avoiding becoming entrenched in a single stance (whether learner or combatant) that they can check details of grammar, gather tips on repairing window shutters and chastise those who object to the direction in which they're taking the thread, while they discuss American justice and French attitudes to change. The border-crossing engaged in here is as much between speaking positions as between languages and cultures. Thus successful participation is not simply a question of starting off on the right footing, but of adapting one's footing throughout an exchange. On the 'Indy', characterized by the digressiveness typical of UK sites, this adaptability and deftness can play out as moves from topic to topic within what is ostensibly the same discussion. As we will see in Chapter 9, on the topic-driven French forums, where digression is avoided, changes of footing still characterize successful interactions but take a different form.

Implications for language learners

Positioning strategies

The implications for language learners are twofold. The first reinforces the conclusion drawn in the previous chapter regarding the importance of developing a range of self-presentation strategies. 'Learner' needs to be considered as only one possible footing among many available in a second language. It need not be the entry point to an exchange unless it lends weight to the discussion underway, but can become a salient facet of one's identity when a particular opportunity for learning arises. Through experimenting with a range of speaking positions highlighting aspects of the self other than their foreignness and lack of native language competence, students can learn to position themselves so as to assert their experience and knowledge and participate as equals in intercultural Internet discussion on topics of shared interest.

Repositioning strategies

The foregoing remarks, however, consider the learner in isolation. The second implication moves beyond the opening gambit and considers the alignment in relation to interlocutors as the interaction unfolds. For adopting a particular role is not sufficient to guarantee a successful intercultural exchange. Footing cannot be decided unilaterally; it is relational and must be negotiated through interaction. Aligning oneself as an interculturalist, keen to exchange cultural perceptions, is one thing; having that role acknowledged and confirmed in responses such that the discussion can continue down that path is another. It is thus important not only to be able to participate in discussion in roles other than those of learner and polemicist, but also to be able to shift footing in response to the various uptakes of one's messages, and to find or create opportunities for one's footing to be recognized and responded to by others.

Let us examine three examples from the forums discussed above where footing is renegotiated in response to feedback from other participants.

Parousia

Parousia's thread on the Unilang French learner's forum provides an example of a determined attempt to adjust frame and shift footing. Self-identifying as both an American seeking to understand cultural difference and as a language enthusiast, Parousia is repeatedly positioned by her respondents as first and foremost a language learner. Rather than ignoring their responses or pointing out their failure to satisfy her desire for debate, she engages with them. She responds in learner mode, graciously accepting and commenting on all corrections, but nonetheless refuses to accept this as her only speaking position. Shifting her footing, she relaunches questions of culture designed to tempt JunMing and others into a response that goes beyond the language lesson.

FDevraie and frogoff

FDevraie on the 'Indy' board, on the other hand, adopts a less resolute, but equally fruitful approach: she takes up an invitation to shift footing provided by another participant. Although FDevraie's first posting is a lengthy grumble in English about French hypocrisy (#41), frogoff responds to the evidence that she knows French by sending her a message – partly in French – about her cultural origins (*'Etes-vous Breton perhaps?'* [Are you from Brittany perhaps?] #42). This is the only aspect of her identity – indeed of her posting – that frogoff takes up and she adjusts her footing to meet it, abandoning her anti-French position and recasting herself as an British expatriate with split allegiances, which leads to a prolonged intercultural exchange about adapting to life across the Channel.

Frogoff's message shows that a strategic intervention can open a space for intercultural exchange. For while an individual participant may be unable to determine the uptake of their own messages in public cyberspace, they can select both the correspondents to whom they reply and the aspects of those correspondents' identities that they affirm in their response. Frogoff identifies FDevraie as a speaker of both French and English like himself and creates an opportunity for her to realign herself by filling the speaking position he opens for her.

SickofRosbif and sarahg26

A parallel opportunity is offered and taken up by SickofRosbif, in what is perhaps the most telling example of a productive shift in footing. SickofRosbif is a paradoxical participant on the 'Indy' forum: on the one hand, his pseudonym is a mix of English and French, suggesting an interculturalist attitude, but on the other hand it positions him as anti-English – *'rosbif'* [roast beef] is a French epithet for the English – suggesting a propensity to rant. Further combining the contradictory profiles of language enthusiast and monocultural ranter, he rails at the Anglophones in their own language, or at least his approximation of it, using rant as a vehicle for language practice (#146, #147, #202, #228). SickofRosbif's first forays on the 'Indy' forum are most unpromising: word-for-word translations from the French make comprehension difficult; he seems to be following the conventions of French forums in assuming that a thread will still relate to the topic question some 144 messages from its beginning; and he takes up the position of defender of France to launch into debate. But despite the language difficulties, the mismatch in genre expectations and his combative initial stance, SickofRosbif is drawn into a fruitful intercultural exchange.

Although no one attempts to correct the obvious deficiencies in his English, his points are taken up patiently by interculturalists FDevraie (#155) and sarahg26 (#229). Sarahg26's message opens an opportunity for him to reposition himself. She presents herself to SickofRosbif as wounded by French-bashing (highlighting what they have in common) and signs off with Viva le France (*sic*, #229). This prompts SickofRosbif to shift footing. He ceases his tirade against Anglo-hegemony, and in turn confirms and mirrors Sarah's alignment as a language and culture enthusiast by picking up a grammatical error (*le* instead of *la France*). He aligns himself as an interculturalist to give a flirtatious lesson on French gender which evolves into a conciliatory commentary on Franco-American relations (#230, see Table 8.1).

And sarahg26 continues the dialogue. Thus with a bit of fancy footwork – shifting footing in response to others – even such an unpromising starter as SickofRosbif is able to engage in a congenial intercultural exchange.

These three examples shed light on the mechanics of intercultural encounters. We see seasoned participants (frogoff and sarahg26) offering opportunities for others to realign themselves; we see FDevraie and

Table 8.1 Message #230 of the 'Indy' forum: 'Are the French Awakening?'

From: **SickofRosbif** 6-Nov 2003 03:02
To: **sarahg26**   21373.230 in reply to 21373.229

Merci, ma belle!
mais c'est VIVE LA FRANCE, et non 'LE'!
LE, mean France is a male! and beep, wrong it's a female!
But if you say grande bretagne, it's female! if you say Royaume Uni, it's male!
We say VIVE LA grande bretagne, and Vive le Royaume UNI!
and Vive Les Etats UNIS D'Amerique, or Vive L'amerique, female!
Unconsciently French people give a sex to things!
Female is seen as more intelligents, sweet and rational, Male ares more stupids
and arrogants irraztional pulsions!
so when french ares against USA they say 'A mort Les etats unis' male!
and when they ares happy and congratulate, they say 'Vive L'Amerique'
female! [...]

SickofRosbif taking up those opportunities; and we see Parousia striving
to reposition herself without cooperation from her interlocutors.

The fact that these exchanges occurred in Internet discussion means
that a record of them is available, and we can trace the moves made
and learn from them. But, in fact, the lessons to be drawn from these
examples are applicable more widely. The ability to position oneself
strategically in relation to others, to avoid tethering oneself to a defensive and/or subordinate position and to shift position in response to
feedback are vital skills, not just in Internet forums but in intercultural
interaction more generally. Indeed they are important in all communication, but we tend to take them for granted in intracultural communication and in interaction in our native tongue. Our exploration of the
default speaking positions for cultural outsiders in the forums, however,
indicates that these skills are not automatically transferred to a second
language.

Conclusion

We conclude by retracing the arc of our arguments on identity presented
in the last three chapters. We saw that acceptance on discussion forums
meant engaging with them as a specific genre, and that this entailed
entering as a debater. This immediately raised questions about identity,
and specifically the inadequacy of the role in which one gestures from
the sidelines for language practice. Identity, we proposed, was more

usefully understood as a tool, rather than a given, as something to be used or indeed challenged as a means of advancing one's argument. By the end of the previous chapter, then, it seemed relatively straightforward: play the genre, and use identity to play it, with identity no longer a singular item laid out in an introductory message but rather a collection of implements brought out to suit specific aspects of the discursive terrain. One might foreground one's sympathies as a Committed Recycler, before voicing one's opinion as a Generation X-er here and as a music enthusiast there, depending on the forum topic. The current chapter leads us to complicate that picture somewhat.

In this chapter we left the precisely defined identities of the previous paragraph to look at the default identities most readily available on forums, identities painted with broad brushstrokes. Firstly, for learners whose contact with a linguaculture has always been, precisely, as learners, this is the default position from which they always speak when speaking in their own voices (as opposed to those of role-play characters). The counterpart to the learner role is that of the teacher, and just as children will play at schools, so can 'learners' take their turn at teaching without leaving the world of the classroom – we see learners dispensing information about language and/or culture.

Why is it so hard to break away from the cosy dyad of classroom discussion? Firstly, because life on public discussion forums has its own default positions. And so we encounter the villainous ranter, who flouts generic convention but seems a part of it, whose gestures towards dialogue are nothing but bait and who is particularly attracted to topics relating to cultural specificity. Now, although we have said that being a cultural outsider should not restrict one to topics of cultural difference and specificity, it remains that these topics are likely to be of interest. The neophyte/student/outsider who ventures into such discussion, perhaps hoping to speak in the voice of the teacher (instructing about 'my culture'), can easily find himself/herself speaking instead in the voice of Cultural Champion, the ranter's natural prey. And so a genuine and at times well-founded trepidation about public discussion forums fuels a preference for learner sites where learner and teacher roles can flourish.

This narrative, where learner sites are seen as retreats, might lead one to expect that a victorious ending would be a definitive casting aside of one's learner identity. But this is not the case. Our final case study, applying Goffman's notion of footing to intercultural discussion on the 'Indy', shows learner and ranter positions as part of a repertoire. Successful interaction, we see, is not about adopting one triumphant identity but rather involves continual negotiation of one's speaking position.

Forum discussion, then, is not a game of solitaire where one's strate-gies can be adopted without reference to other players but rather a game where self-positioning also depends on that of the other participants in the debate. That is, it is not just a matter of activating aspects of iden-tity which confer authority where the debate at hand is concerned, but also one of being aware of the more subtle shifts in positioning vis-à-vis one's interlocutors. And this is how one might not only meet the generic objectives but also subvert them slightly to one's own aims, enticing other participants into providing feedback on language or culture, for example.

Again, it might seem simple. But our experience of forums shows that it is not and that the intercultural terrain, in particular, can be tricky. If our 'Indy' contributors perform so well, it is because they already have long years of experience as intercultural operators – they bring online some of the skills they have honed elsewhere, exploring the transfer of them to this new genre (see frenchval's delight in using his language skills to flout the automatic censor). But what of students, for whom the intercultural encounters on discussion forums are situated nearer the outset of their learning journey? How can they learn to survive and thrive in online discussion? Although forums offer unparalleled oppor-tunities for cross-border exchanges, taking advantage of these is not necessarily easy or self-evident. Our next chapter discusses how these goals might be reached.

9
Using Public Internet Forums to Develop French Argumentation Skills

The context

Argumentation skills – the ability to present and defend logical and well-structured arguments – are highly valued in French. They require not only linguistic proficiency, but also culturally specific techniques for articulating one's ideas and engaging with those of others.

Mastering these skills in both written and spoken genres is the focus of a final-year course for undergraduate French majors at the University of Queensland, Australia. In previous years, much of the course had been devoted to learning to write in the French genre of *la dissertation*, but student enthusiasm for this activity (and indeed for the goal of mastering this highly codified genre) appeared low. When an opportunity to redesign the course presented itself in the February–June semester of 2007, the decision was made to incorporate the use of public Internet forums, which offered the prospect of a more engaging and interactive means of achieving many of the linguistic and intercultural aims of the course. For while the genre of *la dissertation* is undoubtedly critical for those students intending to pursue studies in Francophone universities (and is not neglected in the course), the advantage of teaching argumentation through and for discussion forums is that it equips all students for immediately available, ongoing contact with the language.

This chapter explores the questions raised by this experiment, and in particular the extent to which it facilitated achievement of the inter-cultural objectives of the course. After some initial discussion of the integration of forum participation into the course, it analyses the way in which students engaged with the activity and the learning opportunities provided by the responses their messages attracted.

The course

The course in question is at third-year university level, and corresponds approximately to level C1 of the Common European Framework of Reference for Languages. It aims to equip students to present cogent arguments and participate in vigorous debates in written and spoken French.

More specifically, students are required to

- learn to use appropriate French connectors to express, for example, logical progression, cause and consequence, concession and opposition, intention, justification;
- learn the cultural conventions of argumentation and discussion in French, and understand the differences with respect to discussion among Anglophone Australians (and/or among those of their own cultural background);
- familiarize themselves with the arguments and vocabulary of topical debates in French current affairs.

The course is conducted entirely in French.

Now, the primary aim of participation in French public Internet forums intersects neatly with the course goal of expressing ideas coherently and persuasively in written form. Moreover, the websites of the French newspapers/news magazines *Le Monde*, *Libération*, *Le Figaro*, *L'Express* and *Le Nouvel Observateur* all offer public forums dedicated to discussion of current affairs. As seen in previous chapters, these attract a large number of participants with a range of viewpoints, exclude chat and aspire to quality debate. While many messages across these sites are quite informal, others are composed in exemplary formal prose, illustrating French conventions of written argument. The forums thus provide multiple opportunities to observe the efforts of native speakers and others at argumentation in French and to try one's hand at these same skills.

Taking advantage of these opportunities, however, means integrating forum use into the course in such a way that students participate appropriately and learn from the experience. As Roberts argues in relation to email activities, computer-mediated exchanges that are simply 'add-on' measures appended to a course do not encourage sustained student interest or learning.[1] The course was thus largely rebuilt around forum participation: it was incorporated into the assessment design, and supported both by preparatory work and by discussion in class of particular exchanges.

Assessment design

Students were required to post at least five substantial (minimum 300-word) contributions to forums of their choice (a length appropriate both to the French forums targeted and to expectations of student proficiency), under their chosen pseudonym which was to remain constant for the semester. The messages were to be copied to the teacher for marking, together with the link (URL) to the web page where the message appeared online. The work was due in alternate weeks, commencing in Week 4 of the 13-week semester. This represented 40 per cent of the total mark for the semester (other components being weekly participation in oral discussions, tutorial preparation work on the current affairs theme for each week, and written and oral exams at the end of the semester).

Since student effort is largely assessment driven, the criteria for grading the forum contributions were crafted to encourage students both to comply with the conventions of the forums and to reflect on their use of the argumentation techniques studied in the course.[2] There were four criteria:

- coherence (requiring ideas to be logically structured and articulated with use of appropriate connectors);
- positioning and interaction (requiring messages to acknowledge other viewpoints and take a position in relation to them, for example by affirming, conceding or refusing points of argument);
- genre (requiring messages to conform to forum conventions such that they did not seem out of place);
- linguistic accuracy (requiring the use of appropriate vocabulary and standard grammar).

In this way, students were guided towards standard written expression, which is also recommended in the official guidelines provided by these forums. Although carelessly edited messages certainly appear on the forums, as do occasional postings in text-messaging style, students were not rewarded for following these examples.

The student cohort

Thirty-two students enrolled in the course, ranging in age from 18 to 32 years, with all but four students aged from 20 to 22 years. Many were completing their final year of university study, in programmes including humanities, law, engineering, journalism, economics, business management, hospitality and tourism, and education. Two students were international exchange students (from the Czech Republic and the US); two students had partially Francophone backgrounds; four had Asian-language backgrounds; and the remainder had Anglophone (and mostly Australian) backgrounds. Many of the students studied another foreign language at university.

At the outset of the course, their skills in written French clustered around the B2 and C1 levels of the Common European Framework of Reference for Languages. Ten students had already spent more than six months in a Francophone country (France, Belgium, New Caledonia, Vanuatu), and another nine students had spent between one and six months.

Preparatory work

The initial reactions of students to the proposed work on forums were a mixture of enthusiasm (we're going to be involved in real debate), resignation (whatever it takes to pass the course) and apprehension (but what if people attack what we say?). Whatever the student's attitude, however, skills training was essential for the activity to be successful. As Schneider and von der Emde remark in relation to telecollaboration, online communication by students is 'not simply a matter of "plug-and-play"' (2006, p. 178). Preparation tasks, for completion both in class time and outside class, were therefore designed to prevent technical hitches, to sensitize students to the genre and purpose of forum participation, to alert them to some of the pitfalls for language learners in this situation and to encourage them to reflect on the possibilities open to them with regard to how they wanted to be seen by others on the forum (see Table 9.1).

Task 1

The first homework task was for the students to familiarize themselves with forum conventions, by choosing a particular topic and examining how it was debated on a couple of the sites (selected from *Le Monde, Libération, Le Figaro, L'Express* and *Le Nouvel Observateur*). Students were given a list of features to look for, which included political leaning, length of messages, digression, formality and correctness of language, and what participants revealed about themselves.

The findings were compiled into a wiki (collaborative authoring tool) available on the Blackboard student-learning platform used by the university and were also the subject of class discussion. Eleven students

Table 9.1 Activities in preparation for forum participation

Preparatory tasks focused on

– sensitivity to genre
  o observation of conventions of French forum debate
    ▪ language and register
    ▪ argumentation techniques
    ▪ inclusion and use of personal information (explicit and implicit)
– strategic self-presentation
  o range of positions available in a given debate
  o language structures for positioning oneself
  o de-centring world view of home culture
  o reflection on use of pseudonyms
– technical competence
  o practice in forum navigation
  o online registration

---

contributed (anonymously, and in French) to the wiki, and many of their comments were perspicacious. In particular, they noticed

– variation in the length of messages and responses;
– that participants generally pursued the debate when their messages received responses;
– enormous variation in register and linguistic accuracy, ranging from text-message and colloquial styles to sophisticated formal language;
– a range of quality of argument, with a contrast between clear, well-constructed messages and some less logically argued that leave implicit the conclusion to be drawn;
– the absence of personal information unless it was pertinent to the argument.

A number of detailed observations were also made with regard to the way arguments were formulated:

– that personal experience was often used to justify an argument and boost one's position as an expert on the subject;
– that many discussions seemed to be anti-American, but that negative views were also expressed about France and French culture, provoking fierce debate;

- that dispassionate argument was possible even on such an emotive subject as religion;
- that participants seemed to enjoy playing devil's advocate, reformulating questions and adding new questions to the debate – in short, they enjoyed the practice of debate;
- that rhetorical questions were frequently used.

This observation work was an extremely valuable learning exercise in sensitizing students to the range of practices considered acceptable on forums and to French cultural norms of written argumentation. Furthermore, the comments showed that students were already starting to make judgements regarding the quality and relative merit of the postings they were reading, effectively selecting models for their own practice. And from the outset, students were confronted with the diversity of opinions held by French speakers on any given topic, preventing them from imagining the existence of a monolithic French viewpoint, just as they were dissuaded from the belief that one (high) standard of literacy and expression prevails amongst 'the French'.

For less advanced students, this observation task could be undertaken in class, by providing students with specific samples of forum debate and asking them to identify variations in register and characteristics of debate.

Task 2

The second preparatory activity workshopped strategies for entering debate. We started by looking together in class at the examples of English and American learners of French on the forums of *Le Monde*, discussed in Chapter 6, pondering why David and Laura were more successful than Eleanor and Fleurie, leading the students to analyse the issues of genre and purpose, and draw conclusions for their own practice.

This led to discussion of strategies for presenting oneself. One student had shown considerable insight in the following contribution to the wiki:

'*Les gens ne donnent pas les détails personnels sauf si c'est important pour leur avis. Leur âge, où ils habitent, s'ils ont des enfants, s'ils sont un homme ou une femme – ces choses ne sont pas mises sur les forums sauf si c'est un fait pertinent par rapport à l'argument.*' [People don't give personal details unless it's important to their opinion. Their age, where they live, if they've got children, if they're a man or a woman – these things aren't put on the forum unless it's relevant to the argument.]

Equipped with this hypothesis, we studied messages from the *Libération* forum '*Réchauffement climatique: la lutte au quotidien*' [Global warming: the daily struggle] to see how participants revealed information about themselves in order to take up a position in the debate. Examples included the following:

- '*Le problème c'est qu'en France nous n'avons pas...*' [The problem is that in France we don't have...]
- '*Je suis végétarienne, je contribue donc à économiser...*' [I'm a vegetarian, and so I contribute to saving...]
- '*Je ne bois en RP que de l'eau du robinet avec toute ma famille (6 personnes)*' [My entire family and I (6 people) drink only tap water in the Paris region].

More general discussion of identity issues and of strategic uses of identity ensued: in what contexts was it useful or desirable to present oneself as a language learner or as an Australian, and in what contexts was it superfluous or even counterproductive? And to what extent was it possible to portray oneself other than as a language student from Australia? This question was more easily answered by older students with experience of the workforce, and those studying in disciplines such as law and engineering, who could readily assert other aspects of their identity. For all students, however, it was an opportunity to consider the kinds of expertise and experience they could draw on to make a point.[3]

In conjunction with this discussion, we revised language structures other than '*Je suis*' [I am] for positioning oneself strategically:

- '*En tant que femme, ...*' [As a woman, ...]
- '*Bien que végétarienne, ...*' [Although a vegetarian, ...]
- '*Fille d'immigré moi-même, ...*' [Myself the daughter of an immigrant, ...]
- '*Non-fumeur depuis longtemps, ...*' [A longstanding non-smoker, ...]

To put all these lessons into practice, students then worked in pairs to devise a response to a message on the forum of *L'Express* on the topic '*Internet vous donne-t-il plus de pouvoir?*' [Does the Internet give you more power?]. The messages they crafted were posted on the Blackboard site

Table 9.2 Features of forums of French press websites

Forum host	L'Express	Le Figaro	Libération	Le Monde	Le Nouvel Observateur
Trail from home page to discussion facility	'Débats Blogs' → 'Forums'	'Pratique' → 'Forums'	'Interactif' → 'Forums'	'Perspectives' → 'Forums'	'Forums et débats' → 'Débats'
Registration	No registration necessary; visitors can post directly.	Pre-register username and password.	Pre-register username, receive password within minutes.	Subscription required (6 euros/month).	Pre-register username and password.
Ease of use	Easiest navigation. Messages appear promptly.	Messages may take a day or two to appear.	Relatively easy navigation. Most messages appear promptly.	Subscription gives access to the full edition of the online newspaper but cost effectively precludes student use. Easy navigation.	Problems with messages not appearing on forums not recently active. Accents may appear as symbols making messages difficult to read. No 'threading' of messages (to see who replies to whom)

Distinct URL for each message	Yes	Yes	URL links to debate on given topic, but not to individual message.	Yes
Possible to read in digest mode (multiple messages on one screen)	Yes	Yes	Yes	First lines of several messages visible on one screen.
Other relevant features	Can choose to be alerted by email if a response to your message appears.		Can choose to allow other registered users to contact you by email.	

and discussed in class. They showed the students being vigilant about the way they presented themselves overtly; for example,

> '*En tant que citoyen qui vient de commencer à voter, mais qui appartient à une génération qui est habituée à la vitesse de la technologie moderne, je comprends comment utiliser l'Internet pour m'informer sur le monde politique.*' [As a citizen who has just started voting, but who belongs to a generation accustomed to the speed of modern technology, I understand how to use the Internet to keep abreast of politics.]

On the other hand, students were less aware of more implicit self-positioning, writing of '*la dernière élection fédérale*' [the last federal election] and *le gouvernement*, for example, without pausing to realize that a global Francophone audience would not immediately make the connection to the Australian political context. Clearly there was a need to think about the lack of shared assumptions about where 'here' might be in an Internet forum. Furthermore, it was going to be important to consider the level of knowledge of and interest in Australian events that could be assumed of other forum participants. Events in a far-flung island nation were going to have to be *made* relevant (rather than presumed to be of interest) if they were going to be discussed.

Through examination of these examples, the work on self-positioning led to a realization of the need to decentre the world view of one's home culture, an important precondition for developing intercultural competence (cf. Byram's identification of the need for 'a willingness to suspend belief in one's own meanings and behaviours, and to analyse them from the viewpoint of the others with whom one is engaging', 1997, p. 34).

Task 3

During the following week, students were asked to choose their pseudonym for the semester, reflecting on what it revealed about them and how it would inflect the way others read their post. They were also asked to explore the mechanics of posting online in a forum of their choice, and to register their pseudonym and password if required by the site (see Table 9.2). This task exposed the falsity of the belief that today's 20-year-olds are all 'digital natives' (Prensky, 2001), at ease with technology and adept at website navigation. Some students were clearly less skilled in this area than others, and it would have been useful to schedule this activity in class, where students could have helped each other.

Ongoing integration of forum work

Forum work continued to be supported by class work throughout the semester, with

- language work not only on means of expressing agreement and disagreement, but also on ways of qualifying arguments and making concessions, drawing attention to the range of positions beyond simply for and against a proposition;
- ongoing exercises on the use of connectors to articulate the points of an argument;
- regular workshopping of extracts from student postings to the forums (covering points of language, argumentation, intercultural communication).

The exchanges: Student postings

The value of the preparatory exercises was clear from the first messages posted by the students, and subsequent class workshopping and individual feedback resulted in rapid progress (in language use, argumentation, cultural appropriateness and confidence) over the first three contributions to forum debate. (This suggests three as a minimum number of exchanges when designing a course incorporating forum use.)

Forums chosen

Students avoided the forums of *Le Monde*, now open only to paying subscribers, in favour of those of *Libération*, *Le Figaro*, *L'Express* and *Le Nouvel Observateur*. The most common choices of topic were those that were either being discussed in class (the environment, *'la banlieue'* [the suburbs], the debate over the wearing of the Islamic headscarf at state schools and so forth) or ethical debates also current in Australia (euthanasia, the death penalty, homosexual marriage, anti-smoking legislation). Some students, however, researched more widely and ventured their opinions on more culturally specific issues such as the French wealth tax or the presidential elections. Others drew on their studies in different fields to bolster messages about foreign policy and international affairs.

A few students, however, sought out forums not hosted by the newspaper sites but devoted to their particular areas of interest, be they films, music or track shoes. Here they discovered opportunities to assert their knowledge and expertise before a specialized audience, and to participate in discussions they were genuinely passionate about. By hijacking the forum exercises to their own purposes in this way, these students were clearly taking up speaking positions in line with aspects of their identity beyond that of language learner. The benefits reaped by these students were less tangibly linked to the final grade for the course (the oral and written exams requiring discussion of a current affairs topic), but were clearly considered personally worthwhile: taking on board the lessons about identity in a second language, the students worked to present themselves as they wished others to see them.

Technical issues

Students were asked to provide their lecturer with a copy of each of their messages together with a URL linking to its appearance online. Some students only provided a link to the debate (rather than the individual message). And in many cases (around a third!) the message did not appear on the forum at all, and it was never entirely clear whether this was a technical slip-up (whether on the part of the student or the forum hosts) or whether the student had decided not to bother with posting the message publicly, and simply sent it to the teacher.

There was also a problem with postings to *Le Nouvel Observateur* in the last few weeks of the semester, to the point where we wondered whether messages from our domain name were being blocked for some reason. *L'Express* and *Libération*, on the other hand, were reliable in displaying messages promptly.

A measure to overcome technical difficulties experienced by students is to assist them in posting their messages online in computer laboratory sessions. Overcoming student reluctance to post messages publicly may be addressed through fine-tuning the assessment mechanisms. The solutions trialled in the 2008 iteration of the course proved effective in solving these difficulties. Students had the option of posting their message during the collective computer laboratory session (where help was available from peers/the teacher if needed). Moreover, for their first forum message, they received one mark (out of ten) if they could provide a URL linking to the web page where the message appeared online. This seemed to set the tone for the rest of the semester, and these measures resulted in almost all messages appearing publicly on the forums throughout the semester.

Pseudonyms

Plenty of imagination and ingenuity went into the choice of pseudonyms. Some were indecipherable, but nine used a variation of some aspect of their name or initials, three drew on other languages studied (xiao j, parami, sinverguenza), many alluded to interests, and several to connections with France and French culture. There were three disguised allusions to country of origin, and one more obvious one. Only the latter – '*LePetitKangarouBleu*' (The Little Blue Kangaroo, with the capitals and misspelling revealing an Anglophone influence) – could be seen as pre-positioning the participant as the wide-eyed foreigner and, significantly, was chosen by a student who had been absent for some of the preparation tasks. This suggests that the class discussions of identity issues were effective in diverting students from the default position of the learner and cultural outsider.

Self-presentation

Similarly, the only message that opened with the classic self-presentation of the language learner (cf. Chapters 6 and 8) was the opening posting by a student who had been absent during the first two weeks of the semester:

> '*Bonjour, je suis un étudiant de français et des affaires internationales en Australie. C'est ma quatrième année à l'université, j'apprends du français, des sciences politiques, des économiques et des affaires internationales.* [...]' [Hello, I'm a student of French and international business in Australia. I'm in my fourth year at university, and I'm studying French, politics, economics and international business.]
>
> (draft message, *Le Nouvel Observateur*)

The fact that this was the only example of such self-presentation simultaneously confirms the likelihood of students launching their messages in this way if they are not alerted to forum conventions, and confirms the usefulness of the preparatory exercises in drawing attention to other possibilities for asserting identity online.

The lessons about decentring one's world view had clearly been absorbed. In a *Figaro* forum on the environment, Gem223,[4] introduces the example of the water shortage in Australia in the fifth of six paragraphs. Tmac, on a *Libération* forum, spends three paragraphs engaging with another's opinions on the use of nuclear energy before bringing in an Australian example. These students have avoided simply responding along the lines of 'Well, in Australia, what's happening is...', having understood that the priority in exchanges presented as debate is to engage with the preoccupations of their interlocutors, before leading them towards any point of comparison.

Such examples suggest that the work on speaking positions has an intercultural pay-off: not self-identifying from the opening line as an Australian, choosing a primary role other than that of the foreigner, not only means that one avoids pre-positioning oneself as a defensive representative of one's culture (as discussed in Chapter 8). It also means that one is less likely to take an accusatory role, simply to judge French practices from an outsider's point of view, or indeed tell the French how to run their country (although this did occur in one memorable example – that of M&M – discussed later in the chapter).

The exchanges: Feedback from other forum participants

Over the course of the semester, 108 of the students' messages appeared online, and these were taken up in various ways by other forum participants (see Table 9.3).

Types of response

Some messages attracted no response, but this too needs to be considered as a form of feedback. Unlike telecollaboration, where a lack of response is easily blamed on one's partner, in an Internet forum one is forced to take some responsibility oneself, and to look at one's own strategies if a message attracts no replies.

In some cases, lack of response could be explained by the fact that students had chosen to post on a 'cold' thread, a topic that had been

Table 9.3 Types of feedback

Responses to messages

- no response
  - o   cold thread
  - o   ideas already explored
  - o   nothing to add
- continuation of discussion
  - o   springboard for ideas of others
- individual feedback
  - o   compliments/congratulations
  - o   engagement on topics
  - o   linguistic feedback
  - o   attack

---

inactive for some months and therefore attracted few visitors. In other cases, it was because the message reiterated ideas that had already been explored earlier. And some messages were perhaps not seen as worthy of response. But often, and especially if a student was responding to an earlier posting, lack of response simply meant that the particular point had been sufficiently debated, and that, however relevant the contribution, no reply was deemed necessary.

Continuation of discussion

Often messages acted as a springboard for further discussion. That is to say, the responses they attracted contributed to debate on the topic and offered opinions but did not necessarily engage with the specifics of the student's message. This was the case, for example, with a message by ellamack (*Le Figaro*, 14 May 2007) lamenting an increasingly utilitarian attitude towards education, and giving the example of the under-funding of the humanities in Australian universities. The message opened a new thread, and over the next four days, 15 replies were posted, all debating the purpose of education. Whilst none referred specifically to the points raised by ellamack, they nonetheless provided opportunities for intercultural learning: they demonstrated the level of interest in the topic and the range of views current among Francophones, and simultaneously affirmed the student's ability to contribute effectively to Francophone discussion.

Individual feedback

These functions were also apparent in the responses that directly engaged with the students' individual messages: 35 messages attracted a total of 49 such replies. Feedback took the form of

- engagement with the specific arguments presented (whether agreement, disagreement or qualification of the points made by the student) (in 41 replies);
- compliments, congratulations, thanks, salutations (11);
- feedback on language use (6);
- light-hearted remarks, wordplay (3);
- attack (2).

Several replies realized more than one of these functions.

Contrary to early student fears of being publicly pilloried, the replies were overwhelmingly good-humoured, with far more congratulatory messages than aggressive ones. Indeed, they were sometimes effusive in their praise, with compliments referring to both content and form:

- '*Votre série d'articles devrait se trouver en tête de toute loi cherchant à améliorer notre Education Nationale.*' [Your series of postings should appear in the preamble to all laws seeking to improve the national education system] (allmen67, *Le Figaro*, 21 March 2007).
- '*Vos articles pleins de bon sens devraient être lus par tous les candidats à l'élection présidentielle* [...]' [Your sensible postings should be read by all the presidential candidates] (nolas, *Le Figaro*, 22 March 2007).
- '*Ferdinand bonjour, J'ai adoré votre post plein de bon sens et de sagesse.* [...]' [Hello Ferdinand, I loved your posting full of good sense and wisdom] (Roger, *Le Figaro*, 22 May 2007).
- '[...] *PS avant de sortir: très beau post.*' [PS before I go: very fine message] (Pul-e-Charkhi, *Libération*, 19 May 2007)
- '*Du propos de L'esprit27. Lequel est bien réfléchi et tourné.* [...]' [With regard to l'esprit27's message. Which was well thought out and expressed.] (rvlulu, *Le Nouvel Observateur*, 23 March 2007).
- '*Ca fait plaisir de voir pour une fois une 'contre' dont le discours est calme et cherche à être objectif* [...]' [It's a pleasure to see for once an 'against' where the language is calm and tries to be objective] (Peacebird, *Le Nouvel Observateur*, 10 May 2007).
- '[...] *Juste une question: vous étiez où en France? A paris étudiante à la sorbonne?*' [Just one question: where were you in France? In Paris as a student at the Sorbonne?] (MichelleL, *Libération*, 2 April 2007).

Only the last of these messages refers to the fact that the writer is not French (and in this case, the student's speaking position was explicitly that of someone who had recently visited France). In the other cases, it is either not obvious, not pertinent, or both.

While such complimentary remarks are clearly gratifying and confirm one's proficiency in the language and the genre, messages offering serious engagement with one's ideas are equally inspiring of confidence. Whether the reply agrees or disagrees with the point of view presented, the student's opinions are being taken seriously: he/she is regarded as an informed writer of French whose ideas are worth pursuing. Students are thus able to rehearse identities in French other than that of the foreigner/language learner and receive feedback from other participants that signals successful communication.

An increase in confidence was palpable over the first three postings, as students became accustomed to participating on an equal footing with others in the forums.

Feedback on language use

Feedback on linguistic accuracy was expected not from the forum but from the teacher, who was sent a copy of the message to correct once it was posted on the forums. There were, however, examples of forum participants commenting on and even correcting specific aspects of language use. Although few in number, the responses that included corrections of the French are revealing, in that the purpose invariably goes beyond that of correction to make a point in the debate. Firstly, we might note that, faithful to the French tendency to avoid digression, debate is never derailed by metalinguistic discussion. Furthermore, the fact that replies are never simply a language lesson demonstrates both that linguistic imperfections do not disqualify one from debate and also that they can be so much more than simple formal slips which might annoy the teacher but have limited repercussions in the real world.

Writing of divorce and shared custody of children, student smiley13 concludes,

> '*Sinon, les enfants peuvent être les victimes innocentes d'une guerre chez eux, qui était auparavant bonne et aimante.*' [Otherwise the children can be the innocent victims of a war at home, which was previously good and loving.]
>
> (smiley13, *Libération*, 23 April 2007)

Unfortunately, smiley13 makes an error in adjectival agreement, and so the sentence reads that it was the war rather than the home that was good and loving. Lagaullerie responds,

> '*Bien que vous ne l'ayez pas écrit volontairement, j'aime beaucoup votre «guerre bonne et aimante». Celà résume bien mon vécu durant les trois années qui ont précédé le départ de mon épouse. Elle me livrait une «guerre» bonne et aimante pour obtenir la «garde» de nos enfants. Petite boutade mise à part, je partage entièrement votre analyse [...]*' [Although you didn't mean to write it, I really like your 'good and loving war'. It encapsulates my experience during the three years that preceded my wife's departure. She engaged in a good and loving 'war' with me to

get custody of our children. Jesting aside, I entirely agree with your analysis.]

(Lagaullerie, *Libération*, 26 April 2007)

Far from gratuitous or pedantic, the correction is used to introduce the writer's experience on the topic. The lesson for the student is that adjectival agreements are not merely a grammatical obligation but determine the meaning of a sentence.

A rather different form of language feedback is provided to nabanga2. One of the strongest students in the class, nabanga2 writes French with a high level of linguistic accuracy. In the message in question, however, an attempt to achieve an intellectual style results in vagueness and unintelligibility. A *Figaro* participant replies,

'*On dirait du français, mais ce n'est pas du français. Traduction ???*'
[It looks like French, but it's not French. Translation ???]

(Caton l'Ancien, *Le Figaro*, 8 May 2007)

Once again, the language feedback focuses on meaning, rather than accuracy for accuracy's sake. What the student needs to understand from this response, one of the most brusque received, is the importance of structure and clarity in French argumentation. Without these, even exemplary vocabulary and grammar are insufficient to get the message across.

While teachers can certainly explain to students that adjectival agreements are not merely decorative, or that one needs to write in structured paragraphs, the direct experience of misunderstanding – as in the examples above – can reinforce these lessons in a particularly memorable way.

A different lesson awaits la pokin, who writes in support of the French law recently introduced against smoking in public places. The short response by tabacophile starts by drawing attention to the errors of French, then defends smoking and concludes by complaining of American influence in the legislation:

'*sous prétention : sous prétexte les apprendre : leur apprendre etc etc etc .... Je fume 2 paquets par jour depuis plus de 20 ans et je me porte comme un charme et je ne suis pas la seule... Encore un diktat US!!!!!!*'[under pretension: under the pretext, learn them: teach them etc etc etc .... I've been smoking 2 packets a day for more than 20 years and I enjoy perfect health and I'm not the only one ... Another US diktat!!!!!!]

(tabacophile, *L'Express*, 3 April 2007)

In this case grammar correction is used to score a point in the debate. The clear inference is that la pokin's errors – coupled with her opinions – identify her not simply as a non-native speaker or even as an Anglophone, but as a North American and therefore part of the perceived problem. The lesson here is that one's non-native errors – like one's accent in an FTF encounter – take on the value of a sign of cultural belonging, and that on a topic where an Anglophone country is identified with a particular position, the attribution of identity has an impact on debate. Here indeed it may be valuable to identify one's speaking position more precisely. In this case, la pokin replies graciously – '*Merci de m'avoir corrigé ces erreurs de français* .... *mais cela ne change rien par rapport à mon argument*' [Thank you for correcting the French errors, but that doesn't change anything with respect to my argument, 17 April] – and in a laudable instance of flexible footing repositions herself not in terms of nationality, but in terms of personal experience of tobacco-related illness, before reaffirming her point of view.

It is significant that Tmac attracts a similar complaint about US influence in France when she cites '*des chercheurs américains*' [American researchers] in her message supporting the anti-smoking legislation. Once again, Tmac is assumed to be if not American then at least pro-American, but this time it is not a language error that leads to this interpretation but the source that Tmac cites. Students can learn here how an argumentation strategy assumed to be neutral can appear as anything but neutral in a different cultural context.

Finally, the 2008 iteration of the course provides a further example where the combination of linguistic errors and subject matter (the US primaries) in a message on a *Libération* forum is interpreted as indicative that the writer is American. This time, however, American-ness confers uncontroversial authority on the topic at hand, and the respondent defers to the supposed inside knowledge of Becciej08, who is actually an Australian student of French. Ironically, the presumption of the accuracy of the political perspective is derived from the inaccuracies in the French. While the student's French does have room for improvement, we again see that less then perfect French does not disqualify one from debate – here it is the reverse which is true.

Intercultural lessons from feedback

The above examples already demonstrate opportunities for intercultural learning on questions of identity (learning to anticipate how one's non-native errors or the sources one quotes may be interpreted) and the conventions of argumentation (the importance of structure in French argumentation).

Many further lessons concerning cultural values are available from the feedback. Students were often attracted to topics on which French and Australian opinions tend to differ along cultural lines, such as the French law banning religious clothing and symbols (such as the Islamic headscarf) from state schools. A response from daniel28 (*Libération*, 29 April 2007) to LePetitKangarouBleu (16 April) challenges her view that this is a question of personal freedom of expression, explaining the history of the struggle to separate Church and State in France. He argues that the value at stake for the French is understood to be secularism in this instance. *'La liberté'* is not, however, a neglected value, but in this case, as xiberb (17 April) attests in another response, it is the freedom to resist community pressure to wear the headscarf that is seen to be the issue. But not all Francophones are in agreement. In response to smiley13 (*Libération*, 1 May 2007) on the same topic, sol_weintraub (2 May) also argues against the law, disagreeing, however, with smiley13 that it is anti-Muslim, contending instead that it stems from a more general anti-Arab sentiment.

Exchanges such as these provided evidence of the range of points of view generally taken by French speakers and the values used to justify them. Other hot topics on which students tended to disagree with other forum participants included drug laws, immigration, cultural identity and genetically modified food.

Just as valuable, but less obviously expected by the students, were the insights the responses provided into (once again) French norms of argumentation and identity issues. The response from sol_weintraub (see above) was one of many that justified arguments by citing precise statistics, and by the end of semester students were more likely to use this technique rather than state vaguely 'research has shown...'.

RatRouge, student, (*Le Nouvel Observateur*, 28 April 2007), arguing against the legalization of soft drugs, received a 2000-word point-by-point rebuttal from Peacebird (10 May), complete with fully referenced statistics and quotations. In discussing the exchange, the student saw this response as a keenness that approached 'fanaticism' and as evidence of 'French passion' (personal email, 17 May). The example nicely underlined the analogy drawn in class between French attitudes to debate and Australian attitudes to sporting contests.

Responses to a posting on the same topic from a student who is a native English speaker from Singapore were equally revealing. CJ6340's carefully argued message (*Le Figaro*, 28 August 2007)[5] against the legalization of soft drugs attracted three substantial replies in the hours following the posting, all disagreeing with her. Bearing in mind the heavy penalties for drug use in Singapore and the fact that France has one of the highest rates of cannabis use in Europe, the difference in opinions is perhaps predictable. The respondents, however, cannot perceive this as a cultural difference in values given that the student's French is native-like. Striking in their replies, however, are the repeated references to their own cultural values to justify their arguments: they invoke *liberté* and *logique*, supported by *'bon sens'* [common sense], *'réalité'* [reality] and *la République*, with one of the replies accusing the student of being moralistic and swayed by sentiment, and another claiming her ideas lack coherence. Clearly reason is valued over emotion, but what becomes evident in this exchange – in which the original message is at least as well argued as the replies – is the rhetorical value of accusations of illogicality and sentimentality in French debate.

Conflict and learning

Despite initial fears among students that they might be attacked for their opinions, such attacks were very rare. There were three examples, in response to messages by CJ6340 (cited above), Aurore57 and M&M.

Aurore57 (*Le Nouvel Observateur*, 1 May 2007) mounts an ethical case against voluntary euthanasia, but is attacked by supermomo for ostensibly hiding a religious affiliation (2 May). Internet anonymity means that assumptions about identity are made on the basis of language use and the arguments made. In this case, the student is assumed to be French, and in the French context, the position he/she supports identifies him/her with a particular subculture. This is no doubt a useful thing to know, but the danger is that the student will simply recoil from the attack and disconnect from intercultural engagement.

In M&M's case, however, disconnecting from intercultural dialogue seems to be the cause rather than the result of conflict. The angry response to M&M follows an ill-conceived posting on the sensitive subjects of immigration, racism and national identity. The most basic problem is evident in the fact that the student writes *about* France and

The French rather than *to* a Francophone audience (for example, *'La France peut être considérée qu'un pays qui n'est pas très multiculturel ni très tolérante'* [France can be considered as a country which is neither very multicultural nor very tolerant]). And the problem is compounded when much of the message consists of statements about what The French need to do to lift their game (*'les françaises ont besoin de garder à l'esprit que la France n'est pas le seul pays qui existe ni le centre du monde'* [The French need to keep in mind that France is not the only country that exists, nor the centre of the world]) (M&M, *L'Express*, 1 May 2007).

There are a considerable number of errors in the French that identify the writer as a non-native speaker, and the response to the posting is predictable:

'que faites vous en France alors ? pourquoi etes vous encore ici si c est si penible?' [so what are you doing in France? why are you still here if it's so bad?]

(beliaal, *L'Express*, 14 May 2007)

M&M's unproductive approach can be contrasted with that of another student. Like M&M, smiley13 (*Libération*, 21 May 2007) deplores racism in France but does not adopt an 'us versus them' position to do so. Indeed she starts out by appealing to and identifying with the values of *liberté* and *égalité*. Numerous errors in the French identify her as non-French, but the message attracts a considered reply from Orion2 (4 June) that provides further background information on living conditions in the suburbs.

In their article 'Conflicts in Cyberspace: From Communication Breakdown to Intercultural Dialogue in Online Collaborations', Schneider and von der Emde argue that conflict (between those who hold different beliefs and values and follow different conventions, for example) can be 'a valuable component of intercultural learning' (2006, p. 178), and is not simply something to be avoided at all costs. In analysing intercultural student exchanges involving conflict, they point to the way that 'each side is unwittingly interpolated into representing their own national cultures' (p. 188).[6] Such conflict, they argue, should not be automatically viewed as a failure of communication (p. 197), but as a potentially productive encounter from which one can gain insights into the different positions and values at stake in the exchange.

It is certainly the case that there are valuable lessons to be learned from the instances of conflict cited above, and indeed from the more benign cases of disagreement and difference of opinion that occurred regularly in the forum exchanges. As teachers, however, we have a responsibility to ensure that those lessons are not simply made available, but are teased out, that the students do not merely encounter conflict, but learn to interpret it, and thus profit from the encounter.

In the French course, individual guidance was offered to help interpret the responses in the cases of personal attack. More generally, however, the class as a whole needed guidance in deciding what constituted animosity and what needed to be considered simply as vigorous debate in the French messages. This formed part of a major learning objective in the course: understanding differences in cultural norms of discussion. While workshopping exchanges in class, we returned frequently to the sporting analogy: students were required to learn that, in France, the aim of debate is not to achieve consensus or compromise, any more than the aim of tennis is for both parties to hit the balls in the same direction. Rather, energetic volleys and a robust exchange of views are the marks of quality debate in French.

Lessons for future use

Student reactions

While the mid-semester evaluation of the course by students showed that oral discussion sessions were the preferred activity of the majority of participants, five students singled out forum participation as the most valuable aspect of the course, citing the authenticity of the activity. The open-ended comments of the anonymous post-course evaluation also included the following:

- 'The forum assessment is a great idea to help relate argumentation to real-life situations and authentic material.'
- 'The forums [...] really helped my French heaps. This course took French out of the classroom for me.'
- 'Writing on the forums was very educational.'

These were balanced by three negative reactions (in the section asking for suggestions for improvement to the course) indicating

- Technophobia: 'No computers !'
- Problems with access to technology: 'Less reliance on internet and blackboard[7] or perhaps time to use internet in class.'

- And disinterest in moving beyond classroom communication: 'Forget posting on a real forum, just hand them in. Wasted time sorting out how to use forums I'll never use again.'

Tellingly, while the students generally appreciated the opportunity to use French in an authentic context, none specifically mentioned the opportunity for feedback from others in the forum. This points to what can be seen as the major weakness in the use of discussion forums in this iteration of the course: the relative lack of attention students paid to the feedback available from other forum participants.

Encouraging use of feedback

During the course, it became evident that students were not necessarily spontaneously motivated to look for replies to their messages. Once the assessment requirements were fulfilled, many students moved on to start thinking about their next forum posting.[8] The teacher constantly needed to draw students' attention to the replies they were receiving (involving a considerable investment of time locating them) and also give guidance in interpreting them by workshopping particular exchanges in class. For while rich and varied intercultural lessons are available from the exchanges, students are not necessarily able to integrate these lessons spontaneously, but need to be trained to do so.

Students, then, need to be guided both to look for feedback and to learn from it, as neither of these actions occurs automatically. Both of these omissions can, however, be addressed through modifications to course and assessment design, such that interpreting replies becomes an explicit focus of forum work. Students can be asked to prepare a reflective diary, essay, presentation or group discussion in which they analyse the responses to their forum postings. Guiding questions can include the following:

- Does the response agree with/disagree with/qualify/add information to what I wrote?
- What assumptions are being made about me from what I wrote?
- What cultural values underlie the responses? what seems to be important?
- Are any criticisms made of my message? are they valid? what do they tell us about French argumentation?
- What conventions of argumentation (as discussed in class) are used?

- Is this response typical of messages/exchanges on this forum?
- Can I find any feedback about my language use? any corrections? any phrases used instead of the ones I use?
- Does the response invite a reply from me? how could I reply?

Alternatively, assessment criteria for forum participation can be designed to reward engagement with responses. Awarding marks to messages that elicit responses may counteract the temptation to write an essay as a forum posting, the essay being a known genre for the student, but one that does not necessarily invite interaction. The danger is that this may encourage outrageously provocative messages, sure to attract replies, rather than thoughtful postings.

The solution used in the 2008 course worked very effectively in focusing student attention on feedback from other forum participants: students received one mark out of ten for submitting a supplementary paragraph analysing the responses they had received to their previous message, or indeed analysing why they had not received any responses (see Table 9.4). This small reward was sufficient to motivate students

Table 9.4 Assessment criteria proposed for advanced French argumentation course

---

Structure et cohérence [Structure and coherence]

2   *Texte cohérent et logique, soutenu par l'utilisation variée des connecteurs appropriés*
    [Coherent, logical text, using a variety of appropriate connectors]
1   *Texte cohérent, avec utilisation appropriée des connecteurs étudiés*
    [Coherent text, using appropriate connectors]
0   *Manque de structure OU manque de connecteurs appropriés pour enchaîner les idées*
    [Lack of structure OR lack of connectors linking ideas]

Prise de position dans l'interaction [Taking a position in the discussion]

2   *Position claire par rapport aux autres; reconnaissance et négociation d'autres positions dans le débat (concession, refus, etc.)*
    [Clear position taken in discussion; recognition/negotiation of positions taken by others]
1   *Reconnaissance d'autres positions*
    [Recognition of other positions]
0   *Ne tient pas compte des interlocuteurs*
    [Ignores interlocutors]

Table 9.4   (Continued)

Lexique et connaissances culturelles [Vocabulary and cultural knowledge]

2   *Emploi d'un vocabulaire varié et approprié; connaissance des arguments courants de ce débat; message conforme aux conventions culturelles du forum*
[Varied, appropriate vocabulary; understanding of common standpoints on this topic; message conforms to the cultural conventions of the forum]

1   *Emploi d'un vocabulaire approprié; allusions aux idées courantes de ce débat*
[Appropriate vocabulary; awareness of common ideas on the topic]

0   *Manque de familiarité avec le vocabulaire et les positions courantes de ce débat OU Message qui paraît déplacé dans le contexte du forum*
[Unfamiliar with the vocabulary and ideas of this debate OR message appears out of place in the forum]

Précision du français [Grammatical accuracy]

3   *Grande précision grammaticale, avec très peu de fautes*
[High level of grammatical accuracy; very few errors]

2   *Langage courant, acceptable, sans barbarismes*
[Acceptable level of grammatical accuracy; few anglicisms]

1   *Langage compréhensible, mais avec de nombreuses fautes*
[Comprehensible, but contains numerous errors]

0   *Langage parfois incompréhensible, et/ou avec beaucoup de fautes élémentaires*
[Sometimes incomprehensible and/or many elementary errors]

Analyse des réponses (à partir de la Semaine 6) [Analysis of responses (from Week 6)]

1*   *Un paragraphe supplémentaire analysant les réponses reçues au message précédant (ou analysant le manque de réponses)*
[An additional paragraph has been submitted, analysing any responses to the previous message (or the lack of responses)]

0   *Pas d'analyse des réponses reçues*
[No analysis of responses to previous message]

---

* For their first forum message, students received a point for providing a URL linking to their message online. For subsequent postings, the mark was awarded for analysing the responses received.

to seek out the feedback their messages had attracted, and notice, for example,

- the assumptions being made about their identity (American rather than Australian);
- comments about genre: '*Je crois relire une copie de 1ere ES d'une élève qui ne fait que reprendre les questions sans donner de réponse*' [This sounds

like an essay from a high school student who rehashes the question without giving an answer];
- the fact that they were posting on a topic that was no longer topical.

Although this model of assessment has resulted in significantly more attention to feedback from the forum, it does not remove the need to workshop some of the exchanges in class, so that students direct attention to intercultural issues, learning to recognize and interpret them, and so that the forum work is fully integrated with class content. One of the great advantages of forum work is that a digital record remains of the transactions between participants, ripe for reflection and analysis leading to learning.

Our final example from the course comes from just such a piece of reflection. Analysing the replies received, a student writes of her pleasure at the uptake of her ideas by her respondent, Orion2, and at the fact that there was real discussion. This positive affective response, we can note, is sparked by Orion2 addressing not the student but her ideas, by Orion2 providing not helpful language practice or correction or even personalized chit-chat, but rather serious engagement with the case she has presented. Orion2 hasn't even twigged that she is there as a learner. And indeed she isn't: even if physically she sits in the computer laboratory, or at her desk at home with the criteria sheet in front of her, online she is already positioned as a discussant in a world of discussion.

10
Forums for Learning: Language, Culture and Identity

Forums for a variety of language learning contexts

The course described in Chapter 9 is one example of the integration of Internet discussion forums into the teaching of language and culture. In this case, a pre-existing course on argumentation in French was renovated to include what is, for many forum users, an everyday genre of argumentation. Participation in public discussion forums was used as a means to work towards the course objectives (linguistic and intercultural). The media websites chosen aligned themselves not only with the aims of the course, but also with the linguistic competence of the majority of the students. And while the conventions of forum participation had to be the subject of preparatory work, the students were able to comply with them. In this way, performing the genre posed an achievable challenge.

What can we take away from this case study and apply elsewhere regarding the use, in language courses, of public Internet discussion forums which were not originally set up for learner use? We have emphasized the integration of the activity with other aspects of the learning context. This demands not only careful choice of the forum(s) targeted but also judicious framing and sequencing of the tasks to be accomplished, including pre- and post-task activities (that is, preparation and reflection).

Choice of forum in relation to learners, tasks and objectives

Just as the language level and cognitive maturity of learners will guide the choice of a forum in which they could participate, the learning activity itself needs to be framed in such a way that it dovetails both with the forum conventions and with learning goals relevant to the class.

In other words, care must be taken to match learner proficiency, genre requirements and learning objectives.

Whereas third-year university students of French can be asked to contribute 300-word postings of carefully structured argument to a French newspaper forum, this would not be an appropriate task for learners of English posting to a site such as that of *The Guardian*. Such messages would predestine their authors to marginality to the usual business of a message board where shorter, more conversational postings are the norm (cf. Chapter 3). Tasks involving brief, less formal exchanges of opinions, however, would be suitable in this case. In other words, thought needs to be given to devising tasks and assessment criteria that will encourage an authentic performance and not detract from the realization of the target genre.

Similarly, the media sites chosen for the university French course would not correspond to all cohorts of students. Younger learners, for instance, might have difficulty engaging with the ethical and political issues which are the meat of the discussion on these sites, and may also be more vulnerable to punchy counter-posts. However, current affairs forums attached to newspaper websites are far from being the only kinds of public Internet forum available. There exists such richness of discussion boards catering to so many interests[1] and age groups that it should be possible to apply the principles seen in Chapter 9 to reap the benefits of authentic forum exchange. And this vast choice – from sites hosting quick question and answer forums on everyday practical matters to those proposing in-depth discussion of weighty issues – means that forum participation is not restricted to advanced language learners.

Numerous websites, including the home pages of search engines such as Yahoo (available in a variety of languages), call for reminiscences, life stories or just answers to questions (ranging from pet care through domestic dilemmas to wider social problems)[2]. For beginner adult learners, the wide-ranging and ever-changing line-up of enquiries could be of interest. The challenge here is to be sure of a sufficient number that are suitable and relevant, and will remain active for course requirements.

For language programmes targeting the acquisition of functions such as giving advice or instructions, we also suggest the numerous tourist information sites (for example, the forums hosted by the various language websites of *Lonely Planet*). Typically this would involve the learner offering advice to a native speaker of the target language – either already in country or contemplating a visit – who has posted a question: while the learner's foreign-language skills may be limited, it is he/she who has the upper hand where local knowledge is concerned.

Forums also exist for children and adolescents in many languages. For younger learners of French, authentic discussion forums such as those offered by the 'Momes' site provide opportunities for informal social exchange, for sharing ideas and advice on questions such as *'Comment convaincre mes parents d'avoir un chien?'* [How can I convince my parents to get a dog?], but also for discussion of social issues such as *'Le Coran et la biologie'* [The Koran and biology], *'Sans abris'* [The homeless] and of more specifically young adult phenomena such as rave parties. Learners of English over 13 years of age can join in the discussions of news items on the Kids Forum on the US site 'Topix', which also has a facility for creating polls or surveys. The German site 'Kidopia' offers discussion of a multitude of topics including films and television programs, holiday plans, star signs, eating disorders, piercings, school, homework, animals, and also offers a mechanism to create polls or surveys. Here opportunity exists for school-aged learners of German to communicate with native speakers and simultaneously practise language functions including describing, giving opinions, offering advice and forming questions.

Just as important as the possibilities for participation, however, is the knowledge to be gained from studying the postings already on these sites. Insights into the communicative behaviour, cultural perspectives, daily routines and range of opinions of teenagers from France, the US and Germany, for example, can be gleaned from the above sites at the same time as students familiarize themselves with the vocabulary they will need to post their own information, opinion or question.

The list of sites could go on, each with its own distinguishing features suggesting particular language-and-culture-related activities. And all of these discussions are continuously available in the target language, with no need for teachers to find partners or coordinate groups and time-tables. The point we wish to emphasize, however, is that to be successful, use of these forums cannot be a simple 'add-on' activity for students, but needs to be integrated carefully both with the specific goals of study and with related learning activities.

Preparatory and reflective tasks

Although Internet forums offer unparalleled opportunities for cross-border exchanges, taking advantage of these is not readily achievable without adequate preparation on the part of potential participants (including teachers, in the case of institutional learning). A public discussion forum is not a neutral space, a *tabula rasa* inviting language training, but a cultural practice, with specific conventions and patterns of behaviour. The prerequisites for successful participation, then, are the study of general cultural patterns and expectations in online discussion and an understanding of the specific constraints and possibilities of a given forum.

Does this mean then that every pedagogical exploitation of forums needs to be preceded by the kind of extensive cross-cultural study which is the stuff of the first part of this book? Not necessarily. But it does require familiarity with the genre in the target culture. Happily, in addition to providing opportunities for students, forums also offer a useful way for teachers themselves to maintain the currency of their linguistic and cultural expertise: time spent online familiarizing oneself with a forum for teaching purposes can also be of personal benefit.

Where students are concerned, preparation needs to include the technical aspects of forum access – in Chapter 9 we saw the coexistence of technologically savvy and technologically resistant elements in the same demographic – but access in itself does not suffice. It cannot be assumed that learners will 'get' the genre on their own – although we noted the ability of students (Chapter 9) to make perspicacious observations and to apply them when encouraged to do so. This 'noticing' needs to include the features of the genre (purpose, length, register, topics, turn-taking, use of personal information, ways of starting and finishing messages) and the cultural assumptions being made. In addition to these observations of the forum as it goes about its business, learners need to reflect ahead of time on possible modes of interaction with the chosen forum(s): How they will establish their presence in the forum? How are they likely to be viewed? What, if any, evidence can they see of how the forum deals with 'outsiders'? Decentring exercises can be useful here to help students imagine how messages will be understood and how they themselves will be seen by native speakers participating in the discussion. Such discussion takes on particular urgency when it is foreseeable that aspects of the students' likely online identity may at times provoke controversy (such as the fact of being American on a French forum).[3]

Just as convenors of study-abroad programmes have found it unwise to abandon students once they are in country, so too does a course using forums need to provide some form of ongoing scaffolding for students once they have gone online: class workshopping of student interventions, both successful and otherwise, will provide support, counsel and guidance, and quite simply, raise student awareness of the learning opportunities available to them.

Whatever choice of forum is made, the same issues of generic specificity (purpose, length, topics, turn-taking, use of personal information) and discursive and cultural position will arise and need to be taken seriously. Through consideration of such factors, and application of their conclusions to their own actual postings on the sites, learners can claim their place in the rhetorical practices of their 'target' culture.

Conclusion: Language, culture and identity

Since the early 1990s, foreign-language teaching has been reshaped by a new focus on intercultural learning and by growth in the use of communications technologies in education. Increasing interest has arisen in ways of bringing these two elements together such that ICTs serve the development of intercultural competence. To date, efforts in this direction have largely been applied to projects partnering language learners in different countries.

The use of public Internet discussion forums brings a new dimension to the task of harnessing ICTs to intercultural learning, in drawing students beyond classroom cultures and learner-to-learner communication. Such forums provide opportunities to join in an authentic cultural practice in the foreign language on its own terms, for neither teachers nor students determine the rules and conventions of the online community. This offers great potential for experiential learning in the intertwined areas of language, culture and identity.

There are those who imagine that the ever-widening reach of global communications networks will lead to the disappearance of cultural differences over time. Our data suggest the opposite: even when similar technologies – those allowing Internet discussion forums in this case – are made available, we find them used for culturally differentiated purposes (Chapter 3) which lead them to evolve in different directions (Chapter 4). Our view is that cultural difference is endemic and potentially enriching, and that our task as educators is to draw attention both to the existence of difference and to the means of understanding and dealing with it.

Online public discussion in a foreign language offers the potential for learners to experience cultural difference unfettered by physical location. And it provides a venue for language learners and teachers to focus *not* on language *and* intercultural communication but on language *as* intercultural communication. In this asynchronous textual genre, there is time between messages to interpret and negotiate cultural norms in the matters not only of attitudes expressed, but of the purpose of communication, rhetorical strategies, forms of politeness and turn-taking.

While for many of the language learners encountered in the course of these pages the issue of linguistic performance overshadowed all others, time and again we have seen that discussion forums are also the site of profound and often personal challenges in the performance of identity.

The issue of the development of L2 identities has risen to prominence only in the last decade, since Firth and Wagner's landmark 1997 essay identified a tendency within Second Language Acquisition to focus on the learner as learner 'at the expense of other potentially relevant social identities' (p. 228). Block (2007) traces the rise of questions of identity in the intervening years, pointing to a growing recognition that language learning needs to be understood as a social as well as a cognitive process.[4] More particularly in the field of language learning and technology, Warschauer (2000, 2002; Warschauer, El Said, & Zohry, 2002), Lam (2000, 2003, 2004) and Nguyen and Kellogg (2005) have demonstrated the ways in which various modes of online communication lend themselves to the exploration of identity by language learners.

Our work has found students often mired in a learner identity that is hard to shake off and that appears underpinned by certain classroom practices. Once performing in their L2, many seem unwilling to assert themselves as multifaceted interesting people, preferring to present primarily as learners and thus anchor their identity to a notion of linguistic deficiency. Supporting this restrictive identity is the ease with which they rehearse the genre of self-presentation inculcated in language classes.

We have seen how rarely this type of introduction, the staple of the beginners' class, is used in public discussion forums. That neat recitation of personal details, although seen as essential in launching telecollaboration activities (O'Dowd, 2007, p.29), is actually quite a rare genre in everyday communication, and not the universal key to interactional success that learners may unwittingly be led to expect. Whilst it may provide material for game show introductions or personal fact sheets for Olympic athletes, it is not normally appropriate in initial conversations of either a social or a professional nature. A first step in exploring sustainable L2 identities is, then, to wean oneself from this genre closely associated with the language learner, and from using the self-portrait to attempt to initiate dialogue.

Cultivating viable identities through which to engage in communication in a second language is not an automatic process. Lantolf and Pavlenko (2000), in their analysis of memoirs of acculturation, see it as entailing growth into new subjectivities in a new language. They focus on the immersion situation of life in a new country, but while the negotiation of L2 and transcultural identities may be less urgent for language learners in other contexts, it is nonetheless an important measure of (inter)cultural competence.

Lantolf and Pavlenko's research points to the role of writing in shifting the projection of one's self: 'At first the new voice is often captured in writing' (2000, p. 168). And they emphasize that identities are reformulated through interaction: 'The new linguistic identities, just as the original, are co-constructed with others' (p. 169, cf. Antaki & Widdicombe, 1998). Both these determinants – writing and interaction – are characteristic of public Internet discussion forums, where asynchronous written exchange takes place in the cultural space of the native speaker, that is in the context of the cultural practices of the other.

Discussion forums for the general public thus offer particular opportunities for reflecting on and experimenting with different modes of establishing oneself in an exchange. Here one can try out a discursive position where identity is asserted as part of a point of view rather than an exposition of personal interests (for all that personal interests may motivate engagement with discussion). The self constructed and performed on Internet discussion forums is immediately trialled with a real and vocal audience. And the forums provide a textual, often searchable, record of interaction, with the consequent opportunities to reflect on particular instances of engagement with cultural others, in all their different facets (self-positioning, rhetorical markers, grammatical accuracy, cultural knowledge). They are, in other words, a focus for reflection on language, culture and identity.

This kind of exploration of speaking positions has wider application than the ability to type off salvos expressing agreement/disagreement with other readers of a particular newspaper. It is a means not only of developing interactional skills in a second language, but also of constructing and investing in a range of viable identities in L2 through which to engage in intercultural communication.

We have insisted throughout this book on the desirability of language students moving beyond the confines of the classroom. At the same time, we have emphasized the need for students to be supported by the back-up team of teacher and fellow students facilitating – through course design and classroom discussion – this move to engage with a practice of the target culture. As we conclude, we reiterate the fact that this teacher-guided engagement should be designed to yield skills transferable to other situations as well as familiarity with a genre in which learners can participate autonomously. Beyond the learning they offer in company with classroom support, Internet discussion forums can provide rich opportunities for ongoing, further development as an interculturalist.

The exciting world outside the classroom beckons. And it's not a borderless world. It's a world of cultural specificities and regulated online communities. Back on the discussion forum of *The Independent* (Chapter 8), that site of lively intercultural debate, AlainRudaz signs off a posting with 'Vive le global-bled!' (Independent Argument, 2003–2004, #104). *Le global-bled* is the global village, unromanticized. It suggests not seamless connectivity, but a world-wide-web of insular communities (*bleds*), a paradoxical combination of isolation and connection, of exclusion and inclusion. Public Internet discussion is a way of getting to know some of the locals in the global village, but it will mean doing so not only in their language but largely on their terms. The effort to negotiate one's inclusion, however, is a learning journey worth taking.

Notes

2 Culture and Online Communication

1. See, for example, Dery (1996), Shields (1996), Porter (1997), and Bell (2001; Bell and Kennedy, 2000) on cybercultures; Surratt (1998) and Smith and Kollock (1999) on online communities; Turkle (1995) on identity; Kolko, Nakamura, and Rodman (2000) on race; Spender (1995), Harcourt (1999) and Cherny and Weise (1996) on gender; Stone (1995) on gender identity and disability; Loader (1998) on class; Cooper (2000) on cybersex; Tsagarousianou, Tambini, and Bryan (1998) on cyberdemocracy.
2. Special issues include the following:

   - *Language Learning and Technology* 7.2 (2003) 'Telecollaboration';
   - *International Negotiation* 9.1 (2004) on ICTs and international negotiation;
   - *Journal of Computer-Mediated Communication* 11.1 (2005) 'Culture and Computer-Mediated Communication'; and
   - AAUSC annual (American Association of University Supervisors and Co-ordinators) (2006) *Internet-Mediated Intercultural Foreign Language Education* (eds. Belz and Thorne).

3. See, for example, Siebenhaar (2006, p. 485), whose hypotheses regarding the regional origins of Swiss Internet relay chat users are based on their language use.
4. The discourse of the 'borderless world' persists in talk about the global economy, but is seriously challenged by, among others, Goldsmith and Wu (*Who Controls the Internet?: Illusions of a Borderless World*, 2006), who argue that powerful economic interests will continue to rely on territorial governments for support in their cross-border enterprises.
5. While we recognize that conventions, practices and values are not simply equivalent, the literature tends not to distinguish between them in consistent ways. Our discussion will therefore move between referring sometimes to one and sometimes to all of these types of cultural regularities.
6. They give the telling example of HIV-prevention campaigns, where typically high-context African cultures may be quite explicit, whereas Australian campaigns are unusually implicit and allusive (1997, p. 144).
7. For similar findings, see Twu 2007, p. 250.
8. While these interpretations of Ma's data may seem to veer back towards hypothesis 1 (the Internet removes cultural difference), the argument is more nuanced. There is no expectation that the Internet necessarily eliminates all cultural difference; rather, it might offer an opportunity to break with certain cultural conventions, not all. And – as Ma's work suggests – cultures will both take up this possibility differently and, we contend, continue to interpret

others' online behaviour according to their own culturally determined
expectations.

9. Frow's (2005) critical exploration of genre approaches the concept in a
   similar way to Freadman and Macdonald.
10. In Chapter 4, we discuss the changes that take place over time with respect
    to discussion forums, and show that such changes do not necessarily move
    in the direction of convergence between cultures.
11. Thorne's (2003) subsequent work on 'cultures-of-use' broadens a Hallidayan
    conceptualization of genre to embrace an ethnological approach to the way
    communicative genres and the technologies they employ are embedded in –
    and shape – wider cultural practices. Communications technologies are seen
    as 'artefacts', not simply material but imbued with cultural meaning arising
    from their 'histories of use' (p. 40) by particular communities, histories that
    continue to evolve. This is entirely consistent with our use of genre theory
    as the basis for understanding cultural practices.

3 Debate or Conversation? French and British Public Internet Discussion

1. See also the connections made by Colin and Mourlhon-Dallies (2004)
   between the *'courrier des lecteurs'* (Letters to the Editor) and the public
   discussion forum.
2. Studies by Gubman and Greer (1997), Tankard and Ban (1998), Peng,
   Tham and Xiaoming (1999) and Greer and Mensing (2004) offer similar
   statistics.
3. Cowen (2001) asserts that '[w]ebsites such as the Electronic Telegraph and
   Guardian Unlimited rank as some of the most well-known in Britain'
   (p. 190), while Estela (2000) notes the high position of the daily press among
   the 20 most visited French websites (p. 24).
4. Even in 2003 the proportion of new users at the BBC website remained significant, as the BBC Director of New Media and Technology reported: 'And,
   of the 25 million adults and children online in the UK, 7%, two million, said
   they'd been motivated to log on to the Internet for the very first time due
   solely to the BBC's website' (Highfield, 2003, np).
5. *The Times*, which might have seemed an obvious British counterpart to *Le
   Monde*, did not incorporate a forum facility until well after the other sites,
   with none available in 2002.
6. 'BBC News online receives 660 million page impressions a month, with 9.1
   million UK users reading it (around 30 million worldwide). Compare this
   with its nearest rival – Guardian Unlimited – that has 80 million page impressions a month and 7.2 million users, many from outside the UK. All other
   newspapers' sites are at least a third the size of the Guardian's.' (McCarthy,
   2003, np).

   'User contributions have continued to show steady growth in recent years
   (from an average of 112,310 registered users in November 2002 to 244,963 in
   November 2003; message boards attracted over 7 million page impressions a
   week in November 2003)' (Graf, 2004, p. 27).

7. *Les Echos, L'Equipe* and *Télérama* are dedicated to, respectively, business, sport, television and the arts. Figures sourced from 'Médiamétrie-eRatings' and based on Nielsen//NetRatings (Panel Home and Work. Report France – September 2002), cited in Santrot (2002).

8. The title '*Le Nouvel Observateur* from day to day' distinguishes the frequently updated online version from the paper weekly.

9. Some forums (such as the Middle East forum at *Le Monde*) and some users (participants whose messages have been removed previously, new participants in BBC forums) are pre-moderated; that is, messages must be approved before they appear on the forum.

10. The possibility of launching a debate on a topic of one's own choice was introduced later.

11. The change was part of the redesign of *Le Monde* forums of late 2000.

12. '*[O]n espère que vous participerez à nos petites castagnes amicales*' [we hope you will participate in our friendly little punch-ups] is the greeting posted to a self-identified foreigner on the '*Autres sujets*' forum (Baguette, '*les etrangers, sont-ils bienvenus?*' [are foreigners welcome?], 21 July 1999).

13. Our distinction between 'debate' and 'conversation' parallels the opposition between 'discussion' and 'conversation' in the literature on verbal interaction. We have, however, retained the terms adopted on the sites studied, since 'discussion' is clearly not used by British participants in the technical sense of competitive, topic-driven, monitored public treatment of a subject (Bublitz, 1988, p. 20, cited in Tabensky, 2000, p. 50). Indeed it is construed on both French and British sites in culturally determined ways. Furthermore, as we shall see, the importance of the distinction – the extent to which debate and chat might share the same space – similarly differs along cultural lines.

14. In quoting postings to the sites, we make no attempt to standardize grammar or spelling, nor to reproduce non-standard expression in our translations.

15. While all the forums, French and British, exclude racist, defamatory and advertising messages, the forums of the French national daily *Libération* also explicitly exclude '*les messages non argumentés*' [messages with no argument] (*Libération*, 2005).

16. It is worth noting that Light and Rogers's 1999 article on 'The Debating Chamber' (the site set up by *The Guardian* for discussion of the 1997 UK elections) is entitled 'Conversation as Publishing'.

17. The existence of this thread, and the sentiments expressed on it further serve to underline the extent to which interaction on the British sites enacts conversational conventions: 'Closing down a conversation is a potentially face-threatening act' (Döpke, Brown, Liddicoat, & Love, 1994, p. 22, referring to the work of Laver, 1981).

18. This exchange is discussed in detail in Chapter 6.

19. Cf. Labbe and Marcoccia (2005), who argue that digital genres are initially variations on existing genres, before emerging as new genres in their own right.

20. See Herring (2002) and Adams (1996) on the demographics, origins and purposes of UseNet newsgroups.

4   *Plus ça change . . .* : Are Online Cultural Differences Fading Over Time?

1. The website for the *Daily Telegraph* and the *Sunday Telegraph*.
2. Dialogue was, however, reintroduced in April 2007, with the launch of 'my.Telegraph', which enables users to write blogs, and to post comments on the blogs of others.
3. Similarly, discussion on prominent US newspaper sites has been curtailed and focused: the *Washington Post* has replaced its forums with fifteen 'discussion groups', each hosted by an individual moderator who launches the daily question for discussion, and in April 2007 the *New York Times* closed the majority of its forums, leaving only those on crosswords and games, opera, classical music, books and 'human origins'. It invited readers instead to 'express your views on our blogs, answer our daily question and submit questions for *Times* editors in our "Talk to the Newsroom" feature' (*New York Times*, 2007).
4. 'Re: Exploitation des forums du *Monde*' [Using the *Le Monde* forums], '*Les forums – Vos questions*' [The forums – your questions].
5. This proposal had surfaced independently on a thread on the 35-hour week, when one participant saluted the contribution of another:

   Je trouve que les modérateurs de ce forum devrait mettre ce texte en exergue quelque part dans leur journal, par exemple avec ce titre 'La pensée du mois de notre forum', qu'est-ce que vous en pensez?

   [I think that the moderators of this forum should put this text as a quotation somewhere in their newspaper, for example with this title 'Thought of the month from our forum', what do you think?]

   (navarin, '*Dans l'actualité Les 35 heures en question*' [In the news – Challenging the 35 hour week], 13 October 2002)

5   Public Discussion Forums as a Tool for Language Learning

1. Cf. O'Rourke (2007, p. 49) on the various degrees of integration of tandem learning into institutional learning.
2. Lists of further sites facilitating online student exchanges can be found in O'Dowd (2007, pp. 174, 202).
3. Although impressions of novelty may not be shared by all students: see, for example, Thorne (2003, p. 56) on student rejection of the medium of email as outmoded.
4. We recognize that these may not be their native language and culture.
5. For further discussion of these issues, see O'Rourke (2007, pp. 57–59).
6. For one thing, the generic specificity of Internet discussion forums evidently limits what can be taught through them: Chapter 9 presents a case study of French media website discussion forums used in a course on '*argumentation*'.
7. Here we refer of course to monolingual sites. An example of an explicitly intercultural and multilingual site, not restricted to language learners, Wordreference.com, is given later in this chapter.

8. Thorne notes elsewhere that 'Research on learning in non-institutionalized digital environments is in its relative infancy' (Thorne & Black, 2007, p. 149).
9. For a discussion of the constraints of the language classroom, see Cowley and Hanna, 1997.
10. 'Getting to know each other' (Cultural Discussions) created by moderator GenJen54, 1 June 2006. By September 2007, 233 replies had been posted to this exceptional questionnaire where, for once, readers were invited to reveal personal details.
11. Cf. Little (1991, pp. 3–4); Lamy and Hampel (2007, pp. 147–148).
12. This possibility is discussed in detail in Chapter 8.
13. Cf. Lam (2000, 2003, 2004), whose case studies show how non-standard varieties of English can be used to construct viable English-language identities for online communication.

6 A Funny Thing Happened on the Way to the Forum: Learners' Participation Strategies

1. A subscription which includes the right to post to the forums costs 6 euros per month at the time of writing (2008).
2. See also discussion in Chapter 3. *'Autres sujets'* was replaced by *'Tous sujets'* [All topics] in late 2000.
3. Another significant change in 2001 was the creation of the forum *'Questions sur ce forum'* [Questions about this forum], catering for technical and other 'how to' questions regarding online discussion previously found on *'Autres sujets'*. By 2008, this has simply become *'Vos questions'* [Your questions].
4. Cf. the argument of Kollock and Smith (1996) concerning the ongoing need to negotiate rules in computer-enabled communities:

> Even if a community has developed a good set of rules, there is the task of teaching new members about those rules. [...] New members are tempted to wade into a newsgroup without first learning the local culture by reading the documents that have been prepared by other members or by observing the group for a period of time before attempting to participate.
> [...] Even in newsgroups that have produced a FAQ, many of the rules and institutions that are present remain informal, undocumented and difficult to enforce. As a result, there are certain chronic problems that are difficult to resolve through these informal means. For example, groups routinely wander off of their declared topics, and are frequently invaded by those who are either ignorant of the goals of the group or who actively seek to disrupt them.
>
> (p. 122)

5. Whilst the contributions of these four writers form part of the data for our study, the subjects themselves (David, Laura, Eleanor and Fleurie) do not. We are not acquainted with them, and the nature of their online participation means that all we know of their personal, pedagogical and institutional situation is what they choose to reveal about themselves in their messages.
6. In his subject line, Grossefatigue alludes to a celebrated incident at the battle of Fontenoy (1745), where the English invitation to the French to begin firing

was met with a reply commonly cited as '*Messieurs les Anglais, tirez les premiers!*' [After you, gentlemen: shoot first!] and gallantry cost the French their front line.

7. This episode is echoed in Paramskas' experience with the discussion list '*Causerie*' [Chat] both in the kinds of introductory messages posted by unwitting students and in the lack of continued participation by these novices:

> Every once in a while, a French teacher will discover *Causerie* and push his or her students on to it, resulting in multiple messages of the type:
>
> Hi,
> I'm XXX, and I'm learning French and I would like to talk to you.
> Write to me!
>
> This is perhaps not the best use of the medium, but 'the Cause' takes it all in good stride. Someone always speaks up to welcome the class members, who tend to fade away given the volume of messages. *Causerie* was not set up as a pedagogic tool, but certainly can serve that function well.
>
> (Paramskas, 1995, p. 167)

8. Laura's attempt at textual pastiche here doesn't quite work in translation and her self-positioning as the scary but ultimately harmless wolf may be missed.

9. This is something that Chen (1998) was belatedly required to take into account when he attempted to use a highly codified form of debate as the format for email exchange among students from various countries.

7 Face Off: Identity in Online Debate

1. The famous case, recounted by Stone, of a prominent New York male psychiatrist who participated in a CompuServe chatroom under the guise of a disabled female neuropsychologist and the betrayal felt by those who had befriended her is but one example of the tenacious belief, despite everything, in online sincerity (Stone, 1995, pp. 65–82).

2. As noted in Chapter 4, the majority of the *New York Times* forums were closed and removed in April 2007 (*New York Times*, 2007).

3. For an overview of these developments and their application to the study of online communication, see Thurlow, Lengel and Tomic (2004, pp. 95–105).

4. See, for example, Burkhalter (1999), Donath (1999), Revillard (2000).

5. The *Nouvel Observateur* site accommodates the production of a name for every forum: participants in a debate on Microsoft therefore include Bill Portes and Bill Guette (respectively, a translation and phonetic transposition of the name Bill Gates). (See *Nouvel Observateur*, 2007, to consult the rules.) Such made-to-measure names were at one point possible on the *Le Monde* site, where regulars also rang playful changes on recognizable pseudonyms. If the same person has multiple names, which cannot be traced back to the same address, online and offline worlds might seem to diverge, but we must remind ourselves that other written genres also allow multiple pseudonyms and it is entirely possible to ring talk-back radio or – why not – to talk to strangers on buses under different guises. Although increased policing of the

Le Monde site saw, between 2000 and 2002, an enforcement of the principle of unitary identity – one address, one pseudonym – a further development in 2003 disturbed it. This was when the right to contribute was restricted to subscribers to the online edition. According to discussion on '*Coin détente*' [Relaxation corner], this brought about the formation of forum couples and other groupings, as contributors united under the one name and the one subscription. It has not, however, meant a complete repudiation of the notion of individual identity, as members of these consortia tend to sign their contributions with individual names/pseudonyms.

6. For a discussion of identity cues in newsgroups, see Donath (1999).
7. See also Donath (1999, p. 30).
8. The shift in gender may well be due to the sharing of a subscription to *Le Monde* as mentioned in note 5 above: the point is, however, that no one seeks to clarify this tangential issue.
9. On this point, see Chapter 3. Our investigations into cross-cultural difference in online debate suggest that the focus of discussion on US sites is also about making a case, but that this tends to be through the presentation of conflicting personal views and experiences, rather than through engagement with the arguments of others. This tendency is consistent with Donath's observation (1999, p. 50) that the most usual kind of identity manipulation seen on newsgroups is that of status enhancement, to cast oneself as the authoritative speaker. Debate on French sites is notably less grounded in the personal.
10. Queensland University of Technology unit HHB066, French 6, 2002.

8 Towards Intercultural Discussion: Getting Off on the Right Foot(ing)

1. Our study did not encompass the private sphere of personal contacts between friends, family and colleagues. In the private domain, we would expect the incidence of productive intercultural exchanges (or sustained exchanges that do not degenerate into abuse) to be significantly higher.
2. The distinction Dery makes between 'flaming' ('Exchanging insults electronically', 1994, p. 322) and 'rant' ('On-line demagoguery in which users give themselves over to inspired hyperbole and wild, zany capitalization and punctuation', p. 324) is principally one of length. We will use 'rant' to refer generally to online verbal abuse.
3. Most discussion sites are moderated to some degree; however, in general, contributions appear online immediately (if they pass the automatic censor checking for offensive language), but may be removed subsequently by a moderator if they do not conform to the site's code of conduct.
4. Herring's discussion refers to English-language forums. Examination of the codes of conduct of forums based in a variety of cultures and languages, however, suggests that the inflammatory nature of public Internet discussion is a widespread issue, not restricted to Anglophone cultures.
5. The performance of identity according to a classroom model is similarly noted by Dooly (2006). She presents a striking example of the gap between the construction of an online identity for a pedagogical task (bland self-presentation corresponding to classroom conventions and/or imagined

teacher expectations) and the same individual's online identity performed through her personal webpage with much use of graphics, humour and colour.

6. See Benson (2002) on the distinction between autonomy and self-access.
7. Unilang also offers five such forums, separate from the 'Virtual School of Languages', but only in English. These 'non-language forums' include 'Politics' and 'Cultures'. Here the learner speaking position is abandoned, but although intercultural discussions certainly occur in these forums, the propensity to rant is once again a factor, with prominent warnings about behaviour and the exclusion of users who breach the guidelines.
8. After a lull in activity, the thread was twice revived (11 December 2003–8 January 2004, 137 messages; 12 February–8 April 2004, 48 messages) before being archived on 6 May 2004.
9. In fact, Francophones furnished 147 (36.7 per cent) of the 401 messages; however, 88 of these were by 'frogoff', a Frenchman educated in England and seemingly equally at ease in both languages.
10. Numbers prefaced by # refer to individual messages within the thread.
11. Or as Kuhnheim (1998) succinctly puts it, 'Boundaries are inherent to the definition of subject positions, and a border identity is no exception' (p. 25).
12. Similarly, Park (2007) notes the way in which non-native speaker identity is invoked temporarily at particular moments in the informal, small-group conversations between US, Spanish and Korean college students and graduates that she analyses.
13. Cf. Rosello's (1998) work on the need to 'decline' stereotypes.

9 Using Public Internet Forums to Develop French Argumentation Skills

1. Bruce Roberts, posting on IECC-discussion@stolaf.edu, 22 March 1994, cited in Warschauer, 1995, p. 95.
2. In designing the assessment regime, the instructor had to consider many of the issues which are also raised by Lamy and Hampel in their discussion of assessment (Lamy & Hampel, 2007, pp. 88–101). However, while Lamy and Hampel situate most of their discussion of the assessment of online production in the context of collaborative projects, our solutions relate to the creation of a culturally authentic product. As will be seen later in the chapter, the subsequent requirement that students provide commentary on the production and reception of their successive postings means that there is also a process-based element to assessment.
3. Cf. the example of Kanduhn (Australie) at the end of Chapter 7.
4. The pseudonyms are those chosen by the students for use in the forums.
5. This example comes from a repeat of the course in the following semester.
6. See our discussion of default speaking positions and that of champion of one's culture in Chapter 8.
7. 'Blackboard' here indicates the web-based teaching and learning platform.
8. The situation was different, however, for students posting to *L'Express*, who received an email whenever there was a response to their message, making this a user-friendly destination for student contributions.

10   Forums for Learning: Language, Culture and Identity

1. The use of search terms such as X + forums + discussion (where X is a field of interest, terms translated as necessary) reveals a choice of forums in commonly taught languages on cooking, pets, films, sports, jobs, science and so on.
2. Comparable sites include the Japanese-language site 'AllAbout' and the sites '12chat' and 'Rongshuxia' in Mandarin.
3. And yet we have seen in Chapter 6, with the cases of Laura and David Dalton on *Le Monde*, that American participation can also be warmly welcomed.
4. Key volumes relating language learning to identity issues include Block (2006), Kramsch (2003), Norton (2000), Pavlenko and Blackledge (2004).

References

Adams, C. (1996). *The 1996 Internet counterrevolution: Power, information, and the mass media.* Paper presented at the INET '96 Conference, Montreal, Canada.

Anderson, B. (1983). *Imagined communities: Reflections on the origin and spread of nationalism.* London: Verso.

Antaki, C., & Widdicombe, S. (Eds.). (1998). *Identities in talk.* London; Thousand Oaks, CA: Sage.

Archer, C. M. (1986). Culture bump and beyond. In J. M. Valdes (Ed.), *Culture bound* (pp. 170–177). Cambridge: Cambridge University Press.

Atifi, H. (2003). La variation culturelle dans les communications en ligne: Analyse ethnographique des forums de discussion marocains. *Langage et société,* (104), 57–82.

Atifi, H., & Marcoccia, M. (2006). Communication médiatisée par ordinateur et variation culturelle: Analyse contrastive de forums de discussion français et marocains. In P. von Münchow & F. Rakotonoelina (Eds.), *Discours, cultures, comparaisons* (pp. 59–73). Paris: Presses Sorbonne Nouvelle.

Basharina, O. K. (2007). An activity theory perspective on student-reported contradictions in international telecollaboration. *Language Learning & Technology,* 11(2), 36–58. http://llt.msu.edu/vol11num2/basharina/

BBC. (2002a). *Messageboards.* Retrieved April 24, 2002, from http://www.bbc.co.uk/messageboards/

BBC. (2002b). *The great debate: World views.* Retrieved April 24, 2002, from http://www.bbc.co.uk/cgi-perl/h2/h2.cgi?x=y& board=greatdebate

BBC. (2007). *House rules.* Retrieved January 25, 2007, from http://www.bbc.co.uk/messageboards/newguide/popup_house_rules.html

Béal, C. (1990). It's all in the asking: A perspective on problems of cross-cultural communication between native speakers of French and native speakers of Australian English in the workplace. *Australian Review of Applied Linguistics, Series S*(7), 66–92.

Bell, D. (2001). *An introduction to cybercultures.* New York: Routledge.

Bell, D., & Kennedy, B. M. (Eds.). (2000). *The cybercultures reader.* London; New York: Routledge.

Belz, J. A. (2001). Institutional and individual dimensions of transatlantic group work in network-based language teaching. *ReCALL, 13*(2), 213–231.

Belz, J. A. (2002). Social dimensions of telecollaborative foreign language study. *Language Learning & Technology, 6*(1), 60–81. http://llt.msu.edu/vol6num1/belz/

Belz, J. A. (2003). Linguistic perspectives on the development of intercultural competence in telecollaboration. *Language Learning & Technology, 7*(2), 68–117. http://llt.msu.edu/vol7num2/belz/

Belz, J. A. (2005). Intercultural questioning, discovery and tension in Internet-mediated language learning partnerships. *Language and Intercultural Communication, 5*(1), 3–39.

199

Belz, J. A., & Müller-Hartmann, A. (2003). Teachers as intercultural learners: Negotiating German–American telecollaboration along the institutional faultline. *The Modern Language Journal, 87*(1), 71–89.

Belz, J. A., & Thorne, S. L. (Eds.). (2006). *Internet-mediated intercultural foreign language education*. Boston, MA: Heinle & Heinle.

Benson, P. (2002). Rethinking the relationship of self-access and autonomy. *Self-Access Language Learning* (5), 4–10.

Benson, P., & Voller, P. (Eds.). (1997). *Autonomy and independence in language learning*. London; New York: Longman.

Biesenbach-Lucas, S. (2007). Students writing emails to faculty: An examination of e-politeness among native and non-native speakers of English. *Language Learning & Technology, 11*(2), 59–81. http://llt.msu.edu/vol11num2/biesenbachlucas/

Bloch, J. (2004). Second language cyber rhetoric: A study of Chinese L2 writers in an online Usenet group. *Language Learning & Technology, 8*(3), 66–82. http://llt.msu.edu/vol8num3/bloch/

Block, D. (2006). *Multilingual identities in a global city: London stories*. Basingstoke; New York: Palgrave.

Block, D. (2007). The rise of identity in SLA research, post Firth and Wagner (1997). *Modern Language Journal, 91*(5), 863–876.

Bolter, J. D., & Grusin, R. (1999). *Remediation: Understanding new media*. Cambridge, MA: MIT Press.

Breton, E. J.-L. (2001–2002). *Extraits de débats (archives 2001–02)*, from http://societe2. monblogue.branchez-vous.com/liste.php

Brown, J. S., Collins, A., & Duguid, P. (1989). Situated cognition and the culture of learning. *Educational Researcher, 18*(1), 32–42.

Bublitz, W. (1988). *Supportive fellow-speakers and cooperative conversations*. Amsterdam; Philadelphia: John Benjamins.

Burkhalter, B. (1999). Reading race online: Discovering racial identity in Usenet discussions. In M. A. Smith & P. Kollock (Eds.), *Communities in cyberspace* (pp. 60–75). London: Routledge.

Byram, M. (1997). *Teaching and assessing intercultural communicative competence*. Clevedon, UK: Multilingual Matters.

Cakir, H., Bichelmeyer, B., & Cagiltay, K. (2002). Effects of cultural differences on e-mail communication in multicultural environments. In F. Sudweeks & C. Ess (Eds.), *Proceedings of the Cultural Attitudes towards Technology and Communication Conference, 2002 (CATaC'02)* (pp. 29–50). Perth: Murdoch University Press.

Callahan, E. (2005). Cultural similarities and differences in the design of university websites. *Journal of Computer-Mediated Communication, 11*(1). http://jcmc.indiana.edu/vol11/issue1/callahan.html

Chase, M., Macfadyen, L. P., Reeder, K., & Roche, J. (2002). Intercultural challenges in networked learning: Hard technologies meet soft skills. *First Monday, 7*(8). http://firstmonday.org/issues/issue7_8/chase/index.html

Chen, G.-M. (1998). Intercultural communication via e-mail debate. *The Edge: The E-Journal of Intercultural Relations, 1*(4). Retrieved October 18, 2006, from http://cms.interculturalu.com/theedge/v1i4Fall1998/f98chen.htm

Cherny, L., & Weise, E. R. (Eds.). (1996). *Wired women: Gender and new realities in cyberspace*. Seattle, WA: Seal Press.

Chiou, J.-S., & Lee, J. (2008). What do they say about 'Friends'? A cross-cultural study on Internet discussion forum. *Computers in Human Behavior, 24*(3), 1179–1195.

Clyne, M. G. (1987). Discourse structures and discourse expectations: Implications for Anglo-German academic communication in English. In L. E. Smith (Ed.), *Discourse across cultures: Strategies in world Englishes* (pp. 73–83). New York; Sydney: Prentice Hall.

Colin, J.-Y., & Mourlhon-Dallies, F. (2004). Du courrier des lecteurs aux forums de discussion sur l'internet: Retour sur la notion de genre. In F. Mourlhon-Dallies, F. Rakotonoelina, & S. Reboul-Touré (Eds.), *Les discours de l'internet: Nouveaux corpus, nouveaux modèles?* (pp. 113–142). Paris: Presses Sorbonne Nouvelle.

Convertino, G., Zhang, Y., Asti, B., Rosson, M. B., & Mohammed, S. (2007). Board-based collaboration in cross-cultural pairs. *Lecture Notes in Computer Science* (4568), 321–334.

Cooper, A. (Ed.). (2000). *Cybersex: The darkside of the force.* Philadelphia: Branner-Routledge.

Coverdale-Jones, T. (1998). Does computer-mediated conferencing really have a reduced social dimension? *ReCALL, 10*(1), 46–52.

Cowen, N. (2001). The future of the British broadsheet newspaper on the World Wide Web. *Aslib Proceedings, 53*(5), 189–200.

Cowley, P., & Hanna, B. E. (1997). Is there a class in this room? *Australian Review of Applied Linguistics, Series S*(14), 119–134.

Crystal, D. (2001). *Language and the Internet.* Cambridge, UK: Cambridge University Press.

Daft, R. L., & Lengel, R. H. (1984). Information richness: A new approach to managerial behavior and organizational design. In L. L. Cummings & B. M. Staw (Eds.), *Research in organizational behavior 6* (pp. 191–233). Homewood, IL: JAI Press.

Davies, B., & Harré, R. (1990). Positioning: The discursive production of selves. *Journal for the Theory of Social Behavior, 20*(1), 43–63. http://www.massey.ac.nz/~alock/position/position.htm

Dery, M. (1994). *Flame wars: The discourse of cyberculture.* Durham, NC: Duke University Press.

Dery, M. (1996). *Escape velocity: Cyberculture at the end of the century.* New York: Grove Press.

Dinev, T., Goo, J., Hu, Q., & Nam, K. (2006). User behavior toward protective technologies: Cultural differences between the United States and South Korea. In J. Ljunberg & M. Andersson (Eds.), *Proceedings of the Fourteenth European Conference on Information Systems* (pp. 1815–1826). Goteborg.

Donath, J. (1999). Identity and deception in the virtual community. In M. A. Smith & P. Kollock (Eds.), *Communities in cyberspace* (pp. 29–59). London: Routledge.

Dooly, M. (2006). *Online partners and ICC: Convergences and conflicts.* Paper presented at the IALIC Seventh Annual Conference: Culture and Context, Passau, Germany.

Döpke, S., Brown, A., Liddicoat, A., & Love, K. (1994). Closings in talkback radio: Institutional effects on conversational routines. *Australian Review of Applied Linguistics, Series S*(11), 21–46.

Dovidio, J. F., Gaertner, S. L., & Kawakami, K. (2003). Intergroup contact theory: The past, present and the future. *Group Processes and Intergroup Relations*, 6(1), 5–21.

Dragona, A., & Handa, C. (2000). Xenes glosses: Literacy and cultural implications of the web for Greece. In G. E. Hawisher & C. L. Selfe (Eds.), *Global literacies and the World-Wide Web* (pp. 52–69). London: Routledge.

ePals. (2007). *ePals global community*. Retrieved January 23, 2007, from http://www.epals.com/

Ess, C. (2001). What's culture got to do with it? Cultural collisions in the electronic global village, creative interferences, and the rise of culturally-mediated computing (Introduction). In C. Ess (Ed.), *Culture, technology, communication: Towards an intercultural global village* (pp. 1–50). Albany, NY: State University of New York Press.

Ess, C. (2002). Computer-mediated colonization, the renaissance, and educational imperatives for an intercultural global village. *Ethics and Information Technology*, 4(1), 11–22.

Ess, C., Kawabata, A., & Kurosaki, H. (2007). Cross-cultural perspectives on religion and computer-mediated communication. *Journal of Computer-Mediated Communication*, 12(3), 939–955.

Estela, J.-L. (2000). *Une typologie des stratégies web dans le secteur de la presse*. Unpublished chapter of doctoral dissertation, Université des Sciences et Technologie de Lille. http://christophe.benavent.free.fr/recherche/estella_typowebstrat.PDF

Evans, D. S. (1998). The cultural challenge of the information superhighway in France. *European Business Review*, 98(1), 51–55.

Fischer, G. (1998). *E-mail in foreign language teaching: Toward the creation of virtual classrooms*. Tubingen, Germany: Stauffenburg.

Freadman, A. (1998). Models of genre for language teaching. *South Central Review: Journal of the South Central Modern Language Association*, 15(1), 19–39.

Freadman, A., & Macdonald, A. (1992). *What is this thing called 'genre'?: Four essays in the semiotics of genre*. Mt Nebo, Qld: Boombana Publications.

Friceau, B. (2000). *Les Sites Internet de la presse quotidienne nationale d'informations générales et la cannibalisation: Quelles complémentarités entre édition traditionnelle et édition électronique? Cas pratique: Libération*. Unpublished Maîtrise d'information-communication, Université Bordeaux III, Bordeaux. http://www.benbef.com/memoire_bfriceau.pdf

Froomkin, A. M. (1995). Anonymity and its enmities. *Journal of Online Law*. Art. 4. http://web.wm.edu/law/publications/jol/95_96/froomkin.html?svr=law

Frow, J. (2005). *Genre*. London; New York: Routledge.

Gallois, C., & Callan, V. J. (1997). *Communication and culture: A guide for practice*. Chichester, UK; New York: Wiley.

Gerritsen, M., & Verckens, J. P. (2006). Raising students' intercultural awareness and preparing them for intercultural business (communication) by e-mail. *Business Communication Quarterly*, 69(1), 50–59.

Goffman, E. (1959). *The presentation of self in everyday life*. New York: Doubleday Anchor Books.

Goffman, E. (1981). *Forms of talk*. Oxford: Blackwell.

Goldsmith, J., & Wu, T. (2006). *Who controls the Internet?: Illusions of a borderless world*. Oxford; New York: Oxford University Press.

Gorman, G. E. (2006). Of Orrefors and Noritake: Or, has Geert Hofstede something to say about web site design? *Online Information Review, 30*(4), 337–340.

Gottlieb, N. (2003). Language, representation and power: Burakumin and the Internet. In N. Gottlieb & M. McLelland (Eds.), *Japanese cybercultures* (pp. 191–204). London; New York: Routledge.

Graf, P. (2004). *Report of the independent review of BBC Online.* London: Department for Culture, Media and Sport. http://www.culture.gov.uk/reference_library/publications/4591.aspx

Greer, J., & Mensing, D. (2004). The evolution of online newspapers: A longitudinal content analysis, 1997–2003. *Newspaper Research Journal, 25*(2), 98–112.

Guardian (2002). Guardian Unlimited Talk policy. Retrieved August 15, 2002, from http://www.guardian.co.uk/talkpolicy/0,5540,66799,00.html

Gubman, J., & Greer, J. D. (1997, July–August). *An analysis of online sites produced by U.S. newspapers: Are the critics right?* A paper presented to the annual meeting of the Association for Education in Journalism and Mass Communication, Chicago, IL.

Gunawardena, C. N., Nolla, A. C., Wilson, P. L., Lopez-Islas, J. R., Ramirez-Angel, N., & Megchun-Alpizar, R. M. (2001). A cross-cultural study of group process and development in online conferences. *Distance Education, 22*(1), 85–121.

Gunske von Kölln, M., & Gunske von Kölln, M. (1997). E-mail tandem network I & II. In T. Boswood (Ed.), *New ways of using computers in language teaching* (pp. 94–97). Alexandria, VA: Teachers of English to Speakers of Other Languages.

Hall, E. T. (1976). *Beyond culture.* Garden City, NY: Anchor Press Doubleday.

Hall, S. (1990). Cultural identity and diaspora. In J. Rutherford (Ed.), *Identity: Community, culture, difference* (pp. 222–237). London: Lawrence and Wishart.

Hanna, B. E. (2002). Plus ça change…: Social change and new cultural practices: The case of French Internet fora. In B. E. Hanna, E. J. Woodley, E. L. Buys, & J. A. Summerville (Eds.), *Social change in the 21st century: Conference proceedings.* Brisbane: Centre for Social Change Research, Queensland University of Technology. http://www.humanities.qut.edu.au/research/socialchange/docs/conf_papers2002/HannaBarbara.pdf

Hanna, B. E. (2006). *Look both ways: Intercultural spaces on the Internet.* Paper presented at the IALIC Seventh Annual Conference: Culture and context, Passau, Germany.

Hanna, B. E., & de Nooy, J. (2003). A funny thing happened on the way to the forum: Electronic discussion and foreign language learning. *Language Learning & Technology, 7*(1), 71–85. http://llt.msu.edu/vol7num1/hanna/

Hanna, B. E., & de Nooy, J. (2004). Negotiating cross-cultural difference in electronic discussion. *Multilingua, 23*(4), 257–281.

Harcourt, W. (1999). *Women@Internet: Creating new cultures in cyberspace.* London: Zed Books.

Hart, W. B. (1998). Intercultural computer-mediated communication (ICCMC). *The Edge: The E-Journal of Intercultural Relations, 1*(4). Retrieved October 18, 2006, from http://cms.interculturalu.com/theedge/v1i4Fall1998/f98hart.htm

Heaton, L. (1998). Talking heads vs. virtual workspaces: A comparison of design across cultures. *Journal of Information Technology*, *13*(4), 259–272, also available from *The Edge: The E-Journal of Intercultural Relations*, *1*(4). Retrieved October 18, 2006, from http://cms.interculturalu.com/theedge/v1i4Fall1998/f98heaton.htm

Heaton, L. (2001). Preserving communication context: Virtual workspace and interpersonal space in Japanese CSCW. In C. Ess (Ed.), *Culture, technology, communication: Towards an intercultural global village* (pp. 213–240). Albany, NY: State University of New York Press.

Herring, S. C. (1996). Posting in a different voice: Gender and ethics in computer-mediated communication. In C. Ess (Ed.), *Philosophical perspectives on computer-mediated communication* (pp. 115–145). Albany, NY: State University of New York Press.

Herring, S. C. (1999). Interactional coherence in CMC. *Journal of Computer-Mediated Communication*, *4*(4). http://jcmc.indiana.edu/vol4/issue4/herring.html

Herring, S. C. (2001a). Foreword. In C. Ess (Ed.), *Culture, technology, communication: Towards an intercultural global village* (pp. vii–x). Albany, NY: State University of New York Press.

Herring, S. C. (2001b). Computer-mediated discourse. In D. Schiffrin, D. Tannen, & H. Hamilton (Eds.), *The handbook of discourse analysis* (pp. 612–634). Oxford, UK: Blackwell Publishers.

Herring, S. C. (2002). Communication and collaboration: Computer-mediated communication on the Internet. *Annual Review of Information Science and Technology*, *36*(1), 109–168.

Hewling, A. (2004). Foregrounding the goblet: Moving on from geographic/nationality based frames of reference when looking at culture in the online classroom. In C. Ess & F. Sudweeks (Eds.), *Proceedings of the Cultural Attitudes Towards Technology and Communication Conference, 2004 (CATaC'04)* (pp. 543–7). Perth: Murdoch University Press. http://eduspaces.net/anneh/files/-1/2410/CATaC'04Hewling.doc

Highfield, A. (2003). *Speech given at a Westminster media forum on the Department for Culture, Media & Sport review of BBC online services.* http://www.bbc.co.uk/pressoffice/speeches/stories/highfield_westminster.shtml

Ho, M. L. C. (2000). Computer-mediated communication: A selected review of literature. *Journal of Online Learning*, *11*(2), 14–18.

Hofstede, G. (1980). *Culture's consequences: International differences in work-related values.* Beverly Hills, CA: Sage Publications.

IECC. (2008). *Intercultural E-mail Classroom Connections.* Retrieved September 9, 2008, from http://www.iecc.org/

Independent Argument (2003–2004). *Are the French awakening?* http://forums.delphiforums.com/id-argument/messages/?msg=21373.1

Independent Argument (2004). *Thank you and farewell.* Retrieved April 14, 2005, from http://forums.delphiforums.com/n/main.asp?webtag=id-argument&nav=messages&msg=22600.1&prettyurl=%2Fid%2Dargument%2Fmessages%2F%3Fmsg%3D22600%2E1

Jarvenpaa, S. L., & Leidner, D. E. (1998). Communication and trust in global virtual teams. *Journal of Computer-Mediated Communication*, *3*(4). http://jcmc.indiana.edu/vol3/issue4/jarvenpaa.html

Jauréguiberry, F. (2000). Le moi, le soi et Internet. *Sociologie et sociétés, 32*, 136–152. http://www.erudit.org/revue/socsoc/2000/v32/n2/001364ar.pdf

Johnston, K., & Johal, P. (1999). The Internet as a 'virtual cultural region': Are extant cultural classification schemes appropriate? *Internet Research: Electronic Networking Applications and Policy, 9*(3), 178–186.

Kaplan, R. B. (1972). Cultural thought patterns in inter-cultural education. In K. Croft (Ed.), *Readings on English as a second language* (pp. 245–262). Cambridge, MA: Winthrop.

Kawabata, A., & Tamura, T. (2007). Online-religion in Japan: Websites and religious counseling from a comparative cross-cultural perspective. *Journal of Computer-Mediated Communication, 12*(3), 999–1019. http://jcmc.indiana.edu/vol12/issue3/kawabata.html

Kern, R. G. (2000). *Literacy and language teaching*. Oxford: Oxford University Press.

Kern, R., Ware, P., & Warschauer, M. (2004). Crossing frontiers: New directions in online pedagogy and research. *Annual Review of Applied Linguistics, 24*, 243–260.

Kim, H., & Papacharissi, Z. (2003). Cross-cultural differences in online self-presentation: A content analysis of personal Korean and US home pages. *Asian Journal of Communication, 13*(1), 100–119.

Kim, H., Yu, K.-A., & Sussex, R. (2006). A cross-cultural study of E-mail discourse between Koreans and Australians. *Discourse and Cognition, 13*(2), 79–108.

Kim, H.-S., Hearn, G., Hatcher, C., & Weber, I. (1999). Online communication between Australians and Koreans: Managing the differences that matter. *World Communication Journal, 28*(4), 48–68. Reprinted in Jandt, F. E. (Ed.). (2004). *Intercultural communication: A global reader* (pp. 143–159). Thousand Oaks, CA: Sage Publications.

Kim, K.-J., & Bonk, C. J. (2002). Cross-cultural comparisons of online collaboration. *Journal of Computer-Mediated Communication, 8*(1). http://jcmc.indiana.edu/vol8/issue1/kimandbonk.html

Kim, S., & Lee, Y. (2006). Global online marketplace: A cross-cultural comparison of website quality. *International Journal of Consumer Studies, 30*(6), 533–543.

Kinginger, C., Gourvès-Hayward, A., & Simpson, V. (1999). A tele-collaborative course on French–American intercultural collaboration. *French Review, 72*(5), 853–866.

Ko, H., Roberts, M. S., & Cho, C.-H. (2006). Cross-cultural differences in motivations and perceived interactivity: A comparative study of American and Korean Internet users. *Journal of Current Issues and Research in Advertising, 28*(2), 93–104.

Koda, T. (2007). Cross-cultural study of avatars' facial expressions and design considerations within Asian countries. *Lecture Notes in Computer Science* (4568), 207–220.

Koeszegi, S., Vetschera, R., & Kersten, G. (2004). National cultural differences in the use and perception of Internet-based NSS: Does high or low context matter? *International Negotiation, 9*, 79–109.

Kolko, B. E., Nakamura, L., & Rodman, G. B. (Eds.). (2000). *Race in cyberspace*. London; New York: Routledge.

Kollock, P., & Smith, M. (1996). Managing the virtual commons: Cooperation and conflict in computer communities. In S. C. Herring (Ed.), *Computer-Mediated communication: Linguistic, social, and cross-cultural perspectives* (pp. 109–128). Amsterdam; Philadelphia: John Benjamins.

Kramsch, C. (Ed.). (2003). *Language acquisition and language socialization*. London: Continuum.

Kramsch, C., & Thorne, S. (2002). Foreign language learning as global communicative practice. In D. Block & D. Cameron (Eds.), *Globalization and language teaching* (pp. 83–100). London: Routledge.

Kreef-Peyton, J. (1999). Theory and research: Interaction via computers. In J. Egbert & E. Hanson-Smith (Eds.), *CALL environments: Research, practice and critical issues* (pp. 17–27). Alexandria, VA: TESOL.

Kuhnheim, J. S. (1998). The Economy of Performance: Gómez-peña's New World Border. *Modern Fiction Studies, 44*(1), 24–35.

Labbe, H., & Marcoccia, M. (2005). Communication numérique et continuité des genres: L'exemple du courrier électronique. *Texto!* Dits et inédits. http://www.revue-texto.net/index.php?id=512

Lam, W. S. E. (2000). L2 literacy and the design of the self: A case study of a teenager writing on the Internet. *TESOL Journal, 34*, 457–482.

Lam, W. S. E. (2003). *Second language literacy and identity formation on the Internet: The case of Chinese immigrant youth in the United States.* Unpublished doctoral dissertation, University of California, Berkeley.

Lam, W. S. E. (2004). Second language socialization in a bilingual chat room: Global and local considerations. *Language Learning & Technology, 8*(3), 44–65. http://llt.msu.edu/vol8num3/lam/

Lamy, M.-N., & Hampel, R. (2007). *Online communication in language learning and teaching.* Basingstoke; New York: Palgrave Macmillan.

Lantolf, J. P., & Pavlenko, A. (2000). Second language learning as participation and the (re)construction of selves. In J. P. Lantolf (Ed.), *Sociocultural theory and second language learning* (pp. 153–177). Oxford: Oxford University Press.

Laver, J. (1981). Linguistic routines and politeness in greeting and parting. In F. Coulmas (Ed.), *Conversational routine: Explorations in standardized communication situations and prepatterned speech* (pp. 289–304). The Hague: Mouton.

Leeman, J. (1999). Review of *Un misterio en Toluca. Language Learning & Technology, 3*(1), 31–41. http://llt.msu.edu/vol3num1/review/review4.html

Liang, A., & McQueen, R. J. (1999). Computer assisted adult interactive learning in a multi-cultural environment. *Adult Learning, 11*(1), 26–29.

Liao, C.-C. (1999). E-mailing to improve EFL learners' reading and writing abilities: Taiwan experience. *The Internet TESL Journal, 5*(3). http://iteslj.org/Articles/Liao-Emailing.html

Libération. (2005). *Modération.* Retrieved February 15, 2005, from http://www.liberation.fr/forums/forum.php

Liddicoat, A. (2000). Everyday speech as culture: Implications for language teaching. In A. Liddicoat & C. Crozet (Eds.), *Teaching languages, teaching cultures* (pp. 51–63). Melbourne: Applied Linguistics Association of Australia.

Light, A., & Rogers, Y. (1999). Conversation as publishing: The role of news forums on the web. *Journal of Computer-Mediated Communication, 4*(4). http://jcmc.indiana.edu/vol4/issue4/light.html

Little, D. (1991). *Learner autonomy 1: Definitions, issues and problems.* Dublin: Authentik.

Little, D., & Brammerts, H. (Eds.). (1996). *A guide to language learning in tandem via the Internet.* Dublin: Trinity College Dublin, CLCS occasional paper 46.

Loader, B. D. (Ed.). (1998). *Cyberspace divide: Equality, agency and policy in the information society.* London; New York: Routledge.

Lyotard, J.-F. (1983). *Le différend.* Paris: Minuit.

Ma, R. (1996). Computer-mediated conversations as a new dimension of intercultural communication between East Asian and North American college students. In S. C. Herring (Ed.), *Computer-mediated communication: Linguistic, social, and cross-cultural perspectives* (pp. 173–185). Amsterdam; Philadelphia: John Benjamins.

Mangenot, F. (2002). Communication écrite entre étudiants par forum Internet: Un nouveau genre d'écrit universitaire? *Enjeux, 54,* 166–182. http://w3.u-grenoble3.fr/espace_pedagogique/mangenot-bruxelles.rtf

McCarthy, K. (2003). *BBC news site facing extinction? Tough times for British media institution.* http://www.theregister.co.uk/2003/08/28/bbc_news_site_facing_extinction/

Miller, D., & Slater, D. (2000). *The Internet: An ethnographic approach.* Oxford; New York: Berg.

Mixxer. (2008). *Language exchange online via Skype.* Retrieved September 9, 2008, from http://www.language-exchanges.org/

Le Monde. (2002). *Tous sujets.* Retrieved August 13, 2002, from http://forumselections.lemonde.fr/perl/wwwthreads.pl

Le Monde. (2007). *Mode d'emploi des forums du monde.fr.* Retrieved April 11, 2007, from http://forumselections.lemonde.fr/perl/faq_french.pl?Cat=

Morris, C., & Meadows, M. (2004). Digital dreaming: Indigenous intellectual property and new communication technologies. In G. Goggin (Ed.), *Virtual nation: The Internet in Australia* (pp. 159–176). Sydney: UNSW Press.

Morse, K. (2003). Does one size fit all? Exploring asynchronous learning in a multicultural environment. *Journal of Asynchronous Learning Networks, 7*(1), 37–55.

Müller-Hartmann, A. (2000). The role of tasks in promoting intercultural learning in electronic learning networks. *Language Learning & Technology, 4*(2), 129–147. http://llt.msu.edu/vol4num2/muller/

Murphy, M., & Levy, M. (2006). Politeness in intercultural e-mail communication: Australian and Korean perspectives. *Journal of Intercultural Communication, 12.* http://www.immi.se/intercultural/nr12/murphy.htm

Murray, D. E. (2000a). Protean communication: The language of CMC. *TESOL Quarterly, 34*(3), 397–421.

Murray, D. E. (2000b). Changing technologies, changing literacy communities? *Language Learning & Technology, 4*(2), 43–58. http://llt.msu.edu/vol4num2/murray/

Nakamura, L. (2002). *Cybertypes: Race, ethnicity, and identity on the Internet.* New York: Routledge.

Negroponte, N. (1995). *Being digital.* New York: Alfred A. Knopf.

New York Times. (2007). Readers' opinions. Retrieved April 11, 2007, from http://www.nytimes.com/pages/readersopinions/index.html

Nguyen, H. T., & Kellogg, G. (2005). Emergent identities in on-line discussions for second language learning. *Canadian Modern Language Review, 62*(1), 111–136.

Nishiguchi, M. (1997). The impact of the Internet and the advanced networks on Japanese culture. In P. Crubezy, A. Cresson & K. Dameron (Eds.), *Images, signs, symbols: The cultural coding of communication* (pp. 399–406). Poitiers: SIETAR.

Norton, B. (2000). *Identity and language learning*. London: Longman.

Le Nouvel Observateur. (2007). *Les règles*. Retrieved October 1, 2007, from http://tempsreel.nouvelobs.com/debats/debats-regles.html

O'Dowd, R. (2001). In search of a truly global network: The opportunities and challenges of on-line intercultural communication. *CALL-EJ Online, 3*(1). http://www.tell.is.ritsumei.ac.jp/callejonline/journal/3-1/o_dowd.html

O'Dowd, R. (2003). Understanding the 'other side': Intercultural learning in a Spanish–English e-mail exchange. *Language Learning & Technology, 7*(2), 118–144. http://llt.msu.edu/vol7num2/odowd/

O'Dowd, R. (2006). *Telecollaboration and the development of intercultural communicative competence*. Munich: Langenscheidt.

O'Dowd, R. (Ed.). (2007). *Online intercultural exchange: An introduction for foreign language teachers*. Clevedon, UK: Multilingual Matters.

O'Dowd, R., & Ritter, M. (2006). Understanding and working with 'failed communication' in telecollaborative exchanges. *CALICO Journal, 23*(3), 623–641.

Okamura, J. Y. (1981). Situational ethnicity. *Ethnic and Racial Studies, 4*(4), 452–465.

Opp-Beckman, L. (1999). Classroom practice: Authentic audience on the Internet. In J. Egbert & E. Hanson-Smith (Eds.), *CALL environments: Research, practice and critical issues* (pp. 79–95). Alexandria, VA: TESOL.

O'Rourke, B. (2007). Models of telecollaboration (1): eTandem. In R. O'Dowd (Ed.), *Online intercultural exchange: An introduction for foreign language teachers* (pp. 41–61). Clevedon, UK: Multilingual Matters.

Osman, G., & Herring, S. C. (2007). Interaction, facilitation, and deep learning in cross-cultural chat: A case study. *Internet and Higher Education, 10*(2), 125–141.

Osuna, M. M., & Meskill, C. (1998). Using the world wide web to integrate Spanish language and culture: Pilot study. *Language Learning & Technology, 1*(2), 71–92. http://llt.msu.edu/vol1num2/article4/

Paramskas, D. (1995). Causerie: A cafe campus in French. In M. Warschauer (Ed.), *Virtual connections: Online activities and projects for networking language learners* (pp. 166–167). Honolulu: University of Hawai'i Second Language Teaching and Curriculum Center.

Park, J.-E. (2007). Co-construction of nonnative speaker identity in cross-cultural interaction. *Applied Linguistics, 28*(3), 339–360.

Pavlenko, A., & Blackledge, A. (Eds.). (2004). *Negotiation of identities in multilingual settings*. Clevedon, UK: Multilingual Matters.

Peng, F. Y., Tham, N. I., & Xiaoming, H. (1999). Trends in online newspapers: A look at the US web. *Newspaper Research Journal, 20*(2), 52–63.

Pfeil, U., Zaphiris, P., & Ang, C. S. (2006). Cultural differences in collaborative authoring of Wikipedia. *Journal of Computer-Mediated Communication, 12*(1). http://jcmc.indiana.edu/vol12/issue1/pfeil.html

Porter, D. (Ed.). (1997). *Internet culture*. New York: Routledge.

Prensky, M. (2001). Digital natives, digital immigrants. *On the Horizon, 9*(5), 1–2. http://www.marcprensky.com/writing/Prensky%20-%20Digital%20Natives,%20Digital%20Immigrants%20-%20Part1.pdf

Raybourn, E. M. (1997). Computer game design: New directions for intercultural simulation game designers. *Developments in Business Simulation and Experiential Exercises, 24*. http://www.cs.unm.edu/~raybourn/games.html

Reeder, K., Macfadyen, L. P., Roche, J., & Chase, M. (2004). Negotiating cultures in cyberspace: Participation patterns and problematics. *Language Learning & Technology, 8*(2), 88–105. http://llt.msu.edu/vol8num2/reeder/

Revillard, A. (2000). Les interactions sur l'Internet (note critique). *Terrains & Travaux, 1*, 108–129. http://www.melissa.ens-cachan.fr/article.php3?id_article=36

Rheingold, H. (1993). *The virtual community: Homesteading on the electronic frontier.* Reading, MA: Addison-Wesley.

Rice, C. D. (1996). Bring intercultural encounters into classrooms: IECC electronic mailing lists. *Technological Horizons in Education, 23*(6), 60–63.

Rosello, M. (1998). *Declining the stereotype.* Hanover, NH; London: University Press of New England.

Santrot, F. (2002, October 24). Presse actu en ligne: *Le Monde* et *Les Echos* loin devant. *Le Journal du Net.* http://www.journaldunet.com/ 0210/021024nielsen-mag.shtml

Scheuermann, L., & Taylor, G. (1997). Netiquette. *Internet Research: Electronic Networking Applications and Policy, 7*(4), 269–273.

Schneider, J., & von der Emde, S. (2006). Conflicts in cyberspace: From communication breakdown to intercultural dialogue in online collaborations. In J. A. Belz & S. L. Thorne (Eds.), *Internet-mediated intercultural foreign language education* (pp. 178–206). Boston, MA: Heinle & Heinle.

Schultz, T. (1999). Interactive options in online journalism: A content analysis of 100 U.S. newspapers. *Journal of Computer-Mediated Communication, 5*(1). http://jcmc.indiana.edu/vol5/issue1/schultz.html

Setlock, L. D., Fussell, S. R., & Neuwirth, C. (2004). Taking it out of context: Collaborating within and across cultures in face-to-face settings and via instant messaging. In J. Herbsleb & G. Olson (Eds.), *Proceedings of ACM CSCW04 Conference on Computer-Supported Cooperative Work 2004* (pp. 604–613). New York: ACM. http://portal.acm.org/citation.cfm?doid=1031607.1031712

Shachaf, P., Meho, L. I., & Hara, N. (2007). Cross-cultural analysis of e-mail reference. *Journal of Academic Librarianship, 33*(2), 243–253.

Shields, R. (Ed.). (1996). *Cultures of Internet: Virtual spaces, real histories, living bodies.* London: Sage.

Shih, Y.-C. D., & Cifuentes, L. (2003). Taiwanese intercultural phenomena and issues in a United States–Taiwan telecommunications partnership. *Educational Technology, Research and Development, 51*(3), 82–89.

Short, J., Williams, E., & Christie, B. (1976). *The social psychology of telecommunications.* London: John Wiley and Sons.

Siebenhaar, B. (2006). Code choice and code-switching in Swiss-German Internet Relay Chat rooms. *Journal of Sociolinguistics 10*(4), 481–506.

Slater, D. (2003). Book Review: *On the Internet* by H. I. Dreyfus. *Theory, Culture & Society, 20*(1), 133–138.

Smith, M. A., & Kollock, P. (Eds.). (1999). *Communities in cyberspace.* London: Routledge.

Smith, P., Coldwell, J., Smith, S., & Murphy, K. (2005). Learning through computer-mediated communication: A comparison of Australian and Chinese heritage students. *Innovations in Education and Teaching International, 42*(2), 123–134.

Sotillo, S. M. (2000). Discourse functions and syntactic complexity in synchronous and asynchronous communication. *Language Learning & Technology,* 4(1), 82–119. http://llt.msu.edu/vol4num1/sotillo/

Spender, D. (1995). *Nattering on the net: Women, power and cyberspace.* North Melbourne, Vic: Spinifex.

Sproull, L., & Kiesler, S. (1986). Reducing social context cues: Electronic mail in organizational communication. *Management Science, 32*(11), 1492–1512.

Sproull, L., & Kiesler, S. (1991). *Connections: New ways of working in the networked organization.* Cambridge, MA: MIT Press.

St Amant, K. (2002). When cultures and computers collide: Rethinking computer-mediated communication according to international and intercultural communication expectations. *Journal of Business and Technical Communication, 16*(2), 196–214.

St Amant, K. (2003). Making contact in international virtual offices: An application of symbolic interactionism to online workplace discourse. *IEEE Transactions on Professional Communication, 46*(3), 236–240.

Steiner, P. (1993, July 5). On the Internet, nobody knows you're a dog. *The New Yorker, 69*(20), 61.

Stone, A. R. (1995). *The war of desire and technology at the close of the mechanical age.* Cambridge, MA; London: MIT Press.

Straub, D. W. (1994). The effect of culture on IT diffusion: E-mail and fax in Japan and the U.S. *Information Systems Research, 5*(1), 23–47.

Sugimoto, T., & Levin, J. A. (2000). Multiple literacies and multimedia: A comparison of Japanese and American uses of the Internet. In G. E. Hawisher & C. L. Selfe (Eds.), *Global literacies and the World-Wide Web* (pp. 133–153). London; New York: Routledge.

Surratt, C. G. (1998). *Netlife: Internet citizens and their communities.* Commack, NY: Nova Science.

Swales, J. M. (1990). *Genre analysis: English in academic and research settings.* Cambridge; Melbourne: Cambridge University Press.

Tabensky, A. (2000). Discussion as dyadic interaction: Lessons from a corpus. *Australian Review of Applied Linguistics, Series S*(16), 49–63.

Tan, B. C. Y., Wei, K.-K., Watson, R. T., & Walczuch, R. M. (1998). Reducing status effects with computer-mediated communication: Evidence from two distinct national cultures. *Journal of Management Information Systems, 15*(1), 119–141.

Tandem. (2007). *Language learning in tandem.* Retrieved January 23, 2007, from http://www.slf.ruhr-uni-bochum.de/index.html

Tankard, J. W., Jr., & Ban, H. (1998). Online newspapers: Living up to their potential? In *Proceedings of the 81st Annual Meeting of the Association for Education in Journalism and Mass Communication* (pp. 84–106). Baltimore, MD: Communication Tech and Policy.

Tella, S. (1996). Foreign languages and modern technology: Harmony or hell? In M. Warschauer (Ed.), *Telecollaboration in foreign language learning: Proceedings of the Hawai'i symposium* (pp. 3–17). Honolulu: University of Hawai'i Second Language Teaching and Curriculum Center.

Thatcher, B. (2005). Situating L2 writing in global communication technologies. *Computers and Composition, 22*(3), 279–295.

Thorne, S. L. (2003). Artifacts and cultures-of-use in intercultural communication. *Language Learning & Technology, 7*(2), 38–67. http://llt.msu.edu/vol7num2/thorne/

Thorne, S. L. (2006). Pedagogical and praxiological lessons from Internet-mediated intercultural foreign language education research. In J. A. Belz & S. L. Thorne (Eds.), *Internet-mediated intercultural foreign language education* (pp. 2–30). Boston, MA: Heinle & Heinle. http://language.la.psu.edu/%7Ethorne/thorne_AAUSC2005.pdf

Thorne, S. L., & Black, R. W. (2007). Language and literacy development in computer-mediated contexts and communities. *Annual Review of Applied Linguistics, 27*, 133–160.

Thurlow, C., Lengel, L., & Tomic, A. (2004). *Computer mediated communication: Social interaction and the Internet.* London; Thousand Oaks, CA: Sage.

Toyoda, E., & Harrison, R. (2002). Characterization of text chat communication between learners and native speakers of Japanese. *Language Learning & Technology, 6*(1), 82–99. http://llt.msu.edu/vol6num1/toyoda/

Tsagarousianou, R., Tambini, D., & Bryan, C. (Eds.). (1998). *Cyberdemocracy: Technology, cities, and civic networks.* London; New York: Routledge.

Turkle, S. (1995). *Life on the screen: Identity in the age of the Internet.* New York: Simon & Schuster.

Twu, H.-L. (2007). Computer-mediated communication challenges Chinese teachers' authority. *International Journal of Continuing Engineering Education and Life Long Learning, 17*(2–3), 244–252.

Ulijn, J., O'Hair, D., Weggeman, M., Ledlow, G., & Hall, H. T. (2000). Innovation, corporate strategy, and cultural context: What is the mission for international business communication? *The Journal of Business Communication, 37*(3), 293–316.

Ulijn, J. M., & Lincke, A. (2004). The effect of CMC and FTF on negotiation outcomes between R&D and manufacturing partners in the supply chain: An Anglo/Nordic/Latin comparison. *International Negotiation, 9*(1), 111–140.

von Münchow, P., & Rakotonoelina, F. (2006). L'interrogation et le discours rapporté dans les forums de discussion sur l'environnement en français et en anglo-américan. In P. von Münchow & F. Rakotonoelina (Eds.), *Discours, cultures, comparaisons* (pp. 93–112). Paris: Presses Sorbonne Nouvelle.

Walther, J. (1992). Interpersonal effects in computer-mediated interactions: A relational perspective. *Communication Research, 19*(1), 52–90.

Walther, J. (1996). Computer-mediated communication: Impersonal, interpersonal, and hyperpersonal interaction. *Communication Research, 23*(1), 3–43.

Ware, P. (2005). 'Missed' communication in online communication: Tensions in a German–American telecollaboration. *Language Learning & Technology, 9*(2), 64–89. http://llt.msu.edu/vol9num2/ware/

Ware, P. D., & Kramsch, C. (2005). Toward an intercultural stance: Teaching German and English through telecollaboration. *Modern Language Journal, 89*(2), 190–205.

Warschauer, M. (1995). *E-mail for English teaching: Bringing the Internet and computer learning networks into the language classroom.* Alexandria, VA: TESOL.

Warschauer, M. (2000). Language, identity, and the Internet. In G. Rodman (Ed.), *Race in cyberspace* (pp. 151–170). New York: Routledge.

Warschauer, M. (2002). Languages.com: The Internet and linguistic pluralism. In I. Snyder (Ed.), *Silicon literacies: Communication, innovation, and education in the electronic age* (pp. 62–74). London: Routledge.

Warschauer, M., & Kern, R. (Eds.). (2000). *Network-based language teaching: Concepts and practice.* Cambridge: Cambridge University Press.

Warschauer, M., El Said, G. R., & Zohry, A. (2002). Language choice online: Globalization and identity in Egypt. *Journal of Computer-Mediated Communication,* 7(4). http://jcmc.indiana.edu/vol7/issue4/warschauer.html

Weasenforth, D., Biesenbach-Lucas, S., & Meloni, C. (2002). Realizing constructivist objectives through collaborative technologies: Threaded discussions. *Language Learning & Technology,* 6(3), 58–86. http://llt.msu.edu/vol6num3/weasenforth/

Wong, J. (1995). Two semesters of email keypalling: What works and what doesn't. In M. Warschauer (Ed.), *Virtual connections: Online activities & projects for networking language learners* (pp. 122–124). Honolulu: University of Hawai'i Second Language Teaching and Curriculum Center.

Woodward, K. (1997). Concepts of identity and difference. In K. Woodward (Ed.), *Identity and difference* (pp. 8–29). London: Sage.

Würtz, E. (2005). A cross-cultural analysis of websites from high-context cultures and low-context cultures. *Journal of Computer-Mediated Communication,* 11(1). http://jcmc.indiana.edu/vol11/issue1/wuertz.html

Yang, D., Olesova, L., & Richardson, J. (2008). The impact of cross-cultural differences on learner participation and communication in asynchronous discussions. In K. McFerrin, R. Weber, R. Carlsen, & D. A. Willis (Eds.), *Proceedings of Society for Information Technology and Teacher Education International Conference 2008* (pp. 825–829). Chesapeake, VA: AACE.

Yum, Y.-O., & Hara, K. (2005). Computer-mediated relationship development: A cross-cultural comparison. *Journal of Computer-Mediated Communication,* 11(1). http://jcmc.indiana.edu/vol11/issue1/yum.html

Zhu, P., & St Amant, K. (2007). Taking traditional Chinese medicine international and online: An examination of the cultural rhetorical factors affecting American perceptions of Chinese-created web sites. *Technical Communication Quarterly,* 54(2), 171–186.

Zickmund, S. (2000). Approaching the radical other: The discursive culture of cyberhate. In D. Bell & B. M. Kennedy (Eds.), *The cybercultures reader* (pp. 237–253). London; New York: Routledge.

Zorn, I. (2005). Do culture and technology interact? Overcoming technological barriers to intercultural communication in virtual communities. *ACM Siggroup Bulletin,* 25(2), 8–13.

Internet Forums and Other Websites Cited

12chat (伊乐园中文论坛): http://www.12chat.net/

AllAbout: http://allabout.co.jp/

BBC Messageboards: http://www.bbc.co.uk/messageboards/

   BBC Learning English Messageboards: http://www.bbc.co.uk/dna/mble

Delphi Forums: http://www.delphiforums.com/

   'Idle Chit Chat': http://forums.delphiforums.com/Indiechatters

   'Independent Argument – Redux': http://forums.delphiforums.com/2004election

ePals Global Community: http://www.epals.com/

L'Express, Forums: http://www.lexpress.fr/opinions/forums/

Le Figaro, Forums: http://figaro.concileo.com/user/non-frames/default.asp?

Guardian, The Talk: http://talk.guardian.co.uk/

Independent, Argument: http://forums.indigital.co.uk/id-argument (no longer available)

Intercultural E-mail Classroom Connections (IECC): http://www.iecc.org/

Kidopia: das Forum für Kinder: http://www.kidopia.de/

Libération, Forums: http://www.liberation.fr/forums/forum.php

Lonely Planet,
   Das Lonely Planet Forum: http://www.lonelyplanet.de/forum/
   Foro Lonely Planet: http://www.foro.geoplaneta.es/
   Forum des voyageurs – Lonely Planet France: http://www.lonelyplanet.fr/forum/
   Forum dei viaggiatori: http://www.lonelyplanetitalia.it/forum/
   Thorn Tree Travel Forum: http://www.lonelyplanet.com/thorntree/index.jspa

M6, Les forums de M6: http://forum.m6.fr/

Mixxer: Language exchange online via Skype: http://www.language-exchanges.org/

Momes.net: Premiers pas sur Internet: http://forum.momes.net/

Le Monde, Forums: http://forumselections.lemonde.fr/perl/wwwthreads.pl

New York Times: http://www.nytimes.com/pages/readersopinions/index.html

Nouvel Observateur, Débats: http://tempsreel.nouvelobs.com/debats/

Rongshuxia (榕树下全球中文原创文学论坛): http://www.rongshuxia.com/

Tandem Server Bochum: http://www.slf.ruhr-uni-bochum.de/

Topix: Kids Forum: http://www.topix.com/forum/family/kids

Unilang, Language forums: http://home.unilang.org/main/forum/

Washington Post, Discussion groups: http://www.washingtonpost.com/wp-srv/community/groups/front.html?nid=roll_messboards

Wordreference, Language forums: http://forum.wordreference.com/

TF1, Forums: http://tf1.lci.fr/infos/communautes/lcinautes/

Yahoo Answers:
   http://au.answers.yahoo.com/
   http://answers.yahoo.com/
   http://de.answers.yahoo.com/
   http://es.answers.yahoo.com/
   http://fr.answers.yahoo.com/
   http://it.answers.yahoo.com/
   http://ks.cn.yahoo.com/
   http://uk.answers.yahoo.com/

Index

Note: Page numbers in bold indicate significant discussion